D1411536

The encyclopedia of
CREATIVE

CUISINE

A complete guide to Cuisine Vivante —
preparation, style, presentation.

The encyclopedia of
CREATIVE
CUISINE

A complete guide to Cuisine Vivante —
preparation, style, presentation.

BY HILARY WALDEN

Dishes prepared by Jean-Louis Pollet
Photography by David Burch

CHARTWELL
BOOKS, INC.

A QUARTO BOOK

Published by Chartwell Books Inc.,
A Division of Book Sales Inc.,
110 Enterprise Avenue,
Secaucus, New Jersey 07094

ISBN 1-55521-090-2

Copyright © Quarto Publishing Limited 1986

All rights reserved. No part of this publication may be
reproduced, stored in a retrieval system, or transmitted in any
form or by any means electronic, mechanical, photocopying,
recording or otherwise, without the permission of the
publisher and copyright holder.

First published in Great Britain in 1986 by
Ward Lock Limited, 82 Gower Street,
London WC1E 6EQ, an Egmont Company.
ISBN 0 7063 6419 8

This book was designed and produced by
Quarto Publishing Limited
The Old Brewery
6 Blundell Street London N7 9BH

Senior Editor: Stephen Paul   Photographer: David Burch
Art Editor: Moira Clinch   Illustrators: Lynne Riding, Mick Hill

Editor: Linda Sonntag   Art Director: Alastair Campbell
Assistant Designer: Anthony Bussey   Editorial Director: Jim Miles

Typeset by QV Typesetting, London
Colour origination by
Universal Colour Scanning Ltd, Hong Kong
Printed by Lee Fung Asco Printers Ltd,
Hong Kong

CONTENTS

◆ NOTE

Where the garnish in the photograph differs from that given in the recipe for the dish, it is a seasonal alternative chosen by the chef.

*Jean-Louis Pollet and Hilary Walden relaxing in
the delightful gardens at Frederick's restaurant,
London.*

FOREWORD

As a restaurant chef I have been in as good a position as any to observe the growing success and popularity of Cuisine Vivante. From somewhat elitist beginnings the movement has gone from strength to strength, attracting new followers every step of the way. However, for a number of reasons Cuisine Vivante has remained firmly within the context of restaurant food, and it has come to be regarded by many as a style of cooking that is infinitely complicated and time-consuming. This is a shame not least because it is not entirely true, but also because it has perpetuated the elitist image and has restricted the further development of the cuisine by limiting the number of people who have experience of it.

In this book I was fortunate to have been able to work with Hilary Walden on a large-scale project to introduce Cuisine Vivante to a much wider audience. The aim was not so much to 'popularize' Cuisine Vivante by reducing it to a number of common denominators, but rather to show (through the careful selection of recipes and the explanation of certain basic techniques and preparations) that the 'spirit' of Cuisine Vivante need not be solely the preserve of expensive restaurants.

Cuisine Vivante can be practised at home just as easily as any other cuisine. It can be complicated and time-consuming but it can just as easily be simple and quick. The most important principle to bear in mind is that the quality, flavour and freshness of the food must be given full expression at all times. Every step of the preparation, cooking and presentation must be made with this principle firmly in mind, and there is no reason why the home cook cannot achieve the gastronomic delights that have hitherto largely taken place within the confines of restaurants.

INTRODUCTION

Cuisine Vivante is a new and rapidly evolving style of cooking that offers unprecedented levels of aesthetic and gastronomic pleasure to the diner. It is a style of cooking in which presentation plays an integral role, with dishes receiving a precise and highly original treatment that not only looks superb but also gives full expression to the care and attention lavished on the preparation and to the individual characteristics of the main ingredients.

The essence of Cuisine Vivante lies in the selection of only the finest and freshest ingredients; cooking methods that are sympathetic to the inherent qualities of the ingredients; delicate sauces that complement the taste, texture and color of these ingredients; and finally, a style of presentation that takes all these factors into account and visually underlines them.

The inherent logic of this culinary philosophy has seen the exclusion of traditional flour-based sauces and over-rich dishes where it is often difficult even visually to identify the ingredients let alone identify them by taste. However, Cuisine Vivante is not a slave to dogma, and there are no hard and fast rules. Innovation, experimentation and adaptation are the key concepts, and so long as the spirit of Cuisine Vivante is preserved there is no limit as to the gastronomic heights that may be attained.

The beginnings

The origins of Cuisine Vivante can be traced back to Fernand Point and the "new-style" cuisine of the 1950s. His restaurant, La Pyramide, at Vienne in the Rhône Valley, became the center of French gastronomic innovation as his experiments with a lighter, more delicate style of cooking that was at odds with the classical haute cuisine repertoire of Carème and Escoffier gained widespread acclaim. His ideas were seized upon by the next generation of chefs who were inspired to carry out their own experiments. Sauces were among the first techniques to be revolutionized. Instead of using flour to thicken the sauce, they boiled and reduced them. The result was a sauce that emphasized rather than masked the flavor of the food. This in turn led to a renewed emphasis on the quality of the ingredients used and on light cooking that made best use of this quality.

The presentation of food was the next technique to receive the attention of Fernand Point and his followers, Jean and Pierre Troisgros and Paul Bocuse, now the acknowledged leaders of the "new-style". Having so far strived to do away with the synthetic glamor of traditional haute cuisine in terms of ingredients and preparation, these "new-style" chefs similarly strove to present the food in a different and refreshing way, and for inspiration

◆

OPPOSITE *Paul Bocuse (top) and Jean and Pierre Troisgros (bottom), widely recognized today as the leaders of the "new style". Taking their lead from Fernand Point and incorporating concepts of food presentation from Japan, they have developed a style of cooking worthy of the highest regard.*

◆

Cuisine Vivante aims to stimulate both the eye and the appetite, and this concept is applied to the individual dishes and to the meal as a whole. This selection of dishes — Oysters with watercress, Veal tournedos with mixed peppers, Strawberries and orange crème and a light side salad — demonstrates the qualities of balance, color and flavor progression that are the hallmarks of Cuisine Vivante.

◆

ABOVE *Michel Guérard*
originator of the Cuisine Minceur
that provoked a widespread
reappraisal of food and its
presentation by chefs and
restaurant owners throughout
the world.

they turned to Japan. From the Japanese, the frontrunners of the "new-style" adopted and adapted the precise and ornamental arrangement of dainty portions of food. To these they added a sauce — or even three — not poured over the food to hide it, but to provide background color, a pool of green or pink beneath a white fillet of fish, and to expand the symphony of flavors. The finishing touch was perhaps a scattering of fragrant leaves or a display of colorful julienne vegetables.

Having established the principles of light, sympathetic cooking and subtle saucing, the originators of Cuisine Vivante turned to Japan again for further inspiration — and they found it in the Japanese art of *sashimi* (raw fish). The preparation and serving of raw fish was an explicit manifestation of the spirit of Cuisine Vivante, and was quickly assimilated into the new philosophy. Further inspiration came from South America, where the technique of "cooking fish" by the action of lime or lemon juice was discovered. Slivers of fish were marinated in the juice until they turned opaque — a famous and increasingly popular technique known as Ceviche.

Michel Guérard

The development of the "new-style" cuisine continued apace but knowledge of it remained the privilege of a gastronomic élite until Michel Guérard launched his Cuisine Minceur in the mid-1970s. With its abandonment of all fats and its intensive use of ingredients both expensive and rare, it was too extreme to become a way of eating for many, but because it was extreme it attracted enormous publicity. It started a general revival of interest in food and its preparation, and it caught the imagination of chefs and restaurant owners everywhere. Creativity, originality and individuality in the kitchen were suddenly the order of the day. Chefs hit on new combinations of tastes and textures that often surprised, though at first perhaps did not consistently delight, their customers.

As interest grew and the art mellowed, books and articles were produced and knowledge rapidly spread to a much wider audience. This spreading of knowledge in turn helped to consolidate the foundations of Cuisine Vivante, and went some way toward giving it the international "flavor" it now enjoys. Cuisine Vivante is for people who take a serious interest in their food and who regard cooking as an art itself and not just a laborious means to an end. It calls for a meticulous attention to detail at every stage, from shopping to serving, and it is a style of cooking that can transform the quality of any meal, whether it be breakfast or a bedtime snack.

Cooking and serving a Cuisine Vivante meal perfectly requires a considerable amount of time and thought — and it is this careful attention to detail that will show in the dishes placed before the diner. Although there are no set rules for the combination of dishes and ingredients, experiments are only welcome if they are pleasant to eat. The best way to develop the skill of combining flavors is to experiment on yourself on a small scale.

The aims of Cuisine Vivante

A Cuisine Vivante meal aims to stimulate both the eye and the appetite and should ideally include something that is light and airy, something that has a little more substance, something smooth, something crisp, something creamy, something refreshing, something moist and something dry. A variety of tastes, textures and colors that complement and do not swamp one another is most likely to satisfy the diner. This theme should be carried on throughout the meal — that is in adjacent courses as well as within the same course. Sauces, vegetables and garnishes need to be chosen with care to give balance and aid the progression of flavor, and the meal should have its base in the season's best produce.

The worst sin in Cuisine Vivante, as in any other style of cooking, is monotony. No matter how perfectly it is cooked and presented, a menu of sole timbales with white

BELOW Michel and Albert Roux, widely acknowledged today as the leaders of the 'new style' movement. With over 50 years' experience of cooking in grand houses and in the world's top restaurants, the Roux brothers embody the spirit and excitement of Cuisine Vivante.

*Thoughtful yet innovative
presentation is an integral part of
Cuisine Vivante. The quality of
the food is given full expression in
this varied selection of dishes.*

15

wine sauce followed by poached chicken breasts with potato purée and celeriac purée, and a dessert of vanilla bavarois, will be uninspiring and forgettable. It provides no color to excite the eye, no distinct contrast of flavor and a uniform smooth creamy texture broken only by the tender flesh of the poached poultry.

With a little thought, the same main elements of sole, chicken and bavarois could be turned into a memorable gastronomic experience. A watercress or spinach sauce with the sole would add color, a pleasant sharp edge and slightly more body; crisp snow peas and julienne carrots would lift the chicken in color and texture; and the bavarois could be served with a sauce of raspberry coulis, a garnish of fresh fruit and langues de chat, to give brilliant color, juicy freshness and extra bite, and bring the meal to a mouthwatering close.

Balance is perhaps the first consideration in planning a meal, but there are others that should be taken into account. The time of year affects not only the availability of fresh produce, but the heartiness of appetite, which tends to diminish in hot weather. The activities and tastes of your guests need to be borne in mind. If you are planning an evening meal for someone who has sat at a desk all day and eaten a business lunch, it will need to be lighter than one you would set before someone who had spent an energetic day outdoors. First time guests will appreciate being asked whether there are any foods they avoid eating for reasons of taste, diet or religion.

Finally, but most importantly — consider yourself. You will need to calculate shopping and cooking time and choose as many dishes as possible where all or most of the preparation can be done in advance. Dishes like cold terrines and ice cream can be made beforehand and you can also pre-prepare the base for a mousseline or purée, leaving only the final stages and the decoration for the last minute. It is impractical to imagine that you can cook and present a main course for six and six individual plates of vegetables single handed. Unless you have help, keep the last-minute tasks to a minimum and arrange just one large platter of vegetables, making sure that it includes at least one purée that you can prepare in advance.

Organization of equipment plays a major role in the creation of any meal, and is especially vital with a complicated Cuisine Vivante menu. Before you start to cook, have all the ingredients out and weighed and the equipment ready — the ramekin (individual) dishes in the roasting tray, a sheet of waxed paper nearby, and the kettle filled with water to pour into the roasting tray or to blanch vegetables and take the pressure off the oven. Put all you need, including tongs and plastic wrap, out on the work surface or in a handy cupboard if space is short. The moment you have finished with something, clear it away — if you are using the sink, fill a large plastic bucket with hot soapy

For Two People

ASPARAGUS GATEAUX

BREAST OF CHICKEN WITH
LETTUCE SAUCE AND
THYME

STRAWBERRY COOKIE
GATEAUX

For Four People

GINGER AND LIME SHERBET
WITH MELON

SCALLOPS WITH MUSSEL
PARCELS

SLICES OF LAMB WITH
ASPARAGUS

WINE JELLY WITH PEACHES

For Four People

DUO OF BROCCOLI WITH
LEMON SAUCE

PARCELS OF TURBOT WITH
SCALLOPS

STRAWBERRIES AND
ORANGE CREME

For Six People

TRIPLE VEGETABLE
TIMBALES

NOISETTES OF LAMB WITH
TARRAGON

NOUGAT GLACE WITH
PASSIONFRUIT

For Two People

EGGS WITH LETTUCE AND
SORREL AND CHAMPAGNE
SAUCE

STEAK WITH OYSTER AND
MUSHROOM FILLING

BLACKCURRANT RINGS

For Four People

CRAB AND FINE JULIENNE
VEGETABLES SET IN
LIGHT ASPIC

MEDALLIONS OF HARE
WITH BEETS

MANGO SHERBET

For Six People

CHILLED BEET
CONSOMME

MEDALLIONS OF VEAL
WITH ZUCCHINI AND
LEMON

PILLOWS OF FRESH PEAR

For Four People

PEAR VINAIGRETTE WITH
SMOKED SALMON MOUSSE

FILLET OF BEEF WITH
PARSLEY

KIRSCH ICE CREAM IN
COUPELLES

water and stand it in the corner of the kitchen. Clearing clutter and vanquishing chaos eases tension, as well as making valuable space for the plates to be laid out when you come to arranging the food.

Even perfectly cooked food can look unappetizing unless it is presented with neatness and a touch of flair. Choose plain rather than patterned plates, so the eye is not distracted from the food. A sauce slopping clumsily over the edge of a plate is an appetite depressant, as is an overabundance of garnishes. Cuisine Vivante favors understatement — the bunch of watercress gives way to one or two strategically placed leaves.

Garnish is often minimal as the ingredients of the dish themselves are arranged to form an attractive pattern, as in Loin of venison with pears and cranberries (p.295). Complementary vegetables can also be used to decorative effect, eliminating the need for indiscriminate handfuls of parsley that serve no purpose other than to relieve the monotony of the food they conceal. Only use garnishes that are relevant to the food and that are edible. But beware of spending too much time on the finishing touches or the food will be cold before you take it to the table. The most attractive effects can be achieved with the minimum of effort — for example in the judicious placing of a few leaves of herbs on the sauce or around the border of the plate. Cuisine Vivante lends itself to delicacy of presentation because it avoids gargantuan portions, so that the plates don't need to be cluttered with food.

Serving and choosing wines

Serve wines in the logical pattern of light before full-bodied, dry before sweet, young before old and lesser quality before the best, and serve them at the temperature that brings out their particular character. Serve white wines chilled (about 40-50°F/6-10°C). The more full-bodied and better quality wines need less chilling. Red wines should be served at room temperature (60-65°F/16-18°C). There are one or two exceptions to this general rule — for example, a red Loire is more enjoyable served cool. To trap the aroma of the wine, the bowl of the glass should taper gently inwards to the rim. Glasses should be filled to two thirds full and should generally be topped up after half this amount has been drunk.

Choose a wine that complements the food — unless you are serving fine wines of particular note, when the food will be chosen for its restrained elegance, lightness and purity, to complement the wine. A delicate red wine is the ideal partner for a dish of young lamb, and a more full-bodied wine better suits a beef or game dish with a more pronounced character. But complementary does not always mean similar, except in quality. A dish with rich and complex flavors is best set off by a wine of a simpler, more subdued character.

BATTERIE
DE CUISINE

◆ *A good selection of carefully chosen, well made kitchen equipment will bring pleasure as well as efficiency to cooking. Expand your batterie de cuisine as your repertoire grows. When buying equipment a useful rule for the big items is buy the best you can afford. They should last for about 15 years. But when buying small or specialist equipment that may only be used once or twice, be as economical or extravagant as your budget dictates.* ◆

BASICS AND OPTIONAL EXTRAS

For ease of reference the equipment covered in this section has been divided into two groupings — basics and optional extras. The basic kitchen tools used in the preparation of the majority of the recipes in the book are not all vital, and it is perfectly possible to improvise if you don't possess the whole range.

The optional extras are items that make life a great deal easier if your repertoire is more extensive. Even then, they may not all be necessary — if pasta is not something you enjoy, then there is no point in buying a pasta-making machine. Whatever you buy, from a knife to a sorbetière, should be well made and durable.

Knives

A set of good knives can spell the difference between success and failure in the kitchen. The blade of a good quality knife is forged (hammered into shape from hot metal), and not stamped out of a sheet. The blade should be ground all over so that it tapers from the back to the edge and from the handle to the point. It should extend the length of the handle (the extension is called a tang) and be held in place by rivets.

At one time, carbon steel was considered the best material for knife blades because it could be sharpened to a razor-like edge. Unfortunately, it rusts easily and needs care and attention to be kept in good condition. Stainless steel knives, though less demanding, could not be sharpened to a sufficiently sharp edge in the early days, but this drawback has since been overcome and there are now stainless steel knives around that can carry out any chopping or cutting task with proficiency.

Balance and weight are also crucial factors in the selection of kitchen knives. It is impossible to use a knife efficiently if it does not feel right in the hand.

SHARPENING KNIVES

1 Hold the blade at a 30° angle.

2 Draw down to the steel's handle.

There are basically two methods for sharpening knives — a sharpening steel or an oilstone.

To sharpen a knife with a steel, hold the blade at an angle of 30° to the steel (starting at the tip) and draw down to the steel's handle making sure that the whole length of the blade comes into contact. Sharpen both sides of the blade in the same way.

1 Clean the stone with oil.

2 Rub in a circular motion.

To sharpen a knife on an oilstone, first clean and lubricate the stone with cooking oil. Place a cloth under the stone to stop it slipping about. Tilt the blade at a 20° angle to the stone and slowly rub the whole length in a circular motion.

BASIC HAND
UTENSILS
1/2 *Large and small wire*
   whisks
3 *Skimmer*
4 *Ladle*
5 *Fish slice*
6 *Pastry brush*
7 *Measuring spoons*
8 *Knife sharpener*
9 *Small paring knives*

10 *Flexible boning knife*
11 *Flexible filleting knife*
12 *Heavy bladed cook's*
   knife
13/14 *Metal spatulas*
15 *Potato peeler*
16 *Grater*
17 *Lemon squeezer*
18 *Tongs*
19/21 *Wooden spatulas*
20 *Rubber scraper*

BASIC UTENSILS
(above)

1/2 Heavy, flat-bottomed
   sauteuses
3 Chopping board
4 Nonstick frying pan
   with lid
5 Plastic measuring jug
6 Balance scales with
   metric and imperial
   weights
7 Heat resistant mat
8 Liquidizer

BASIC UTENSILS
(right)

1 Mixing bowls
2/3/4 Sieves
5 Colander
6/7/8/9/10 Selection of
   different sized ramekin
   (individual) dishes
11 Roasting pan for cooking
   ramekins
12 Stock pot with lid
13 Large saucepan
14 Bowls

OPTIONAL EXTRAS

1 Steamer
2 Mandolin slicer
3 Tart or cupcake cups
4 Set of aspic cutters
5 Food processor
6 Rolling pin
7 Poultry shears
8 Small mezzaluna and
   bowl

9 Set of plain cutters
10 Flour dredger
11 Meat cleaver
12 Set of dariole molds
13 Baking pan
14 Pasta making machine
15 Canelle knife
16 Zester
17 Melon baller

INGREDIENTS

Quality and freshness are the key words for all Cuisine Vivante ingredients. Even pantry staples, which are not used extensively, should not spend long on the shelves.

When buying fresh ingredients, shop around for the best. Ask for advice and discuss your requirements with the supplier. Don't be afraid to insist on getting what you want. Make a careful selection of fruit and vegetables. If you want the tomatoes from the box on display, don't allow yourself to be served out of a box at the back of the shop you can't see. Ask to inspect the meat that has been cut for you, and if it is not quite right, say so.

VEGETABLES

Vegetables feature prominently in Cuisine Vivante. Their textures and colors make them ideal material for using to decorative effect, and so quality is of paramount importance. Second rate vegetables can ruin a Cuisine Vivante meal.

Spotting top vegetables is not difficult — but tracking them down can cause a problem. Try to be flexible in your choice and pick the vegetables that look the best rather than the ones you had planned to use if these happen to be inferior. Firm tubers, plump juicy tomatoes, crisp hollow peppers, tight headed cauliflower, leafy spinach, should all look fresh, have a good bright color, be unblemished and undamaged. Avoid specimens that are limp or wilting, discolored or damaged and look generally dull and tired.

Flavor is more difficult to determine from appearance than freshness, but the general rule that small equals young, tender and sweet is nearly always a sound one. Buy a vegetable in its natural season and avoid the "forced" varieties. They will almost inevitably be lacking in flavor.

Picture: page 32
1 Pumpkin
2 Leeks
3 Shallots
4 Cherry tomatoes
5 New carrots
with leaves
6 Oyster
mushrooms
7 Butter
mushrooms
8 Asparagus
9 Red pepper
10 Green pepper
11 Potatoes
12 New potatoes
13 Zucchini
with flowers
14 Salsify

Asparagus
There are two main contenders for best asparagus — the fat "whites" and the slim, green variety. Both are delicious, but the tips of the slim green asparagus are better for presentation purposes.

Carrots
Choose slim young ones with their feathery green leaves still intact. They will taste fresher and part of the green stem can be left on to preserve the flavor of the cooked carrot and to make it look more interesting. The leaves can be used separately both for garnishing and for flavor.

Leeks
For flavoring delicate sauces, for garnishing or for serving as a vegetable, use only tender slim leeks. Slightly fatter ones can be used as a flavoring in stocks and more full-bodied meat sauces. Unless specifically called for, remove the green part.

Mushrooms, cultivated
Tiny, tightly closed button mushrooms are useful for garnishing, either sliced or turned, but are very mild in flavor. Flat or open mushrooms have more flavor, but they darken when cooked and give off quite a lot of dark juice. They can be used instead of wild mushrooms when these are not available.

Mushrooms, wild
With the exception of morels, wild mushrooms are one of the treats of autumn. Morels show due consideration and come out in the spring. Very few people pick their own wild mushrooms but rely on specialist vegetable stores and some of the better supermarkets.

Ceps vary in size. They have a strong brown cap and a thick stem. They do not collapse to the same extent as other mushrooms when cooked. They have a meaty flavor and a meaty texture.

Chanterelles or girolles are bright yellow trumpet-shaped mushrooms with a smell that has a hint of apricots to it and a fine delicate flavor. Their slightly chewy texture easily becomes tough if they are not cooked with care.

Morels have caps that look rather like sponges — they are covered with holes. Because of this particular care is needed when cleaning these delicious mushrooms to make sure all the grit is removed.

All these mushrooms are available dried. They must be soaked before they are used and will usually have a stronger but less fresh flavor and a more chewy texture.

Potatoes
Potatoes can be chosen intelligently so that their variety is best suited to the dish you intend to make. More and more stores are marking potatoes with their name, if not their use, so choosing the most appropriate type is now at least a little easier. For purées choose white potatoes, for potato baskets choose Idaho potatoes.

Salsify
Buy salsify and its close cousin scorzonera whenever you can.

They have a delicious delicate flavor and it is always nice to serve something a little different. Both are long slim roots, salsify having a white skin, scorzonera a black one.

Shallots

If you have ever thought that to use shallots rather than onions was merely an extravagance, prepare two simple sauces, one using shallots, the other using onions. Now taste. Shallots will have imparted a sweet delicate flavor, where onions are heavy and dominant. Shallots must always be cooked gently as browning makes them slightly bitter.

Tomatoes

Whenever tomatoes are to be puréed or used in a sauce, make sure that they have plenty of juicy flesh and few seeds and, most importantly, have been basking in the sun. Merely selecting a type that is traditionally grown in the sun is not enough.

Turnips

Avoid the cannonball size, harsh-flavored variety that smacks of institutional cooking in favor of the glowingly white, sweet flavored baby "navets" that appear on spring and early summer tables as "primeurs". As with baby carrots, buy the ones that still have their tops intact.

SALAD LEAVES

The most delicately flavored and textured salad leaves are those that are picked when young. As they grow older they increase in coarseness, their flavor becomes harsher and any tendency towards bitterness more pronounced. With their increase in popularity, many varities are being cultivated under glass. This has the advantage of increasing the yield and extending the natural season, but the disadvantage of producing plants that lack the character of young specimens grown outside.

Picture: page 33
1 Round lettuce
2 Watercress
3 Radicchio
4 Mignonette lettuce
5 Romaine lettuce
6 Belgium endive
7 Corn salad (Field salad)
8 Curly endive (Chicory)
9 Iceberg lettuce

Escarole

Sometimes called batavian endive, this has broader leaves than curly endive. The edges of the leaves have varying degrees of curl to them but they are never as crinkly as those of the curly leaved variety. It has quite a substantial texture with a mild bitterness and a slight pungency. Available in winter.

Chicory

Chicory is also called French endive, and witloof in France. It has blanched white tightly packed cigar-shaped leaves that should be pearly and translucent. The bitter note that is a characteristic of the flavor of chicory is at its finest and most delicate in small leaves. Chicory is available from autumn through to spring.

Corn salad

This is also known as field salad, lamb's lettuce, or mâche in France. It has elongated slightly spoon-shaped leaves that are soft rather than crisp and have a slightly velvety feel to them. They do not form a heart. Corn salad should have a subtle, bitter, earthy flavor. Found growing wild, they are available from late autumn, through winter to the early months of spring.

Romaine or Cos lettuce

This type has long, coarse, crisp leaves with a slightly more pronounced flavor that is sometimes described as nutty.

Curly-leaved endive

This is also called chicory, and chicorée frisée in France. It has a mop of frizzy, crinkly leaves. The outer ones are bright green and the inner ones are almost white.

Iceberg lettuce

The tight, light green compact head of this crisp lettuce is best for cooking as it retains its texture. Available all year round.

Radicchio

This is really a red chicory. The leaves are dark red or maroon in colour or streaky with red and cream. The heads are the same shape as ordinary chicory or they may fall more openly. Available from autumn through to spring.

Round lettuce

Also known as butterhead, Boston or Bibb lettuce, it has soft coarse loose leaves and a mild flavor. Available nearly all the year round.

Watercress

Cuisine Vivante has brought new life to watercress. No longer merely a minor salad vegetable or useful greenery for garnishing, watercress is puréed to add color, texture and a pleasant, slightly piquant flavor to sauces and stuffings and the leaves are used individually to add a simple touch of color.

HERBS

Herbs are one of nature's flavorings and therefore have an important role to play in Cuisine Vivante. But they are used with discretion and not allowed to become too dominating. Even when a herb is the main flavor in a sauce, such as the basil sauce with the medallions of rabbit, its use is carefully regulated. Its character shows, but with subtlety.

Successful traditional combinations, such as mint with lamb, are regarded with respect by Cuisine Vivante, but treated to a fresh approach. Instead of being added to a sharp vinegar dressing (a killer for any wine), the mint appears as an attractive highlight in a warm velvety sauce. Cuisine Vivante cooks are constantly developing original and perhaps surprising combinations of herbs with meat or fish, such as Duck breasts with tarragon sauce (p.268).

There is no comparison between the flavor of dried and fresh herbs. For the very best results, pick small tender sprigs early in the morning after they have spent a brief life basking in warm sunshine with just the right amount of water. Grow them yourself in the garden, a window box or a pot behind a sunny window, but don't pick them while they are hot from the sun. Failing this, buy from a supplier who has a good turnover. Even fresh herbs lose their flavor after a few days. Once picked or bought, keep the herbs cool and moist. Larger sprigs can be placed in a container of cold water, small sprigs and leaves placed between sheets of damp paper towels inside a plastic bag and stored in the salad crisper of the refrigerator.

BELOW *Frozen herbs should normally be finely chopped before freezing. However, if the stems are also required they may be left whole.*

Fresh herbs can be dried at home, but they cannot be dried successfully. A more successful way of preserving them is by freezing. Chop the herb finely, spread it out on a tray, quickly open-freeze, then wrap in plastic bags.

Quantities of herbs specified in recipes can only be approximate because even fresh herbs can vary in the intensity of their flavor. Tasting just before serving is therefore vital.

Picture: page 36/7
1 Mint
2 Rosemary
3 Sage
4 Parsley
5 Bay leaf
6 Summer savory
7 Basil
8 Fennel
9 Lemon thyme
10 Lemon verbena
11 Marjoram
12 Tarragon
13 Chervil
14 Dill
15 Chive with flowers

Basil
The shiny green leaves of basil have a slightly clove-like, warmly pungent flavor. Pick when young and handle gently as the tender leaves bruise and discolor easily. For this reason the leaves should be torn rather than chopped.

Bay
The sweet, resinous, warm and spicy flavor of bay is an indispensable part of a bouquet garni.

Bouquet garni
A bouquet garni is a number of herbs tied together in a bundle in a small cheesecloth parcel with a string attached so that they can be removed easily at the end of cooking. It is used in soups and stocks to give an all around flavor. The traditional herbs in a bouquet garni are parsley, bay and thyme, but they can be varied according to the dish being cooked, eg a sprig of rosemary can be added if the stock is to be used for a lamb dish.

Chervil
The delicate flavour of chervil with its hint of aniseed is so subtle that it has to be used in fairly large amounts. The feathery leaves are popular for garnishing as they look attractive yet do not upset the balance of flavoring within the dish.

Chives
Only the most slender, tender green leaves should be used for a flavor that is mild and delicate with just a suggestion of onion.

Dill
Feathery dill leaves impart an aromatic, slightly sharp yet sweet flavor that has a particular affinity with fish.

Fennel
Sweet herb fennel should not be confused with the bulbous vegetable, Florence fennel. The feathery leaves look very much like dill leaves but have a totally different flavor, having a sweet aniseed note to them. But like dill, fennel goes well with fish.

Mint
Unless the type of mint is specified in a recipe, such as apple mint, use the type that grows so profusely and completely unaided in many gardens. This is spearmint. Use it judiciously as it can be all-pervading.

Parsley
Parsley is the best known herb and the most adaptable. The flat leaved variety has a finer, more pronounced flavor that stands up to cooking in stocks better than the curly leaved type. Use only the leaves to garnish a dish. Keep the stalks for flavoring.

Rosemary
The sweet, spicy flavor of rosemary has an intensity that can be overpowering if it is not used with care. The spiky leaves are much tougher than those of other herbs and must be chopped very finely.

Sage
Use only young, small tender sage leaves, as the fragrant, aromatic flavor becomes more harsh and dominating in larger, older leaves.

Summer savory
Summer savory has a smell that is redolent of thyme but it has its own particular mild aromatic flavor with a pleasant hint of bitterness.

Sweet marjoram
Sweet marjoram (not pot or wild marjoram) is used for its pungent, yet mild, warm, sweet flavor.

Tarragon
The variety with the familiar warm, sweet, vanilla-aniseed flavor is French tarragon. Russian tarragon is altogether different and is dull and disappointing in comparison.

Thyme
The tiny leaves of thyme have a fairly strong, warm, sweet flowery earthy flavor and smell that stands up well in the cooking of stocks.

FRUIT

The affinity of some fruits with some savory foods has long been exploited, both in classical haute cuisine and traditional country cooking. But fruits are used more frequently in Cuisine Vivante than in either of these. Fortunately the initial craze for using fruit with almost anything with seemingly little regard for what a dish was actually like to eat has died away and given way to more thoughtful, and consequently more enjoyable, combinations. A fruit is used when it contributes something — a pleasant contrast of color or flavor, whether it is a juicy sweetness, a tang or a sharpness.

And, of course, fruits are vital in Cuisine Vivante desserts. Simply puréed or sieved they provide sauces that are light, fresh, clean and delicate. They form the basis for ice creams, sherbets and mousses and the filling for pastries. There is now a very wide variety of fruits quite readily available at every season of the year. This is not always a good thing. Strawberries, for instance, are delicious when opened naturally by a warm summer sun, but tasteless in winter when forced by a grower. Many other fruits suffer from not being enjoyed where they are produced. A lemon straight from a tree has a rich, warm, full, tangy aroma and flavor undetectable in a lemon bought in a store hundreds of miles away. Though it is not always desirable to limit your purchases to local fruit or fruit in season, it is best to buy from what is plentiful, as it is then less likely to be an exclusive, out of season crop.

The condition and quality of fruit is easy to assess. There should be no blemishes, it should be undamaged, have a bright clear color and feel heavy for its size.

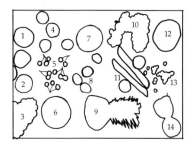

Picture: page 40/1
1 Red apple
2 Golden Delicious and Granny Smith apples
3 Black grapes
4 Limes
5 Cherries
6 Small melon
7 Charantais melon
8 Passionfruit
9 Pineapple
10 Seedless white grapes
11 Rhubarb and apricots
12 Mango
13 Cranberries
14 Pears

Apples
A common enough fruit but of the dessert varieties, pick yellow and red Delicious and Newtown Pippin for the best flavor; of the cooking apples, the choice lies with Northern Spy, Russet, and Greening.

Apricots
A great deal of care is required when buying apricots as all too often the fruit that is offered for sale is hard, dry and lacking in flavor. Apricots should be picked when they have just reached their optimum ripeness. However, at this point they are very fragile and do not travel well, and are consequently harvested when immature.

Depth of color is not necessarily a sign of ripeness as some varieties are always pale skinned. There should not, however, be any tint of green in the color. The fruit should feel heavy for its size, yield slightly to light pressure in the palm of the hand and have a faint, warm, fruity smell. If in any doubt, buy the smallest quantity you can and taste one before buying the full amount required.

Cherries
Cherries are available in a variety of colors, so bear in mind the color of the dish in which they are to be used and select those that will look most effective. However, do not use dark Morello or Montmorency cherries unless they are specifically called for since they have a sour taste.

Cranberries

A small fruit, cranberries have a lustrous skin which varies in color from pink to dark red. The berries have a sharp, slightly bitter flavor and should be firm and smooth. Cranberries are one of the very few fruits that it is worthwhile buying frozen.

Figs

These squat pear shaped fruits are soft to the touch when ripe, and the skin, which is either white, red or purple, has a bloom to it. The juicy pulp is sweet, deep red and heavily seeded.

Grapes

Whenever possible buy grapes in bunches and be sure to avoid any with shrivelled, split or squashed berries, or those which show mold near the stems. The juicy, thin-skinned grapes most widely used in Cuisine Vivante recipes should have a distinct bloom to them.

Kumquats

The sweet/sharp flavor of this small (½-2 in/4-5 cm long) fruit combines well with both sweet and savory dishes, and its bright orange flesh and skin add a splash of color.

The skin is very thin and does not need to be removed before the fruit is eaten as it has a delicious sweet, slightly aromatic flavor.

Mangos

Mangos have the reputation of being the most delicious of fruits. There are several different types of mango with different colored skins, coming from different parts of the world. They may be green, deep yellow, red or dappled.

Melons

When buying melons always touch them to check for ripeness; a ripe melon should yield to gentle pressure applied at the stalk end.

Ogen melons have a yellow/orange skin with faint green stripes. The sweet and juicy flesh is pale yellow.

Charentais melons are small and perfectly round. The skin is yellow/green and slightly rough. The deep orange flesh is faintly scented.

Passionfruit

The skin of this vine fruit should be hard and wrinkled — the wrinkles are a sign of ripeness. The seeds of the passionfruit and the pomegranate are eaten, but those of the pawpaw (papaya) are not.

Pears

Pears, like apples, are divided into dessert and cooking varieties. They are easily bruised and should be treated very gently. Ideally pears should be purchased before they are fully ripe and should be kept in a warm cupboard for 2-3 days. To test for ripeness gently squeeze the stalk end to see if it yields.

Of the dessert varieties Bartletts, Seckels, Anjous and Boscs are probably the best.

Pineapple

Smell a pineapple to judge if it is ripe — if it smells warm, fragrant and fruity it will be ready to eat.

Pineapples are one of the few fresh products that can be bought a day or so in advance as they will safely continue to mature. Generally speaking a pineapple that feels heavy will be the most succulent, and likewise one that is small will generally have the sweetest flavor and the most tender flesh.

Rhubarb

Select slim, pink, crsip sticks of rhubarb as these will have a delicate flavor and flesh that almost smells when cooked. Large sticks tend to have an acidic taste and flesh that is coarse, watery and fibrous.

Strawberries

Although strawberries are available at unusual times of the year, they are best avoided. Likewise strawberries picked at the very beginning of the season should be avoided if possible, since they will not have had sufficient sunshine in which to develop their true flavor.

Choose from fruit that has a bright, clear, uniform color — depth of color is not necessarily an indication of depth of flavor — and that is firm and unblemished with the hulls still intact. Strawberries are extremely perishable and should only be bought from a supplier who keeps them in a cool place away from stong light. Try to buy as near as possible to the time they are to be used and keep them in a cool place after purchase. Remove the hulls at the last moment and avoid washing if possible; wipe it very carefully with a damp cloth.

FISH

Shopping around for fish is a luxury few of us can indulge in. In some areas just finding one fishmonger is enough of a problem. Whether he is good or bad, encourage him, and query poor quality politely. Talk to him about the more unusual varieties, especially if he does not stock them, and keep asking when he is likely to get them.

The first consideration in selecting fish is freshness. Whole fish should be stiff but not frozen rigid, the skin bright and shining with scales that are close together and lying flat against the body. The gills should be hard to open and their insides should have a clear pink-red colour. The eyes should be full and bright with black pupils and transparent corneas. When buying pieces of fish look for flesh with a pearly translucency that doesn't show any signs of milkiness.

Picture: page 44
1 Red fleshed trout
2 Brill
3 Pike
4 Wild salmon

Carp
There are many cousins of carp but the one that is generally considered to have the finest flavor and texture is the true French daurade.

Monkfish (lotte; baudroie)
This is a very ugly fish. It has a large head and a tail that provides firm very white flesh with a texture and taste often considered to be more like lobster than a white fish. Monkfish has a sufficiently good flavor and texture to be judged on its own merits. To see it merely as a substitute for lobster is to do it an injustice.

Pike (brochet)
Pike appears most frequently in Cuisine Vivante as an ingredient in recipes for quenelles, as the flesh has a gelatinous quality that helps to bind the mixture together without making it heavy.

Pickerel
Pickerel has quite a dry flesh, making sautéeing or marinating the best choice for preparation.

Salmon (saumon)
The best salmon is wild salmon from Scotland, and should be cooked quite simply. Less delicate farmed salmon is also delicious poached in a well-flavoured court bouillon.

Salmon trout (fruite de mer)
As the name suggests, this fish combines the characteristics of the salmon with those of the trout. The flesh has the fine flavour and the pale pink colour of salmon, but it is softer and more succulent.

Sea bass (loup de mer; bar)
As with carp the name bass encompasses a number of different fish but the one to use in the context of Cuisine Vivante is the common sea bass.

Sole (sole)
Dover sole has a subtle flavor and beautiful firm white flesh. The light cooking and delicate light sauces placed under the fish in Cuisine Vivante recipes enhance its fine flavor and texture.

Trout (truite)
Rainbow trout is readily available. Brook or lake trout is almost exclusively the prerogative of fly-fishermen. Many rainbow trout on sale are farmed, but it is still important to buy only from suppliers who are known to take particular care over their stock as their flesh easily becomes tainted if the fish feeds off strange-tasting, stagnant or muddy matter.

Turbot (turbot)
The flesh of these large flat fish is creamy white and well flavored. It is delicate yet firm, one of the more substantial fish.

SHELLFISH

Whereas fish should look as if they are almost alive when they are bought, crustaceans (lobster, crab, prawns, crayfish etc) should actually be alive if at all practical and possible, as they deteriorate very quickly. Live shellfish should be animated and should feel heavy in relation to their size.

Molluscs (oysters, clams, mussels etc) must be alive when they are bought, and any specimens that are open should not be bought at all.

Picture: page 45
1 Clams
2 Crab
3 Scallops
4 Lobster
5 Mussels
6 Fine oysters
7 Pacific oysters

CRUSTACEANS

Crab (crabe)
The male crab is generally considered to be the better buy as it contains a higher proportion of white meat. But, like the hen lobster, when female crabs are in season they will provide coral. To distinguish between the sexes, look at the tail flap on the underside — the male's is smaller than the female's.

Crawfish (langouste)
These are lobster-like creatures, but with small claws. There are also some other differences. When live, crawfish are reddish, lobsters dark bluish. When cooked, crawfish are a less brilliant color than the lobster.

Crayfish (écrevisse)
These look rather like miniature lobsters. They are very good for eating on their own — they have delicate, sweet flesh — and also provide a useful and popular garnish for many other fish dishes.

Dublin Bay Prawn (langoustine)
The tails of these miniature lobster-like creatures, also known as Norway lobsters, provide the ubiquitous frozen scampi. But don't let that put you off buying fresh langoustines, as they can be one of the most delicious of seafoods.

MOLLUSCS

Clams (praires)
Open them in the same way as oysters. Remove and discard the black intestinal tube and keep the liquor for fish stock and sauces. Clams are available all the year round but are best during the summer months.

Mussels (moules)
Mussels are available from the fall through to the spring but they are at their best during the winter.

Oysters (huîtres)
Oysters are available all the year round. Those at lower prices do not have the fine flavor and texture of their more costly cousins. The different varieties are distinguished by their shells. Which size oyster to buy depends on how prominent they are in a dish. Oysters have extremely delicate flesh so any cooking must be kept to an absolute minimum.

Scallops (coquilles Saint-Jacques)
Scallops are frequently used in Cuisine Vivante dishes because both the delicate bright white body and the tender brilliant orange coral are delicious to eat and attractive to look at. In theory scallops should be available all the year, but supplies can be erratic as they are affected by the weather. Scallops are opened in the same way as oysters. Once opened, remove and discard the fringe and black intestinal thread, then gently lift the flesh from the shell with a rounded soup spoon. The flesh is almost as delicate and fragile as that of an oyster, so must be cooked with the same degree of respect. The coral cooks more quickly than the body, so the two are often separated.

POULTRY AND GAME

"Poultry" is the term used for birds that are bred in captivity for the table. Poultry can be bought from a poultry farm and game dealer, a market stall or a supermarket. From all but the last outlet fresh poultry, especially chicken, may be on sale resplendent in its feathers and undrawn, although the plucking and drawing should be done for you if you ask. A good supplier will automatically include the giblets with the drawn bird.

"Game" is the term used for wild animals and birds that are hunted for food. The majority of game are protected by law and can only be hunted during an "open" season. This period varies from species to species and from country to country. But most people's source of game is not the shoot but the game dealer. If you are lucky, your butcher may also be a game dealer. A reliable supplier is as vital for game as for ordinary meat. The critical points that can make or mar a game dish are the age of the bird or animal and the length of hanging. Only the flesh from young animals is suitable for Cuisine Vivante recipes, as older animals need longer and slower cooking. However, they should not be too young as their flesh would not have had a chance to develop any character.

The game dealer will tell you how long the game has been hung. If you order game in advance he should hang it for you in just the right conditions — if you live in a heated apartment you will not have anywhere suitable at home — and for the length of time you specify. After hanging he will also skin or pluck and draw for you, possibly for a small fee.

Picture: page 48/9
1 Mallard
2 Teal
3 Hare
4 Wood pigeon
5 Red-legged
partridge
6 Cock pheasant
7 Quails

POULTRY

Chicken

Fresh whole chickens and chicken portions are very popular. But "fresh" does not necessarily mean that the bird has spent its life ranging free and searching for its own food and therefore has superior flavor. "Fresh" may simply mean that the bird has come direct to the supplier from a battery farm. Nevertheless, it should still be more tasty than its frozen cousins because its flavor will be unimpaired by the freezing process — indeed it will have been given a boost by hanging.

Tasty, yellow fleshed corn-fed chickens are becoming easier to find.

With the exception of poussins (young birds weighing only about 1-1½ lb/450-700 g) only the breasts of the bird are popularly used in Cuisine Vivante and although these can be bought as portions, buy whole birds whenever possible and remove the breasts yourself. The legs can be used in more everyday cooking whilst the carcasses will be the foundations of a stock.

Duck

Like chicken, fresh duck is beginning to make a comeback, though, as with chicken, "fresh" does not necessarily mean free range. Again, it is possible to buy the breasts separately, but it makes more sense to buy a whole bird.

Some duck breasts come from specially fattened ducks and are firmer, more meaty and tasty and will have a layer of fat between the skin and flesh.

The ratio of flesh to carcass on some ducks is low, so the best buy is not the smallest and youngest. For a reasonable portion of meat buy a duck weighing about 4 lb/2 kg.

Guinea fowl

These are a relative of the pheasant and at one time were classed as game. But now, with very few exceptions, all the birds offered for sale have been specially reared for the table and are considered as poultry.

Guinea fowl are about the size of a pheasant or a small chicken and may be hung for 2-3 days so that they develop a flavor that is a cross between the two.

GAME

Grouse

Grouse should be eaten in the year of their birth. Young grouse have soft, downy feathers on the breast and under the wings. The outermost large flight feathers should have pointed tips. Hang young grouse for 3-4 days.

Hare

Young hare of under a year is easy to recognise as it will have a white belly, pliable ears that split easily, a very small hare lip and short claws. Hare and rabbit should be hung by the feet of their hind legs (birds are hung by their necks) so that the blood will drain away from the intestinal areas of the body and escape through the mouth. Only the saddle, divided into its two fillets, is used in Cuisine Vivante. It may be sliced along its length or cut into round medallions. Hang for about 3 days.

Partridge

A bird of about 14oz/400g in weight should give the right balance of tenderness and flavor. As with pheasant, look for plump breasts, which provide the majority of the flesh of a partridge, supple skin and smooth, securely attached feathers. The legs of a young partridge will have a yellowish color, becoming slate grey with age, and the outermost large flight feathers will have pointed tips. Hang young partridge for about 4 days.

Pheasant

The male (cock) pheasant steals the show for looks when alive but it is the female (hen) who makes the best eating. She will generally be more plump, succulent and tender. Young birds will have smooth, pliable feet and light plumage, the first wing tip feather will be pointed (it is rounded in an older one) and the spurs of a young cock will be short and rounded. Also look for plump firm breasts, supple skin and smooth, securely attached feathers. Hang young pheasant for about 5-6 days.

Pigeon

Wild pigeon are at their best during the summer months when they are feeding on young shoots and leaves. These wild birds have a darker flesh with a more "gamey" flavor than birds that are bred for the table. They will become tough with age, so it really is important to select young birds if serving wild pigeon, although in Cuisine Vivante only the more tender breast meat is used. If you prefer or if the other flavors in a recipe dictate, use a mellow flavored bred bird instead of a wild one. If you have the chance, opt for a corn-fed pigeon, which is tender, with a delicate yet distinctive flavor.

Quail (also woodcock, plover and snipe)

Choose fresh birds with plump breasts and a pliable skin that shows no signs of dryness. Quail have a delicate flavor and are not hung before being eaten.

Rabbit

The flesh of an animal that has frolicked in the fields will have more color and flavor than a cosseted creature. If you have the choice, which to select is really a matter of taste, but always look for the same signs of youth as in a young hare. A wild rabbit will benefit from a short hanging.

Just the fillets from the saddle are used in Cuisine Vivante. This has a similarity to chicken, but is less dry with a slightly more distinctive flavor.

Venison

Venison is now widely available in the shops as attempts to farm it commercially are showing dividends.

The prime cuts are the fillets from the saddle and the loin. The flesh from the small roe deer is generally considered to be finer than that of the large red deer, but any good quality venison should be a rich dark red and finely grained. The male (buck) is better for eating than the female. Both are at their best when between 18-24 months of age. Hang venison for about a week.

Wild duck

There are several species of wild duck — small teal, slightly larger widgeon and the largest, most commonly used, mallard.

MEAT AND OFFAL

A good butcher or meat department who can be relied on to sell only top quality meat is vital. Undue amounts of fat and gristle are immediately visible, but toughness and flavor, or the lack of it, are a different matter. A sauce may be sublime, but if the meat with which it is served requires more than a moment or two's chewing and tastes of nothing, the whole dish will be doomed to failure.

Given the Cuisine Vivante treatment, offal — liver, kidneys and sweetbreads — provides some of the most delicate, succulent and appetising of dishes. To make good enjoyable eating it really must be fresh and it must be cooked lightly. Overcooking is often responsible for the ruination of offal.

Picture: page 52
1 *Veal steak*
2 *Veal kidneys*
3 *Pork fillet*
4 *Beef fillet*
5 *Calves liver*
6 *Sweetbread*
7 *Rack of lamb*

Beef
Hereford and Aberdeen Angus are highly prized for the quality of their flesh. The flesh of good quality beef has a fine grain and appears moist but not wet. When freshly cut, the color will be bright red, but it becomes dark red, even brownish after several hours. Avoid meat that shows any sign of dryness. The fat should be firm, fresh looking and yellow, but the shade of yellow depends on the diet of the animal. Grass produces a deeper yellow fat than barley.

Kidneys
Although larger than other kidneys, veal kidneys are the most tender and delicate. They are not kidney shaped, but have a unique shape and structure consisting of many small segments joined to a central core. Lambs kidneys weigh only 1-2 oz/25-50 g each. Soaking in milk for an hour or so helps to remove the blood. After soaking, rinse and dry the kidneys thoroughly.

Lamb
The most meltingly tender, delicately flavored lamb comes from milk fed animals, but they are only available during the early spring months. As the year progresses and the animals become larger, their flesh will gain flavor and color but it will also get tougher. The late spring and early summer are considered to be the time of year for the optimum balance between flavor and tenderness.

Because of these differences, the method of cooking the lamb and the flavor of the sauce must be chosen carefully if a dish is to work successfully as a whole.

The most frequently used cuts are loin, which is usually rolled and boned, best end of neck and fillets cut from the saddle. Noisettes are cut from the boned and rolled best end of neck. Medallions are cut from a boned best end of neck. The fat is trimmed off, the meat is rolled up firmly with the eye inside and tied in shape with string. The size of the cuts and the number they serve change noticeably throughout the year.

Liver
Calves liver is the finest of all. It has an excellent flavor, a smooth texture and is exceptionally tender. However, it is always expensive and not always available. More accessible is lambs liver. Its more pronounced flavor can be complemented by a fuller flavored sauce.

Sweetbreads
Calves sweetbreads, and in particular those from milk fed veal, are the sweetbreads to choose for the finest flavor and texture. To get fresh sweetbreads it is usually necessary to order them in advance from the butcher, who will probably sell them in pairs rather than by weight. Allow one pair per person. When they arrive they should be pale, creamy, moist and plump. Frozen sweetbreads are sold in pre-weighed packs, usually of 8oz/ 225g, by some supermarkets.

Soak sweetbreads in frequent changes of cold water to remove all traces of blood, then blanch them in water acidulated with lemon juice to keep them white, enabling the covering membrane and pieces of gristle to be removed easily. After cooking, they should be pressed to help them to keep their shape.

Veal
Milk fed veal from calves slaughtered when they are between 8 and 12 weeks is preferred by Cuisine Vivante chefs. The flesh of tender milk fed veal is a pale pearly pink, whereas the flesh of older, more highly flavored and slightly tougher veal is a darker pink. All veal flesh should be firm and moist, though not wet, and the bones should be bright and translucent.

The cuts that are used are the loin and the fillet. Medallions are cut from the fillet. They should be about 1 in/2.5 cm thick, trimmed and tied into neat round shapes. Escalopes are cut across the grain and come from the top of the leg. They are generally beaten firmly, but not heavily, between two sheets of plastic wrap to flatten them to about ¼ in/6 mm, then trimmed to a neat shape.

MISCELLANEOUS

Picture: page 53
  (top)
1 Fine olive oil
2 Virgin olive oil
3 Sunflower seed
  oil
4 Walnut oil
5 Hazelnut oil

(bottom)
1 White wine
  vinegar
2 Pure red wine
  vinegar
3 Rosemary
  vinegar
4 Lemon wine
  vinegar
5 Raspberry
  vinegar
6 Tarragon
  vinegar

Butter
The butter used in Cuisine Vivante is always sweet. This is partly because it allows for more control over the amount of salt used in a dish, but more importantly for reasons of quality. Only the best quality butter is left unsalted. It will usually taste fresher than salted butter and have a sweeter, more delicate flavor.

Caul
Caul is a lace-like membrane that is wrapped around foods when they are cooked for two reasons. It holds ingredients together which might otherwise disintegrate during cooking and keeps them moist by protecting them from the heat and gently basting them. If it does not melt away during cooking once it has served its purpose, it can be peeled off easily before the food is served. Caul can be ordered from good butchers.

Crème fraîche
Crème fraîche, with its light texture and slightly acidic flavor, gives delicious, fresh tasting results. Many supermarkets and smaller specialist food stores now sell crème fraîche but if you are unable to buy it, a reasonable imitation is easy to make. Blend heavy cream with twice the amount of sour cream or full fat plain yogurt. Heat the mixture gently to 90°C, pour into a container, cover and keep in a warm place (about 75°C) overnight. Stir, then keep in the refrigerator.

Oils
Sunflower oil can be used to sauté ingredients for particularly light, delicately flavored dishes, and it may also be blended with olive oil to produce a salad dressing with a slightly less characteristic flavor.

Olive oil should be your first choice for all fine cooking but it is important to select the right grade of oil for the particular task in hand. The lighter, mildly flavored, less expensive grades are suitable for the majority of Cuisine Vivante recipes but for salad dressings use the rich, green virgin oil from the first pressings of the olives. The very best of these come from Provence and Tuscany — those from Provence have a slightly fruity flavor, while those from Tuscany have a slightly nutty note.

The use of nut oils such as walnut and hazelnut can add an interesting dimension to salads. For a subtle effect they may be blended with a little olive or sunflower oil.

Peppercorns
Buy in quantities that you will use up fairly quickly and grind freshly each time you require pepper as it does lose its strength. Black pepper is more often used because it has a finer, more aromatic flavor than white, which is hotter. White pepper is preferred when specks of black would spoil the appearance of a dish.

Green peppercorns, which are unripe berries, can occasionally be bought fresh, but are more usually sold in cans or bottles in brine. They must be rinsed before they are used. Green peppercorns are crisp and tender with a mild flavor.

Pink peppercorns come from a plant of a different species. They are soft with a surprisingly subtle flavor that lacks the hotness or spiciness of pepper. Pink peppercorns imported from Madagascar are generally considered the best.

Vinegars
Different flavored vinegars have joined the ranks of sherry vinegar, red and white wine vinegars, cider vinegar and tarragon vinegar in the preparation of a number of sauces for meats and fish as well as salads. The most notable are the fruit vinegars, especially raspberry, but there are other herb ones as well. These can easily be prepared at home by steeping the required herb in a good quality white wine vinegar for about two weeks.

Wild rice
Wild rice is not actually a rice but a grass with a deliciously distinctive flavor that to some people is reminiscent of nuts. It is expensive, but well worth using for the right dish on the right occasion. To make the wild rice go a little further mix it with a little brown rice cooked separately. Wild rice is available from delicatessens, specialist food stores and good supermarkets.

Wines, spirits, eau-de-vie
When choosing a wine for cooking, select one that you would be more than happy to drink. A thin acidic wine cannot produce a rounded, well flavored sauce. It is for this reason that medium bodied white wine is frequently specified in the recipes. Too many wines from the lower end of the price scale are too light and unbalanced to withstand boiling down satisfactorily. The same applies to vermouth — do not shop around for the cheapest you can find, but look for flavor and body.

Cognac is usually specified rather than brandy, because not only does this guarantee a certain level of quality, but also a certain type of flavor. There are other brandies of equal quality, but they often have different, individual flavors.

When "Framboise" or "Fraise" are called for, this means the dry, colorless, eau-de-vie — not the sweet, colored liqueur.

TECHNIQUES AND BASIC PREPARATIONS

◆ *The techniques and basic preparations of Cuisine Vivante are not overly complicated, but it is important that they are carried out correctly. The following section details the methods of preparation and cooking that characterize Cuisine Vivante and that are designed with one aim in mind — to preserve and give expression to the quality, flavor and freshness of the food. In addition, recipes are given for the most commonly used basic preparations referred to throughout the main recipe section.* ◆

BASIC PRINCIPLES

◆ The overriding objective when preparing and cooking foods for Cuisine Vivante is always the preservation of the quality and natural flavor and freshness of the food.

◆ The preparation of all ingredients is left to the last possible moment.

◆ All equipment for cutting is sharp.

◆ Meat, if kept temporarily in the refrigerator, is transferred to room temperature about half an hour before cooking.

◆ Nothing is cooked until the last possible moment.

◆ Cooking is light and quick.

◆ A fish slice, spatula or tongs are used to turn or lift meat during and after cooking to avoid piercing the surface and allowing the juices to escape.

◆ Food is served as soon as it is ready.

MEAT, POULTRY AND GAME

With meats, poultry and game the aim is to cook them so they remain moist and, generally, pink in the center. The exceptions are pork and sweetbreads, but this certainly does not mean they should be overcooked, especially in the case of sweetbreads. The source of heat must be preheated and it must be high and the cooking must be brief. The methods favored are roasting and steaming, sautéeing or frying. If a meat is to be cut before it is served it must be left to rest for 10-15 minutes to allow it to settle and the juices to run evenly throughout the meat. In the majority of dishes the meat will be resting while the sauce is prepared. Cut meat cools very quickly, so to keep it warm while the plates are prepared with the sauce and garnish, the slices are put back together and covered with plastic wrap.

Roasting
The meat is usually cooked very briefly on either side, often in a little fat in a hot pan to sear the outside and keep the flesh moist by sealing in the juices before it is put into the hot oven. Leaving the flesh on the bone also helps to keep it moist or, as in the case of veal, it may be cooked in a heavy casserole dish that the piece of meat just fits. Meats that have a tendency to dryness, such as game, can be covered with waxed paper during cooking.

Steaming
This gentle method of cooking is sometimes used for small pieces of meat that are very lean, tender and delicately flavored, such as baby lamb and chicken breasts. The water in the steamer must be boiling so that the meat immediately comes into contact with a high temperature and a steady stream of steam should be maintained throughout the cooking. Mild flavorings such as herbs can be added to the water, or stock can be used instead to give a nuance of flavor to the flesh. The liquid may then be used in the making of the sauce that is served with the meat.

Sautéeing or frying
This is the method most frequently used for cooking meat, poultry and game. Make sure the meat is completely dry, at room temperature, and use a heavy based, flat bottomed pan that the meat will just fit in a single layer. Melt the butter, but do not allow it to get too hot otherwise it will burn. Add the meat, skin side down if it has a skin, and cook it quickly until set and golden brown on the underside, shaking the pan occasionally. Turn the meat over and cook the other side in a similar way. The smaller, thinner or more delicate the cut, the shorter the cooking should be and the closer it should be watched. Small, very delicate pieces, such as diced sweetbreads, kidneys and liver need constant attention.

Duck breasts
Duck breasts are cooked for longer on the skin side than they are on the other side. Fatty ducks are best cooked in a slightly different way. Place the duck, skin-side down, in a hot pan, without any additional fat, and cook it over a high heat until the skin is crisp and golden and the fat runs out. Pour the fat from the pan, turn the breast over and cook the other side more briefly. Fatty duck may also be cooked under a hot broiler.

STEAMING

Steaming is ideal for tender, delicately flavored meat such as chicken. Herbs can be added to the water to bring out the flavor.

FISH AND SHELLFISH

Fish and shellfish need to be prepared and cooked with the utmost care to preserve their delicate texture and flavour. Cooking times are exceptionally short, especially when the fish is to be kept warm while a sauce is made, as gentle cooking will continue during this time. Keep the fish on a warm (not hot) plate over a pan of barely simmering water and cover it loosely. It should not be allowed to dry out.

Steaming and poaching are generally the best cooking methods for fish. Frying or sauteéing are also used occasionally but in a very controlled way.

Steaming
As most cuts of fish are small, a traditional fish kettle is not essential for steaming. The fish can be put in an ordinary steamer over an ordinary pan. The liquid, which must of course be boiling when the fish is put over it, can be plain water, but the careful addition of herbs, the use of wine or a court bouillon or fish stock, will give an additional subtlety of flavor. The liquid can then provide the foundation for a sauce.

Poaching
Poaching liquid should barely shudder and give no more than the occasional bubble while the fish is sitting in it. It is an integral part of the recipe and contributes toward the overall flavor of the dish. The dish may also be flavored by vegetables, principally shallots. They are usually softened first in a little butter, then used as a bed for the fish to sit on, acting as a protective barrier between the delicate flesh and the hot pan.

To skin and fillet flat fish
The fish should be cold. Use a sharp, flexible, long bladed filleting knife. A little salt on the fingertips will stop the fish slipping when you are working on it. The skin of sole is easier to remove before filleting. The fish is often served whole and filleted at the table.

Place the fish with its dark skin facing upwards. Then remove all the fins with kitchen scissors. Mark an incision in the skin just

FLAT FISH

1 Remove the fins with scissors.

2 Hold the tail firmly in one hand.

3 Pull the skin away sharply.

4 To remove the fillets, cut through the flesh on top of the backbone starting from the head and working down to the tail.

ROUND FISH

1 Slit the belly from vent to head.

2 Loosen the lateral bones.

3 Cut the backbone at the tail.

4 Pull the backbone away gently.

5 Remove any remaining bones.

6 Loosen the skin at the tail and push the flesh away.

above the tail and loosen the skin with the thumbnail, working around each side of the fish to the head.

Hold the tail firmly with one hand and pull the skin away sharply. The white skin is removed in the same way.

Remove the fillets by cutting through the flesh at the top of the backbone, allowing the knife to scrape along the bones from the head to the tail to ensure that they are all removed.

To clean, skin and fillet round fish
Slit the belly from the vent towards the head. Open up and remove the entrails. Rinse under cold running water. Use your thumbnail or a knife tip to scrape out the black blood channel down the backbone which would give the fish a bitter taste. Rinse again.

Cut off the heat just below the gills. Use a sharp, flexible knife to ease the top fillet away from the backbone. Use the blade to loosen lateral bones from the top fillet. Pull

it away and cut the skin along the belly to free it completely.

To loosen the bottom fillet, cut through the backbone at the tail end. With the help of a filleting knife, pull the backbone up and away gently. Take as many small bones as possible with the backbone. Any remaining small bones can be removed with pliers or large tweezers.

To skin, lay the fillet skin side down, loosen the skin at the tail, grip it firmly (salt helps) and "push"

LOBSTER

1 Split the lobster in two.

2 Remove the eye 'sac'.

3 Ease the tail flesh away with a knife.

5 Discard the 'dead men's fingers'.

4 Holding the lobster firmly, remove the claws.

6 Remove the claw flesh.

the flesh away. Keep the cutting edge close to the skin and use the flat of the knife to push.

To prepare crabs

To kill a crab plunge the point of a knife through the underside behind the eyes and through the nerve center when the tail flap is held back. If a live crab is put into boiling water it is liable to shed its claws.

To shell a crab lay it on its back and twist off the claws. Then twist off the legs — do not pull them. Prise the apron up by pulling at the pointed end near the mouth to remove the body from the shell.

Remove the "dead men's fingers". These are soft and spongy and are found at the sides of the body and stomach sac which lies behind the head. Strip out any cartilaginous membrane from the shell and discard it.

Remove the brown meat from the shell and put it aside. Do not mix it with the white meat from the body, legs and claws. Remove the white meat from the body, legs and claws. Crack the legs and claws with a hammer or lobster cracker.

Use a lobster pick or skewer to help you extract all the flesh

To prepare lobsters

To kill lobsters plunge them head first and upside down into a pan of heavily salted boiling water. Alternatively, plunge a trussing needle deep into the head between the eyes.

To prepare a lobster place it on a board with the tail spread out flat and push the point of a chopping knife firmly into the cross on the top of the head. Hold the side of the lobster firmly and bring the knife down to where the tail meets the head and split it in two. Remove the gritty "sac" behind the eyes and , if it is visible, the intestine vein in the meat near the tail.

Gently insert the sharp end of the knife into the tail, and with a backwards and forwards movement remove the flesh.

Holding half of the lobster firmly on the board, pull off the claws. Discard the "dead men's fingers". These can be found beneath the shell with the small claws attached.

Crack the claws with a heavy weight and remove the white flesh with a skewer.

To open (shuck) an oyster

Wrap the hand in which you are to hold the oyster in a cloth. Hold the oyster flat side uppermost with the hinge facing you. Insert the end of a short sturdy knife through the seam between the two halves of the shell just beside the hinge. Give a short, sharp twist with the knife to break the hinge (or work at it until you succeed). Slide the knife from right to left, keeping the blade close to the top shell, to sever the muscle. Lift off the flat shell.

To prepare scallops and mussels

Scallops are opened in the same way as oysters. Once opened, remove and discard the fringe and black intestinal thread, then gently lift the flesh from the shell with a rounded soup spoon.

Mussels should be discarded if the shells do not close when tapped sharply. Scrape the shells with a sharp knife and then rinse in cold water.

CRAB

1 Twist off the claws.

2 Remove the body from the shell.

3 Remove the 'dead men's fingers'.

4 Remove any membrane.

5 Extract the brown meat.

6 Extract the white meat.

VEGETABLES

There are two main methods of cooking vegetables — boiling and steaming. Brief boiling — blanching — is a process often used to soften a julienne for garnish. Once cooked, vegetables can be served as they are or puréed. Cuisine Vivante recipes favor small young tender vegetables and brief cooking times. The results are tender-crisp and flavorsome. If you use older vegetables, which are both larger and tougher, they will take longer to cook and will not be as satisfactory.

Whether steaming or boiling vegetables, do not cook too many at a time. The water you use will take longer to come to or return to the boil and steam will not be able to circulate properly.

To prepare vegetables, use a sharp stainless steel knife of an appropriate size. It is very difficult to cut cleanly and quickly with a knife that is either too large or too small. Vegetables that are to be cooked together, whether they are whole or cut, must be the same size to ensure they cook evenly.

Celeriac, artichokes, salsify and scorzonera discolor as soon as they are cut and so must be put immediately into water acidulated with lemon juice or white wine vinegar and cooked in acidulated water. They are often cooked unpeeled, as the skin is easier to remove after cooking.

Asparagus is also cooked in acidulated water, partly to overcome the problem of discoloration, but also for the flavor.

Beets must not be peeled or cut before cooking, or their juices will bleed away.

All vegetables must be drained very well after cooking, then refreshed quickly in cold running water to preserve their color and to stop further cooking. They can then be kept warm in a warm covered dish.

Boiling

Put root vegetables, with the exception of new potatoes, into cold water, bring the water to the boil and time the cooking from boiling point. Put all other vegetables, including new potatoes, into boiling water and time cooking from the moment the water returns to the boil.

Steaming

Place the vegetables in a single layer in the steamer. They should not touch each other. Make sure the water is boiling before placing the vegetables over it. A herb that complements a vegetable, such as summer savory with broad beans, may be added to the water.

Leafy vegetables such as spinach should not be boiled. They will cook in the few drops that cling to the leaves after they have been washed and shaken dry. Cover the pan and cook the leaves until just tender and "fallen", shaking the pan occasionally. Uncover the pan and increase the heat to drive off as much excess water as possible. Drain extremely well. Leafy vegetables may also be steamed.

Purées

A good purée is light and delicate with a clear, fresh flavor and a good bright color. Cook the vegetables for purées beyond the crisp stage but do not allow them to become overcooked or too soft and wet. After refreshing and draining, reduce to a purée in a food processor or blender or pass through a mouli-légumes. For extra smoothness and lightness, the purée can then be sieved.

Drive off any surplus moisture by heating the purée in a clean, preferably nonstick pan until it is dry (some very moist vegetables such as spinach and turnips may also be given a preliminary drying before puréeing).

For really dry purée, leave it to

COOKING TIMES FOR SMALL, YOUNG VEGETABLES		
Vegetables	**Boiling**	**Steaming**
Artichokes (whole)	30-40 minutes	45-55 minutes
Asparagus Tips	3-5 minutes	10-12 minutes
Beans, Lima	4 minutes	6-8 minutes
French	3 minutes	7-10 minutes
Beetroot	40-90 minutes	1½-2 hours
Broccoli	4-5 minutes	6-8 minutes
Brussels Sprouts	3-5 minutes	5-10 minutes
Carrots	5-10 minutes	10-15 minutes
Cauliflower flowerets	2-4 minutes	5-10 minutes
Celeriac	20 minutes	
Cucumber, balls	30 seconds	
turned	30 seconds	
Leek, whole	4-7 minutes	10-15 minutes
sliced	2-3 minutes	5-7 minutes
Peas	2-3 minutes	5 minutes
Potatoes, old	15-20 minutes	20-30 minutes
new	15 minutes	20 minutes
Salsify	20 minutes	25 minutes
Snow peas	30 seconds	4-5 minutes
Spinach	1-2 minutes	2-5 minutes
Turnips	10-12 minutes	15-20 minutes
Zucchini, whole	3-6 minutes	5-9 minutes
sliced	1 minute	3-5 minutes

drain through a sieve lined with cheesecloth then twist to remove the last vestiges of water. Over a low heat beat in warm cream and diced butter for lightness and smoothness.

Purées are delicious in themselves, and they can also form the base of other dishes. Prepare them in advance and add cream or butter at the last minute. The easiest way of doing this is to put the purée in a bowl over a saucepan of hot water to heat through gently.

Glazed vegetables
To glaze baby or "turned" vegetables or chestnuts, melt 1 tbsp/15 g butter and 1 tbsp sugar in 2-3 tbsp water left over from the cooking of the vegetables. Simmer gently until slightly syrupy. Add the vegetables or nuts and cook, shaking the pan frequently, until they are an even, glossy, light golden color.

To skin tomatoes
With the point of a sharp knife, make a small cross in the skin in the end opposite the stalk, then quickly lower the tomato into boiling water

---

PUREES

1 Cook and refresh with iced water.

2 Blend in a food processor.

3 Beat in the diced butter.

4 Blend in warm cream with a wire whisk for lightness and smoothness.

on a slotted spoon or skimmer or in a sieve. Remove after 10-20 seconds depending on the size and ripeness of the tomatoes. Cool the tomatoes immediately in cold water then peel back the skin from the cross.

To prepare concassé tomatoes

Skin the tomatoes and remove the seeds. Cut the flesh into strips, then cut across the strips to make diamond shapes of flesh.

To seed tomatoes

Cut tomatoes horizontally then gently press out the seeds and juice with the thumb. Shake sharply to remove any remaining seeds.

To prepare asparagus

Trim off any woody parts from the stems and cut all the spears to the same length by aligning the tips. Support the spear in the left hand (or right hand, if left handed) with the tip pointing away from you. With a vegetable peeler starting about 1½ inches/3.4 cm away from the tip, remove the little spurs and any coarse fibers.

To prepare artichoke bottoms

Snap off the stalk from the base. Pull the outer leaves outwards from the base, then pull them downwards and off the base. Continue until you reach the pale inner leaves. With a stainless steel knife trim the tops of the inner leaves by one to two thirds the cut edges with lemon juice if they are to be used in a garnish. With the same knife pare away the tough, dark exterior of the base, working in a spiral from the stem. Pull out the central hairy "choke" and remaining leaves. Rub all the cut surfaces with lemon juice.

To skin peppers

Turn the peppers under a very hot broiler until the skin dries out, blackens and blisters. Allow the peppers to cool. The skin will now come away easily.

To turn vegetables

Cut off both ends of the vegetable so they are flat, then trim the sides to make a shape resembling a rectangle. With a small sharp knife trim down the corners to make a smooth oval shape.

TO SKIN TOMATOES

1 Make a small cross in the end. *2 Peel the skin from the cross.*

TO PREPARE ASPARAGUS

1 Trim off any woody parts. *2 Peel away from the tip.*

TO TURN VEGETABLES

1 Square off the sides. *2 Trim the corners to make an oval.*

TO TURN MUSHROOMS

1 Make a series of cuts. *2 Remove a narrow strip.*

TO PREPARE ARTICHOKE BOTTOMS

1 Snap off the stalk.

2 Trim the inner leaves.

TO CHOP OR DICE

1 Slice the vegetable into strips.

2 Stack and cut across.

TO CHOP AND DICE AN ONION

1 Slice into regular widths.

2 Cut across to make small cubes.

TO SLICE VEGETABLES

1 Trim the sides and ends.

2 Slice to required thickness.

To turn mushrooms

Choose large button mushrooms. Wipe the cap if necessary with a damp cloth. Trim the stem level with the cap. With a very sharp knife make a series of cuts, about ½ inch/6 mm apart following the natural shape of the cap from the top to the edge. Remove a narrow strip from each cut.

To slice vegetables

Cut the sides and ends of the vegetable so that they are flat. Hold the vegetable firmly with the fingertips. Work the knife across the vegetable moving the blade up and down just in front of the fingers and moving the fingers, closely followed by the knife, back for a distance that corresponds to the thickness of the slice required after each cut.

To julienne

Cut the vegetable into lengthways slices the width of a matchstick. Cut through the slices to form very fine sticks.

To chop or dice

Cut sliced vegetables into strips of the required thickness, as for julienne, stack the strips neatly and cut across them so they fall into small squares.

To chop and dice an onion

Cut the onion in half through to the base. Place one half cut-side downwards on a firm surface and cut down vertically to the width required, using the slicing action described above, and keeping the base intact. Then cut across the first cuts to make cubes, and continue right across the onion.

TO JULIENNE

1 Cut into slices then fine sticks.

S A U C E S

The foundation of the majority of Cuisine Vivante sauces is a good stock appropriate to the sauce (ie a chicken stock in a sauce to be served with chicken, a game stock for a game dish). Without this it is impossible to achieve the right depth and clarity of flavor, the bright color, glossy appearance and light consistency. A delicate texture is achieved by boiling the sauce until it is well reduced. This makes the addition of large volumes of cream unnecessary and gives a sauce character and distinction. Reducing times and before and after quantities given in recipes can only be guidelines — there is no substitute for tasting and this must be done frequently as the sauce approaches the right consistency so that adjustments can be made.

Once a sauce has been made it should ideally be served immediately; if it is to be served within about five minutes, stand the saucepan on an asbestos mat over a very low heat. Stir the sauce occasionally and on no account allow it to boil, otherwise it will separate and become oily. The safest way to keep a sauce warm for up to half an hour is to pour it into a bowl, cover the surface closely with plastic wrap and place the bowl in a pan of hot water.

ABOVE *To keep a sauce warm put it in a bowl, cover with plastic wrap and stand in a pan of hot water.*

Reduction sauce

Stock or wine is usually stirred into the meat or fish cooking juices (a process known as deglazing) so their flavor can be incorporated into the sauce. Before deglazing the pan remove any burnt sediment and pour out excess fat, even if more is to be added later in the form of butter. A buttery sauce is very different from a fatty one. Always boil down wine added to deglaze a pan to concentrate its flavor. Vermouth has a more pronounced flavor and does not need to be boiled down to the same degree, so it is used in smaller quantities. Its characteristic herby note means that it needs to be used selectively.

Puréed vegetables can be incorporated into a sauce to thicken it, to give flavor and a different type of texture. Always sieve a sauce, especially if it contains a purée or small solids such as pieces of shallot, unless the recipe specifies otherwise. Herbs are usually sieved out after they have softened and given up their flavor. Fresh herbs may be scattered over the sauce when it is served to contribute added flavor and texture and for decoration.

Add butter to sauces in small amounts and gradually, to ensure that it melts without turning oily and so is completely incorporated or emulsified into the sauce. Whether the butter is added over a very high heat or, as is more common, over a very low heat, and whether it is stirred, swirled or whisked depends on the texture and appearance required. A smoother more glossy sauce can be obtained by boiling, and a light, creamy one by whisking over a very low heat.

A small amount of butter is often added at the last moment to sauces that are not ostensibly "butter sauces", just to round off the flavor and give the sauce a sheen.

Beurre blanc

Ingredients
$\frac{1}{2}$ cup/110 g sweet butter
2 shallots, finely chopped
2 bay leaves
$1\frac{1}{2}$ tbsp wine vinegar
$1\frac{1}{2}$ tbsp water
1 tbsp heavy cream

Chill the butter, then cut it into medium size cubes. Keep cold. Put the shallot, bay leaves, vinegar and water into a thick bottomed sauté pan or shallow saucepan. Boil slowly until about 2 tbsp liquid remain.

Slowly add the cream. Using a small wire sauce whisk gradually add the butter cube by cube. When the last of the butter is beaten in, the sauce should be warm rather than hot. (As the proportion of fat to vinegar increases, the danger of separating increases if the sauce is too hot.) The process should take about 4 minutes. Sieve the sauce into a warmed bowl.

REDUCTION SAUCE

1 Pour out excess fat.

2 Add the wine to the cooking juices.

3 Pour in the stock (appropriate to the sauce).

4 Sieve the sauce.

5 Add the butter.

6 Whisk to the required texture.

BEURRE BLANC

1 Add the shallot, bay leaves, vinegar and water.

2 Boil, then add the cream.

3 Whisk in the butter cubes.

4 Sieve into a warm bowl.

MOUSSELINES

Mousselines are delicate mixtures of puréed raw meat or fish bound with egg white and lightened with cream. They are frequently used in Cuisine Vivante recipes.

Puréeing the flesh by hand is not difficult, but it does take time and effort, as it must be done in a pestle and mortar to obtain the right degree of smoothness. But with a food processor or blender it can be done in moments.

All the ingredients must be cold and it is a good idea to put the food processor bowl in the freezer for about an hour before you begin. Pass the purée through a fine sieve even after using a good processor for a really smooth mixture. This will not be necessary if a certain amount of texture is required in the dish. Salt and lemon juice helps to firm up the flesh. Egg white holds the mixture together, but too much can make it rubbery. Mixtures to be poached are in danger of disintegration and need more egg white than mixtures to be used for stuffings.

Pour the egg white slowly into the purée with the motor of the food processor or blender running. Beat the cream in very gradually by hand, with the bowl standing over ice. It is easier to incorporate the cream when the mixture is cold. Up to three times as much cream as meat or fish can be beaten into a mousseline, but usually Cuisine Vivante recipes call for much less.

Test for seasoning, texture and lightness by poaching a teaspoonful of the mixture in salted water for two minutes on each side. Cut open and taste the cooked mixture. It should have a light, just-set texture and be perfectly smooth and creamy. Chill and cover the mixture for at least 30 minutes before cooking. If necessary it can be prepared a few hours ahead of time. Mousseline mixtures that are to be eaten hot or warm should be served as soon as possible after they have been cooked.

MOUSSELINE

1 Purée the fish or meat.

2 Pour in the egg white.

3 Beat in the cream.

4 Poach a teaspoonful of the mixture in salted water to test for seasoning, texture and lightness.

GARNISHES

A garnish is the final touch, the last detail that completes the picture on the plate. The right garnish adds an interesting facet to the flavor, it enlivens the color and gives character to an uninteresting shape. It can also provide texture in an otherwise soft dish. It may be an integral part of the dish or it may be something extra; it may be formal or it may be informal, but it must always be edible and complementary. In Cuisine Vivante a garnish is not something that is picked off and put on the side of the plate before the diner begins to eat.

A garnish should never dominate a dish, be too complicated or ornate, or too abundant. It should look fresh, delicate, simple and appropriate as in salmon eggs with salmon or leaves of herbs dotted on a pool of sauce. If a dish is to be served hot, a garnish such as vegetable diamonds or julienne vegetables should be heated too, or it will cool down the food.

To prepare garnishes for Cuisine Vivante you need good sharp knives. Additional pieces of equipment that may come in handy are a potato peeler, a mandolin, a canelle knife and aspic cutters.

Don't forget before you start the number of plates to be garnished, so that you can allow enough time to do the job properly.

Garnish theory
◆ Choose a garnish that is a different shade of the color of the sauce or main ingredient for a toning effect — such as stronger or lighter green.
◆ Blanched rings or fine julienne of a strong colored vegetable such as red pepper, green leek or snow peas look good on a pale sauce.
◆ Strategically place a single leaf or a small sprig of herbs.
◆ Arrange a few herb leaves in a pattern.
◆ Form blanched vegetables into shapes — small balls or torpedoes.
◆ Make use of feathery leaves, such as dill, fennel or the tops of young carrots to add lightness .
◆ Add fine gratings of orange or lemon peel or stronger strips, perhaps tied into knots or bows.
◆ Knot the tops of scallions.
◆ Make corkscrews from apple peel.
◆ Stack blanched julienne vegetables into neat piles or heap them informally. Use different colored julienned vegetables for greater

impact, where this is required.
◆ Tie small bundles of blanched julienne vegetables together with a strip of chive or of blanched red pepper or lemon peel.
◆ Use crescents or other shapes of crisp pastry.
◆ Add small mounds of purée of toning or contrasting colors.

GARNISHES

Cucumber slices
Score the peel with a canelle knife, then cut into slices.

Cucumber rings
Score the peel with a canelle knife and cut into thick slices. Hollow out the slices, cut a slit in the ring that is left and join the rings together like links in a chain.

Cucumber boats
Cut short lengths of cucumber in half and scoop out the core of seeds to make boats.

Cucumber diagonals
Canelle the cucumber skin, cut it in half lengthways, remove the seeds and cut slices on diagonal.

Cucumber circles
Canelle the cucumber, cut it into slices and cut out the centers with a small, fluted cutter. Use both the centers and the outer circles for garnishing.

Cucumber cones
Thinly slice the cucumber into rings. Cut each slice from center to edge. Hold each side and twist to form a cone.

Cucumber knots
Quarter a short length of cucumber lengthways. Remove the seeds and make two cuts in each quarter, one going from the left not quite through to the right, the other one going the other way. Gently ease the "Z" shape open. Twist the right hand end under the central bar and over the left hand.

SIMPLE GARNISHES

1 Cucumber cones.

2 Cucumber rings.

3 Carrot rolls.

4 Scallion tassels.

Cucumber butterfly

Halve the cucumber lengthways. Cut off a ¾-inch piece. Cut into 4 slices but leave a small hinge. Fold the slices back to the hinge to make wings. Repeat for the other side of the butterfly. Make the body by cutting out the seed channel. Place a length of peel on top. Finish with 2 half slices on either side and use 2 quartered slices for the antennae.

Carrot shapes

Cut decorative shapes out of carrot slices with the point of a sharp knife or aspic cutter, or canelle slim carrots before cutting into slices.

Carrot coils

Pare strips of carrot, coil them around your finger, secure with a toothpick. Put into iced water. Remove the toothpick to serve.

Carrot rolls

Peel strips from a large carrot. Roll each strip to make a curl, secure with a toothpick. Put into iced water. Remove the toothpick to serve.

CUCUMBER BUTTERFLY

1 Fold slices back making wings.

2 Cut out the seed channel.

3 Quarter a slice to make the antennae.

Carrot flowers

Peel and trim the carrot to a bluntish point at one end. Score the surface with a canelle knife. Peel off the outer layer in a circular motion from the pointed end. Remove the "flower".

Tomato roses

Peel the skin from a tomato in a long spiral, as you would an apple. Beginning at the end that was opposite the stem, wind the peel round and round in one continuous strip, winding the center tightly and the rest more loosely. Secure with a toothpick until ready to use.

Tomato tails

Cut a tomato in half lengthwise. Place the cut side downward, with a small sharp knife, make a diagonal cut just off from the middle, toward the center. Make a similar cut in the over side to join the first in the center to form a wedge. Continue making cuts all the way over the surface. Gently ease the wedges outwards so they are staggered.

Egg

Separate the white and yolk of a hard cooked egg and chop them separately. Arrange them in a pattern.

Scallion tassels

To make tassels, trim the vegetable at both ends. With the point of sharp knife cut fine, lengthways slits in the green part. Place in iced water for at least 30 minutes until the strips curl. Dry well before using.

Celery sprays

Cut a long fringe at either end of a short length of celery. Cut out the center from a slice of carrot. Thread the carrot ring into the center of the piece of celery. Place in a bowl of iced water for about 30 minutes or until the celery curls. Dry well before using.

Zucchini fans

To make fans, slice through small, young zucchini lengthwise almost to the end 3 or 4 times. Ease the slices apart.

Apple tails (see tomato tails)

ZUCCHINI FAN *Slice through and ease apart.*	**CANELLED SLICES** *Score and slice.*

CELERY SPRAYS

1 "Fringe" a length of celery.   *2 Slice and core the carrot.*

TOMATO TAILS

1 Make cuts from the center.   *2 "Skin" the wing pieces.*

APPLE TAILS

1 Make cuts from the center.   *2 Cut "wing" sections the same way.*

TOMATO ROSES

1 Peel the skin from one end.

2 Continue in a spiral motion.

3 Wind up the peel into a "rose".

CARROT FLOWERS

1 Peel the outer layer from the end.

2 Continue peeling round the tip.

3 Remove the "flower" from the main section.

BASIC RECIPES

The basic recipes contained in this section feature widely in the Cuisine Vivante recipes that follow. Many of them may be made in advance in order to cut the preparation time of the main recipes.

BROWN VEAL STOCK

INGREDIENTS
2 lb 2 oz/1 kg veal knuckle bones and
   trimmings, chopped
1 tbsp oil
1 onion, sliced
1 carrot, sliced
white of 1 leek, chopped
1 stick of celery, sliced
4 oz/100 g mushroom trimmings
5 fl oz/150 ml full bodied dry white
   wine
1 lb/450 g tomatoes, chopped
bouquet garni of 1 bay leaf, a sprig of
   thyme, 4 parsley stalks and a sprig
   of tarragon

The bones can be browned under a preheated broiler if this is more practical.

Heat the oven to 425°F/220°C.

Put the bones and trimmings into a roasting pan, pour the oil over and turn the bones so they are lightly coated. Put in the oven until browned, turning frequently. Stir the onion, carrot, leek and celery into the bones and return to the oven for about 10 minutes until browned. Stir in the mushroom trimmings, then tip the contents of the roasting pan into a large saucepan over a moderate heat. Stir the wine into the roasting pan to dislodge the sediment and boil until reduced by half. Pour in the saucepan. Add the tomatoes, bouquet garni and about $8\frac{3}{4}$ cups/2 L water. Bring to the boil, remove the scum from the surface frequently and simmer gently for 3-4 hours, until the liquid is reduced to about $4\frac{1}{2}$ cups/1 L.

Pass the stock through a sieve lined with cheesecloth. Leave to cool, then carefully remove all the fat from the surface.

To make meat glaze
Boil brown veal stock slowly, pouring it into progressively smaller pans, until it is reduced to a thick syrupy consistency.

VEGETABLE STOCK

INGREDIENTS
25 g/1 oz butter
2 shallots, finely chopped
white of one small leek, finely chopped
1 small carrot, finely chopped
2 tbsp finely chopped fennel or 1 tsp
   fennel seeds
2 tomatoes, chopped
bouquet garni of 4 parsley stalks,
   1 bay leaf, a sprig of chervil and a
   sprig of thyme
1 tsp white peppercorns
salt

Heat the butter, add the shallots and leek, cover and cook over a low heat, shaking the pan occasionally, until the shallot is soft.

Stir in the remaining ingredients, cover with water and simmer for $1\frac{1}{2}$—2 hours, removing the scum from the surface frequently.

Pass through a sieve lined with cheesecloth, leave to cool and remove the fat that comes to the surface.

FISH STOCK

INGREDIENTS
1½ tsp/20 g butter
1 onion
white part of 1 leek, chopped
1 cup/50 g mushrooms, chopped
1 lb 3 oz/1 kg fish bones, heads and
    trimmings, soaked in cold water for
    3 hours
⅔ cup/150 ml medium bodied dry
    white wine
bouquet garni of 1 bay leaf, 3 parsley
    stalks, a sprig of fennel

Ask the fish store for bones. Do not allow the vegetables and bones to brown when they are being fried as this will color the stock.

_____

Heat the butter, add the vegetables, cover and cook over a moderate heat, shaking the pan occasionally for 4-5 minutes. Stir in the fish bones and trimmings and cook, stirring, for 2-3 minutes. Stir in the wine and reduce by half. Add the bouquet garni and about 7½ cups/1.75 liters water, bring to the boil, remove the scum from the surface, then simmer for 20 minutes, removing the scum from the surface occasionally.

Pass through a sieve lined with cheesecloth. Leave to cool, then remove all the fat from the surface.

To make fish glaze
Boil fish stock slowly, pouring it into progressively smaller pans, until it is reduced to a thick syrupy consistency.

CHICKEN STOCK

INGREDIENTS
2 lb 3 oz/1 kg chicken carcasses,
    necks, wings, feet, giblets except
    the liver, or 1 boiling fowl, chopped
1 pigs trotter or veal knuckle bone,
    chopped
1 whole onion, spiked with 2 cloves
1 carrot, sliced
1 stalk of celery, sliced
white of 2 leeks, sliced
bouquet garni of 1 bayleaf, 4 parsley
    stalks, a sprig of thyme and
    2 sprigs of chervil

Pigs trotters and veal knuckles contain plenty of the gelatinous substance necessary for a good jellied stock.

_____

Put the chicken carcasses, bones and giblets, or the boiling fowl and the pigs trotter or veal bone into a large saucepan. Cover with cold water and bring to the boil. Carefully skim the scum from the surface, add the vegetables, bouquet garni and about 8¾ cups/2 L water. Return to the boil, remove the scum from the surface, then simmer for about 3 hours, removing the scum from the surface occasionally.

Pass through a sieve lined with cheesecloth. Leave to cool, then remove all the fat from the surface.

VEAL STOCK

INGREDIENTS
2 lb 3 oz/1 kg veal knuckle bones,
    chopped
1 onion, studded with 1 clove
1 carrot, chopped
white of 1 leek, chopped
1 stalk of celery, chopped
bouquet garni of 1 bayleaf, 3 parsley
    stalks, a sprig of thyme and a sprig
    of chervil

Blanch the bones for 1 minute. Drain, then place in a large saucepan and cover with about 8¾ cups/2 L water. Bring to the boil, remove the scum from the surface, add the vegetables and bouquet garni and simmer for 3—4 hours or until the liquid is reduced to about 4½ cups/1 L.

Pass through a sieve lined with cheesecloth, leave to cool, then remove all the fat from the surface.

GAME STOCK

INGREDIENTS
2 lb 3 oz/1 kg game carcasses, bones
   and trimmings, chopped
1 tbsp oil
1 onion, studded with 2 cloves
1 carrot, chopped
1 stalk of celery, chopped
6 juniper berries, crushed
6 coriander seeds, crushed
bouquet garni of 1 bay leaf, 4 parsley
   stalks, a sprig of sage and a sprig of
   thyme
2 cups/425 ml red wine
5 cups/1 L veal stock

Venison bones can also be used to make game stock, so it is worth asking the game dealer for bones. If the stock is not needed immediately, it can be frozen for future use.

———————

Heat the oven to 425°F/220°C, or heat the broiler.
   Put the game carcasses, bones and trimmings in a roasting pan. Pour the oil over and turn the bones to coat them lightly. Place in the oven or under the broiler until lightly browned.
   Tip the contents of the roasting pan into a large saucepan. Over a moderate heat, stir the wine into the roasting pan to dislodge the sediment then boil until reduced by a third.
   Pour into the saucepan, add the remaining ingredients, stir in the stock and about 10 cups/2 L water. Bring to the boil, remove the scum from the surface then simmer for 3—4 hours until the liquid is reduced to 4½ cups/1 L, removing the scum from the surface frequently.
   Pass through a sieve lined with cheesecloth. Leave to cool then remove all the fat from the surface.

COURT BOUILLON

INGREDIENTS
1 cup/250 ml medium bodied dry
   white wine
2 tbsp white wine vinegar
2 carrots, chopped
3 shallots, thinly sliced
white of 1 leek, thinly sliced
bouquet garni of 4 parsley stalks, a
   sprig of thyme, a bay leaf, a small
   sprig of fennel
½ tsp crushed white peppercorns
2 coriander seeds, crushed
salt

Court bouillon is an aromatic, slightly acidulated liquid used for poaching fish and seafood and occasionally vegetables or meat.

———————

Bring the wine, vinegar and 4½ cups/1 L water to the boil. Add the remaining ingredients, bring to the boil then simmer for 15—20 minutes.
   Pass through a sieve.

VINAIGRETTE

INGREDIENTS
2 tsp lemon juice
1 tsp sherry vinegar
1 tsp white wine vinegar
salt and freshly ground black pepper
1½ tbsp olive oil
1 tbsp pure vegetable oil
1 tbsp finely chopped chervil
1 tsp finely chopped parsley

The choice of herbs can be varied according to what is available or what will best compliment other flavors.

———————

Whisk the lemon juice, vinegars and seasoning together.
   Very gradually whisk in the oils to make a thick emulsion.
   Stir in the herbs.

CHICKEN ASPIC

INGREDIENTS (makes 4½ cups/1 L)
1 cup/175 g chicken, finely chopped
white of 2 leeks, finely chopped
2 stalks of celery, finely chopped
2 carrots, finely chopped
2 shallots, finely chopped
2 egg whites, lightly whisked
2 egg shells, crushed
3¾ cups/1.7 L chicken stock, brought
   to the boil
3 tbsp gelatin

Mix the chicken, vegetables, egg whites and shells together in a large saucepan. Very gradually pour on the boiling stock, stirring with a balloon whisk. Bring to the boil very slowly, stirring constantly. As soon as boiling point is reached, stop stirring, lower the heat so the stock is gently simmering, and simmer for 1 hour without stirring.

Remove the saucepan from the heat and very carefully remove the scum from the surface. Ladle the stock into a sieve lined with cheesecloth.

Dissolve the gelatin in 4 tbsp of the liquid in a small bowl placed over a pan of hot water. Stir a little more of the liquid into the gelatin, then strain it into the bulk of the liquid. The aspic is ready to use when it has cooled to the point when it has the consistency of unbeaten egg white.

FISH ASPIC

INGREDIENTS
3 egg whites, lightly whisked
½ cup/100 g white fish, ground
2 shallots, chopped
1 carrot, finely chopped
white of 1 leek, finely chopped
4 button mushroom stalks, finely
   chopped
10 white peppercorns
4 parsley stalks
1 bay leaf
a small sprig of thyme
¼ tsp tomato paste
juice of 1 lemon
salt
4½ cups/1 L boiling fish stock
3 tbsp gelatin

Mix the egg whites, fish, shallots, carrot, leek, mushroom stalks, peppercorns, parsley stalks, bay leaf, thyme, tomato paste, lemon juice and salt together in a large, heavy based saucepan. Slowly pour in the boiling fish stock, stirring constantly with a wire whisk. Bring to the boil slowly, stirring.

Reduce the heat, allow the foam to rise, then simmer for 5 minutes. Remove from the heat, cover and leave for 10 minutes.

Make a hole in the surface scum. Carefully ladle out the liquid underneath, taking care to disturb the scum as little as possible, and pour it into a sieve lined with cheesecloth.

Dissolve the gelatin in 4 tbsp strained stock in a bowl over a saucepan of hot water, then strain into the remaining stock. Stir thoroughly, then leave to cool. Remove any fat that rises to the surface.

Use the aspic when it is on the point of setting and very syrupy.

RED SHELLFISH BUTTER

INGREDIENTS
2 cups/100 g red shellfish shells,
   crushed
½ cup + 2 tbsp/150 g butter, softened
salt
cayenne pepper
cognac

Beat the shells and butter together, then heat very gently, stirring constantly, until a froth rises to the surface. Very carefully pour off the clear liquid beneath the froth into a sieve lined with cheesecloth. Leave to set in a cool place then beat in a little salt, cayenne pepper and cognac.

BASIC NOODLE DOUGH

INGREDIENTS
2¼ cups/225 g all purpose flour
a pinch of salt
2 eggs, beaten
1 tbsp olive oil

Sieve the flour and salt onto the work surface and form a well in the center.

Pour the eggs into the well with the oil and about 1 tbsp water. Using the fingertips of one hand draw the flour into the egg and work together to form a soft, but not sticky, pliable dough, adding more water or flour as necessary. Knead thoroughly for 5-10 minutes, until the dough is smooth and elastic and small air bubbles are visible under the surface.

Cover the dough with an inverted bowl and leave to relax at room temperature for at least an hour.

Divide the dough in half. Keep one half covered by the bowl and roll the other half out very thinly on a lightly floured surface using a lightly floured rolling pin and working from the center to the edge.

Roll out the other half of the dough and leave both sheets to dry for about 15 minutes..

Fold each sheet into a long strip, then slice through the dough at approximately ¼ inch/6 mm intervals along its length with a very sharp knife. Leave to dry for at least an hour draped over a clothes horse or between the backs of two kitchen chairs.

Bring a large saucepan of salted water to the boil, add the noodles, bring the water back to the boil and stir well. The addition of 1 tbsp of oil to the water prevents the noodles sticking together. (If a large amount of pasta is being cooked, add it to the water gradually and bring the water back to the boil after each addition.) Cook for about 3-4 minutes or until the noodles are tender but still resilient.

Tip into a colander, rinse with boiling water and drain.

Once dried, pasta dough can be kept for up to a week if wrapped in plastic wrap and stored in the refrigerator.

INGREDIENTS
1 cup/225 g spinach
a pinch of salt
2¼ cups/225 g all purpose flour
2 eggs, beaten
1 tbsp olive oil

Green pasta

Cook the spinach for 2-3 minutes in boiling salted water. Drain thoroughly through a sieve, pressing down well on the spinach to extract as much liquid as possible. Purée, then heat in a nonstick saucepan, stirring, to drive off excess moisture.

Prepare the dough in the same way as the Basic noodle dough (above), adding the spinach with the eggs and omitting the water.

Pink pasta

Add 2 tbsp tomato paste to the Basic noodle dough (above) with the eggs and omit the water.

Red pepper pasta

Skin 1 cup/225 g red pepper, purée the flesh and add to the Basic noodle dough (above) with the eggs, omitting the water.

PUFF PASTRY

INGREDIENTS
1 cup/225 g cold butter
2¼ cups/225 g all purpose flour
a pinch of salt
1 tsp lemon juice

Puff pastry is easy to make provided everything is kept cool — if butter shows even the slightest sign of oozing through the surface of the dough or out of the sides put the dough immediately into the refrigerator or freezer to harden the fat.

Place the butter between 2 sheets of waxed paper or plastic wrap and beat it with a rolling pin until it is soft and malleable. Form it into a square about ½ inch/1.25cm thick. If it becomes too soft, chill it.

Sieve the flour and salt together then form into a soft, pliable but not sticky dough with about 8-10 tbsp very cold water and lemon juice. Transfer the dough to a lightly floured surface and knead lightly. Cover and chill for about 30 minutes.

Return the dough to a lightly floured surface, form into a square then roll it out to a square about ¼ inch/6mm thick around the edges with a slightly thicker "pad" of dough in the center. Place the butter on the "pad" and fold the corners of the dough around it so they meet in the center, like an envelope, and overlap very slightly where they meet.

Gently press the block of dough with the rolling pin at ½ inch/1.25 cm intervals across its surface until it has grown slightly then roll it out to a rectangle, watching to make sure the butter does not break through the surface or out of the sides. Fold the two ends of the rectangle so they meet in the center then fold the whole piece in half, like a book. Cover and chill for 30 minutes.

Repeat the rolling and folding 5 times, chilling the dough after each time. Then roll the dough once more before covering and chilling for at least 2 hours.

PUFF PASTRY CRESCENTS (FLEURONS)

Roll out pastry to about ⅙ inch/4.5 mm thick. Starting at an outer edge cut semi-circles of pastry with a cookie cutter. Carefully transfer to a baking tray with a fish slice, cover and leave in a cool place for at least 30 minutes.

Meanwhile, heat the oven to 450°F/230°C. Brush the tops of the crescents with beaten egg, taking care not to let any drip down the cut edges. Bake for about 10 minutes until golden brown, well risen and crisp.

PATE BRISEE

INGREDIENTS
1¼ cups/125 g all purpose flour
a pinch of salt
2 tsp confectioners' sugar
6 tbsp/75 g butter
1 egg yolk, beaten

In hot weather, make pastry early in the day when the kitchen is cool. Work quickly and lightly and always leave the rolled out dough in a cool place to relax before baking to prevent shrinkage.

Sift the flour, salt and sugar onto a cold counter and form a well in the center.

Pound the butter with a rolling pin to soften it slightly, then chop it roughly.

Put the lumps of butter into the well with the egg yolk, then quickly and lightly blend them together with the fingertips until they are just beginning to come together and look rather like rough scrambled egg.

Sprinkle a little flour over them. Quickly and lightly draw the ingredients together by chopping through them with a cold, round bladed knife whilst at the same time drawing the flour from the edges of the pile into the center in a smooth flowing action.

When all the flour has been incorporated, draw the mixture into a ball with the fingertips. Cover and chill for at least 30 minutes.

Roll out on a lightly floured surface with a lightly floured rolling pin to about ⅛ in/3 mm and cut as required.

PATE BRISEE TARTS

INGREDIENTS
Pastry based on 1 cup + 2 tbsp/100 g
    flour will make about 12 tarts

Roll out the prepared pastry on a lightly floured surface with a lightly floured rolling pin to ⅛ in/3 mm thick. Cut out shapes with a lightly floured cutter, about 1½ in/4 cm. With a fish slice or metal spatula carefully transfer the cut-out shapes to muffin pans and ease them gently into the shape of the pans, making sure there are no air bubbles trapped underneath. Prick lightly with a fork, cover and chill for 20-30 minutes. Heat the oven to 400°F/200°C.

Bake the tart shells for about 10 minutes until crisped and a light golden brown. Leave to cool in the pans for a couple of minutes before removing carefully with a metal spatula.

FILO (PHYLO) PASTRY

INGREDIENTS (serves 4)
2¾ cups/285 g all purpose flour
pinch of salt
1 egg
⅔ cup/150 ml water
1 tsp oil

Ready made filo pastry is available from some supermarkets and Greek speciality food stores. It comes ready rolled and in convenient leaves. It can be frozen.

Sift the flour and salt into a bowl.

Beat the egg and add the water and oil. First with a knife and then with one hand mix the water and egg into the flour, adding more water if necessary to make a soft dough.

Beat the past until smooth and elastic. Put it into a clean floured bowl. Cover and leave in a warm place for 15 minutes.

The pastry is now ready for rolling and pulling.

FILO PASTRY TARTS

Heat the oven to 425°F/200°C. Brush muffin pans with melted butter or oil.

Cut out shapes in sheets of filo pastry with a lightly oiled cutter, about 1½ in/4 cm. With the help of a fish slice or metal spatula, carefully transfer half the pastry rounds to the muffin pans, easing them gently into the shape. Brush with melted butter or oil then cover with the remaining rounds, again using a fish slice or spatula. Bake for about 10 minutes until crisp and golden brown. Remove from the muffin pans carefully with a metal spatula.

CREME PATISSIERE

INGREDIENTS
1 cup/225 ml milk
1 vanilla pod
3 egg yolks
scant ½ cup/85 g sugar
6 tbsp/40 g all purpose flour

If the sauce is not used immediately cover the surface closely with wetted greaseproof paper or cling film to prevent a skin forming.

Pour the milk into a heavy based saucepan, add the vanilla pod and bring slowly to the boil. Remove from the heat, cover and leave to infuse for 15 minutes.

Beat the egg yolks, sugar and flour together.

Remove the vanilla pod from the milk and bring the milk to the boil.

Stir the milk into the egg mixture, pour back into the saucepan then bring slowly to the boil, stirring constantly. Simmer for 2—3 minutes, still stirring.

Strain through a fine sieve.

If it is not to be used immediately, cover the surface closely with waxed paper or plastic wrap to prevent a skin forming.

FIRST
COURSES

◆ *First courses serve a dual purpose in that they should both whet the appetite and take the edge off the diner's hunger while not satisfying it completely. They should flirt with the diner, proffering temptation to the eye and palate, and they should set the tone for, and give a preview of, the dishes to come. If so desired, two first course dishes could, by careful selection, be served in succession to provide a light meal perhaps more suitable for the middle of the day.* ◆

HERB TART

INGREDIENTS (serves 6)
FOR THE PASTRY
4 tbsp cold butter
¾ cup all purpose flour
a pinch of salt
a pinch of sugar
½ egg yolk
⅓ cup cream cheese

FOR THE FILLING
2 tsp butter
1 tbsp finely chopped shallot
¼ crisp lettuce, finely shredded
1½ tbsp mixed finely chopped chives,
*   parsley, tarragon, fennel and*
*   rosemary*
1 tbsp finely grated Parmesan cheese
1 egg, beaten
⅔ cup cereal cream
salt and freshly ground black pepper

FOR THE SAUCE
tomato and pepper sauce (see p.93)

FOR THE GARNISH
small sprigs or leaves of herbs

The tarts can be served individually as suggested in the recipe — with a little sauce on the side — and put at each place setting for the guests when they are at table, or they can be handed around to eat with the pre-prandial drinks. In which case, omit the sauce.

For the pastry, rub the butter into the flour, salt and sugar. Add the egg yolk and cream cheese and quickly and gently bind to a soft dough. Cover and chill for at least 30 minutes.

Roll the pastry out thinly on a lightly floured board with a lightly floured rolling pin. If the dough is a little too sticky to handle roll it out between 2 sheets of plastic wrap, separating the plastic wrap and pastry occasionally to allow the pastry to stretch evenly.

With a lightly floured cutter, cut out circles and use to line cupcake or muffin pans. Cover and chill for 30 minutes.

Heat the oven to 375°F.

Prick the pastry lightly with a fork and bake for 10-15 minutes until lightly colored and crisp.

Meanwhile, heat the butter for the filling, add the shallot and cook over a moderate heat, stirring occasionally, until soft. Stir in the lettuce and cook for about 30 seconds, stirring. Purée then pass through a fine sieve and mix with the herbs.

Lightly beat the cheese, egg and cream together then stir in the herb mixture. Season.

Spoon into the baked pastry shells. Lower the oven temperature to 350°F and bake for about 15 minutes.

Leave the tarts to cool for a few minutes before removing from the pan. Spoon a little of the tomato and pepper sauce over part of 6 warmed plates. Place a tart to one side and garnish with herbs.

SMOKED SALMON FLOWERS

INGREDIENTS (serves 4)
8 tbsp cold fish aspic (see p.77)
4 small, wafer thin slices of smoked
*   salmon*
4 tsp caviar
4 long chives or julienned green part
*   of leek, blanched*
8 smaller chives or julienned green
*   part of leek, blanched*
8 petal shapes of lemon peel
8 small coriander leaves

A 'picture on a plate' with which to welcome each guest to their place at table.

Spoon the aspic over 4 medium size cold plates and leave until just on the point of setting.

Fold the sides of the slices of smoked salmon under and shape each slice into circles. Lightly put in position towards the edge of each plate. Make a well in the center of each piece of salmon. Place a little caviar in each well to form the centers of the flowers.

Make a stem for the flower from the long chives or

julienned leek and make leaves from the shorter pieces.

Place the petal shapes of lemon below the smoked salmon and the coriander leaves at the base of the stems. Leave in a cool place.

CHEESE POUCHES

INGREDIENTS (per pouch)
2 sheets of filo pastry, approximately
  5 inches square
melted butter
1 cube of soft mild goats cheese
2 tsp chopped pecans or walnuts
oil for deep frying
thin strip of green part of leek,
  blanched

Allow one pouch per person if these tasty morsels are to be handed round with pre-prandial drinks — and do provide napkins and plates. Allow two or three per person if they are to be served as a first course.

Brush one side of one piece of pastry with melted butter. Place the other sheet on top. Place the cheese and nuts in the center.

Fold the corners of the pastry over the filling and twist them around so they are sealed and stand at right angles to the filling.

Heat a deep fat frying pan of oil to about 375°F. Lower the pouches into the oil and fry for about 3 minutes until crisp and golden brown. Serve hot with a thin strip of leek tied around the neck.

MUSHROOMS FILLED WITH TOMATO

MOUSSETTES

INGREDIENTS (serves 4)
2 cups mushroom caps
flesh of 4 large tomatoes
1 tbsp tomato paste
1 tbsp medium bodied dry white wine
1 tsp gelatin
⅔ cup whipping cream, lightly
  whipped
salt and freshly ground black pepper
very small basil leaves or finely
  shredded basil

Blanch the mushroom caps in lightly acidulated, seasoned water. Drain very well then dry on paper towels.

Purée the tomato flesh with the tomato paste and wine in a liquidizer, then simmer gently for about 5 minutes. Leave to cool slightly.

Dissolve the gelatin in 1½ tbsp water in a small bowl placed over a pan of hot water. Remove from the heat and cool slightly.

Blend the gelatin into the tomato and leave to cool placed over a bowl of iced water. Stir occasionally.

When almost set, gently fold in the cream. Season.

Spoon tomato mixture onto individual mushroom caps. Leave in a cool place.

Place very small basil leaves or finely shredded basil on top of each moussette to serve.

OPPOSITE *Artichoke mousse in smoked salmon*
Recipe: page 88
ABOVE *Ceviche of salmon*
Recipe: page 89

GINGER AND LIME SHERBET

WITH MELON

INGREDIENTS (serves 4)
3—4 honeydew melons, lightly
*   chilled*

FOR THE SHERBET
bare cup sugar
finely grated rind of 1 lime
1 tbsp very finely chopped fresh root
*   ginger*
juice of 3 limes, strained

FOR THE GARNISH
small lettuce or watercress leaves
julienned lime peel, knotted and
*   blanched*
pieces of lime

Picture: page 90

To taste the full fresh, clean glory of this sherbet do not prepare it more than a few hours in advance. It will then make a delicious, light refreshing first course.

For the sherbet, gently heat the sugar in 1 cup water, stirring until dissolved. Add the lime rind and ginger and leave over a very low heat, covered for 15 minutes. Stir in the lime juice and leave to cool.

Pour the syrup into a shallow metal container. Chill for an hour then cover and place in the freezer until firm, turning the mixture into a cold bowl and whisking well with a cold whisk every 45 minutes. Alternatively, freeze in an ice cream or sherbet maker for 10—12 minutes then transfer to a container, cover and leave in the freezer.

About 30 minutes before serving, transfer the sherbet to the refrigerator.

Cut the melons into halves; the number of melons to use depends on their size. Scoop out the seeds and cut the flesh into slices. Carefully remove the skin from the slices.

Arrange the slices of melon on 4 cold plates. Add scoops of the sherbet, the lettuce or watercress leaves, julienned lime and pieces of lime.

ARTICHOKE MOUSSE IN

SMOKED SALMON

INGREDIENTS (serves 4)
4-6 slices of smoked salmon

FOR THE MOUSSE
2 large artichokes
a squeeze of lemon juice
1 tsp gelatin
1 tbsp dry white wine
salt and freshly ground white pepper
⅔ cup whipping cream

FOR THE SAUCE
2 tbsp finely chopped shallots
4 tbsp tarragon vinegar
4 tbsp butter
1 tbsp crème fraîche
1 cup fromage blanc or yogurt
salt and freshly ground white pepper

Trim the artichokes, then cook in salted, acidulated, boiling water for about 40-45 minutes until tender.

Remove the artichokes and leave upside down to drain. Pull off the leaves, (reserve some for the garnish) and scrape their flesh into a bowl. Discard the hairy choke, chop the base and add to the bowl.

Dissolve the gelatin in the wine and 2 tbsp water in a small bowl placed over a pan of hot water. Remove from the heat.

Purée the artichoke flesh with the seasoning, then mix in the gelatin. Cover and leave in a cool place until very lightly set.

Meanwhile, line 4 individual serving dishes with the slices of smoked salmon, leaving sufficient overlapping the sides of each one to fold over the tops.

Lightly whip the cream, then gently fold into the artichoke mixture. Check the seasoning and add a little lemon juice, if

FOR THE GARNISH
artichoke leaves
tarragon leaves
radicchio leaves
slices of zucchini with carrot
sprigs of dill

Picture: page 86

necessary. Divide between the dishes and fold the overlapping smoked salmon over.

Cover and leave in a cool place to set.

For the sauce, boil the shallots in the vinegar until nearly all the liquid has evaporated. Very gradually stir in the butter, making sure each piece is completely incorporated before adding the next. Stir in the crème fraîche. Remove from the heat, leave to cool slightly. Then stir in the fromage blanc or yogurt. Season.

Unmold the smoked salmon parcels onto 4 cold plates, preferably oval. Arrange 4 or 5 artichoke leaves in a circle to the side of the smoked salmon and place a small spoonful of the dressing in the center. Garnish the dressing with tarragon leaves. Add radicchio leaves, slices of zucchini with carrot and sprigs of dill.

C E V I C H E   O F   S A L M O N

INGREDIENTS (serves 4)
1¼ lb skinless salmon fillets,
*   chilled*
½ cup lime juice
¾ cup lemon juice
½ red chili, seeded
1 bunch of fresh coriander
3 avocados
3 tbsp crème fraîche
2½ tbsp thyme or tarragon vinegar
1 tbsp Dijon mustard
2 tbsp red pepper, julienned
2 tbsp green pepper, julienned
2 tbsp chopped shallot
salt
a squeeze of lemon juice

FOR THE GARNISH
strips of red and green peppers,
*   blanched*
slices of lemon

Picture: page 87

The origins of this dish are rooted in the traditional cuisine of South America.

Cut the salmon into ⅛ in thick slices, about 1 inch square, then lay them in a large shallow dish.

Mix the lime and lemon juice, chili and the stems from the coriander together and pour over the salmon. Cover and leave in a cool place for 4—5 hours.

Drain off the marinade.

Purée the flesh from one avocado and mix with the marinade, crème fraîche, vinegar, 1½ tbsp finely chopped coriander leaves, mustard, peppers, shallot and salt. Pour over the salmon and leave for 10—15 minutes.

Peel and slice the remaining avocados. Brush with lemon juice, then arrange in fan shapes on 6 cold plates. Add the salmon slices.

Adjust the seasoning of the dressing if necessary and spoon a little over the salmon. Garnish with strips of red and green peppers and slices of lemon.

◆

OPPOSITE
Ginger and lime sherbet
with melon
Recipe: page 88
ABOVE   *Crab and fine julienned*
vegetables set in light aspic
Recipe: page 93

P E A R   V I N A I G R E T T E   W I T H   S M O K E D   S A L M O N   M O U S S E

INGREDIENTS (serves 6)
3 ripe pears
⅓ cup white wine vinegar
¼ cup fruity dry white wine
10 mint leaves
10 tarragon leaves
salt and freshly ground white pepper

FOR THE MOUSSE
3 tbsp full bodied dry white wine
½ bay leaf
5 tbsp fish stock
1 tsp black peppercorns, crushed
pinch of cayenne pepper
1½ tsp lime or lemon juice
5 oz smoked salmon, skinned and
    boned
1 rounded tsp gelatin
¼ cup crème fraîche, lightly
    whipped

FOR THE GARNISH
radicchio lettuce
mint and tarragon leaves

Picture: page 94

Peel, core and slice the pears. Place them in a sauteuse or large frying pan, add the vinegar, wine, mint, tarragon, salt and pepper and water to cover if necessary. Poach for 5—10 minutes until just opaque. Leave to cool in the liquid, then remove with a slotted spoon and drain well. Reserve the liquor.

For the mousse, boil the wine, bay leaf, stock, peppercorns, cayenne pepper and lime or lemon juice until reduced by half. Pass through a strainer.

Purée the smoked salmon in a food processor or blender.

Dissolve the gelatin in 2 tbsp water in a bowl placed over a pan of hot water. Remove from the heat, leave to cool slightly, then stir in the reduced liquid.

Mix the gelatin mixture into the salmon, then fold in the crème fraîche. Season, then spoon into lightlyoiled individual molds. Cover and leave to set.

Unmold the mousses onto cold plates. Arrange the slices of pear around and spoon a little of the poaching liquor over them. Garnish with radicchio lettuce, mint and tarragon leaves.

F I L L E T   D E   B O E U F   C R U

INGREDIENTS (serves 6)
½ cup lemon juice
½ cup olive oil
3 tbsp finely chopped shallots
2 tbsp finely chopped parsley
2 tbsp finely chopped watercress
1 tbsp finely chopped tarragon
1 tbsp finely chopped basil
1 tbsp finely chopped chervil
salt and pepper
1 lb fillet of beef, chilled in the freezer,
    wrapped in foil, for about an hour

FOR THE GARNISH
1 carrot, julienned
6 scallion tassels (see p.71), halved
3 inch piece of celery, julienned

The secret of getting really wafer thin slices of beef lies with chilling the meat briefly in the freezer and using a long bladed, razor sharp knife.

Mix the first 9 ingredients together in a blender. Chill.

Slice the beef as thinly as possible across the grain with a very sharp knife. Beat each slice separately between two sheets of plastic wrap. Lay the slices on 6 cold plates.

Trickle the dressing over the slices of beef to form a pattern, then garnish with the vegetables. Serve any remaining dressing separately.

EGGS BEHIND BARS

INGREDIENTS (serves 4)
4 carrots, sliced in ¼ in wide strips
½ cup French beans, trimmed
2 oz thickly sliced smoked salmon,
    cut into ¼ in wide strips
4 sprigs of chervil
butter
3 eggs, beaten
1 cup whipping cream
finely grated rind of ½ lemon
salt and freshly ground black pepper

FOR THE SAUCE
2 tbsp olive oil
3 shallots, finely chopped
1 clove of garlic, crushed
1 large tomato, chopped
1 large red pepper, skinned and
    chopped
bouquet garni of a sprig of thyme,
    ½ bay leaf, 3 parsley stalks, a sprig
    of basil
salt and freshly ground black pepper
½-1 tsp tomato paste
pinch of sugar

FOR THE GARNISH
sprigs of chervil

Picture: page 95

Heat the oven to 325°F.

Cook the carrots and beans separately in simmering salted water until just tender. Refresh and drain very well.

Cut the carrots, beans and smoked salmon to the same height as the mold to be used. Place a sprig of chervil in the bottom of each of 4 well buttered molds. Stand 2 strips of carrot inside each mold and press them well into the butter. Place 2 beans next to the carrots and 2 strips of smoked salmon next to the beans. Repeat until the molds are completely lined.

Lightly beat the eggs with the cream, lemon rind and seasoning. Strain into the molds, place the molds in a baking or roasting pan and surround with boiling water. Cover the molds and place in the oven for about 40 minutes until lightly set.

Heat the oil for the sauce, add the shallots and garlic and cook over a very low heat, stirring occasionally, until soft. Stir in the tomatoes, pepper and bouquet garni. Add 6-7 tbsp water to cover. Season, cover the pan and simmer for 20-30 minutes. Remove the bouquet garni and pass the tomato mixture through a sieve. If necessary, add a little tomato paste to give a good color and adjust the flavor with a pinch of sugar. Reheat gently.

Remove the molds from the heat and leave to stand for about 2 minutes before unmolding towards the side of 4 warmed plates. Spoon a crescent of sauce around the molds and garnish with sprigs of chervil.

CRAB AND FINE JULIENNED

VEGETABLES SET IN LIGHT ASPIC

INGREDIENTS (serves 4)
3¾ cups fish aspic (see p.77)
generous ½ cup cooked white crab
    meat, shredded
¼ cup fine julienned white of leek,
    blanched
¼ cup fine julienned celery, blanched
¼ cup fine julienned peeled, seeded
    cucumber
1½ tbsp finely diced tomato flesh

Picture: page 91

Spoon a little aspic into a small decorative mold then twist and turn the mold around to coat the sides and base in aspic. Repeat with 3 more molds.

Spoon a little of the remaining aspic into a small bowl, add the crab meat and stir it around gently until it is lightly coated. Remove, with a slotted spoon, allowing excess aspic to drain off.

Place some of the crab in the base of each mold. Coat the vegetables in aspic with the same method used for the crab, then arrange some on top of the crab. Repeat the layering until all the crab and vegetables have been used up. Fill the molds with any remaining aspic. Leave the molds to set.

Just before serving, unmold the molds onto the plates.

*Pear vinaigrette with smoked salmon
mousse
Recipe: page 92*

Eggs behind bars
Recipe: page 93

EGGS WITH LETTUCE AND SORREL

AND CHAMPAGNE SAUCE

INGREDIENTS (serves 4)
3 tbsp butter
1 shallot, finely chopped
⅓ cup finely shredded Iceberg lettuce
    leaves
¼ cup finely shredded sorrel
¼ cup finely shredded spinach
⅔ cup dry white wine
¼ cup veal or chicken stock
⅓ cup whipping cream
salt and freshly ground black pepper
4 eggs
champagne sauce (see p.156)

FOR THE GARNISH
individual watercress leaves
caviar
radicchio leaves

Picture: page 98

Heat half the butter, add the shallot, cover and cook over a moderate heat, shaking the pan occasionally until soft. Stir in the lettuce, sorrel and spinach, wine and stock. Cook over a moderate heat until the spinach and sorrel have nearly fallen and are almost tender but the lettuce still has some texture, then increase the heat and boil rapidly until the excess liquid has evaporated. Stir in the cream and simmer for 2—3 minutes, then lower the heat and swirl in the remaining butter. Season.

Meanwhile, poach the eggs in a large shallow pan of salted, acidulated water until the yolks are slightly set. Carefully remove with a slotted spoon and drain on a cloth. Cut to a neat shape with a plain cookie cutter.

Gently warm the champagne sauce.

Divide the lettuce mixture between 4 warmed plates. Place the eggs on top and spoon the champagne sauce around. Garnish the egg yolks with a little caviar and arrange the watercress and radicchio leaves around the outside edge of the sauce.

SLICES OF CUCUMBER FILLED WITH

TROUT MOUSSE

INGREDIENTS (serves 4)
8 oz trout fillets
a squeeze of lemon juice
1 egg, separated
salt and freshly ground white pepper
4 tbsp whipping cream
1 tbsp red shellfish butter, softened
    (see p.77)
1 long straight English cucumber,
    peeled, trimmed and cut into 3
    even lengths

FOR THE SAUCE
2 tbsp finely chopped shallots
flesh of 3 tomatoes, chopped
a sprig of fennel
½ cup medium bodied fruity dry white
    wine
1 cup vegetable stock
⅔ cup crème fraîche
salt and freshly ground white pepper

If shellfish butter is not available, use 1-2 tsp tomato paste. Although the flavor will suffer slightly it will still be a delicious, light first course.

———————————

Purée the trout in a food processor or blender until smooth, then mix in the lemon juice, egg yolk and seasoning, until smooth. Add the cream, then the egg white and shellfish butter, mixing well until smooth. Chill for about an hour.

With an apple corer, remove the seeds from the cucumber and sufficient flesh to leave a ring of cucumber about ¼ inch thick, and leave to dry on paper towels.

Place each piece of cucumber on a piece of foil, fill with the trout mixture then enclose in foil, securing the seams well.

Place the foil parcels in a saucepan, cover with water and simmer for 30 minutes.

Remove the parcels from the pan, open them and carefully drain off any moisture. Leave to cool completely, then chill.

For the sauce, boil the shallots with the tomatoes and fennel in the wine and stock until reduced to ⅔ cup.

FOR THE GARNISH
diamond shapes of tomato flesh
sprigs of dill

Remove the fennel, liquidize the sauce, then pass through a sieve into a clean saucepan. Stir in the crème fraîche and simmer until slightly thickened. Season, leave to cool then chill.

About 15 minutes before serving return the cucumber to room temperature. Cut each length of cucumber into 4, making 12 rings.

Divide the sauce between 4 cold plates. Arrange 3 slices of cucumber with the diamonds of tomato and sprigs of dill in the sauce.

MUSSEL TERRINE

INGREDIENTS *(serves 6—8)*
1 lb mussels in their shells
⅓ cup dry white wine
1 tsp chopped parsley
1 tsp chopped chives
1 lb turbot, chopped and chilled
salt
lemon juice
2 egg whites
2 cups whipping cream, chilled
freshly ground white pepper
1 green pepper, blanched and diced
12 spinach leaves, trimmed and
  blanched
¾ cup cooked shrimp, shelled

FOR THE SAUCE
flesh of 4 ripe tomatoes
1 tbsp tarragon vinegar
1½ tbsp olive oil
1 tsp tomato paste
pinch of sugar
salt and freshly ground white pepper

FOR THE GARNISH
coriander leaves
tomato 'roses' (see p.71)

Picture: page 99

The underrated mussel comes into its own in this terrine, at its best made in late autumn or winter, when mussels are in their prime.

———————————

Cook the mussels with the wine and herbs in a covered, heavy based pan over a high heat for about 5 minutes, shaking the pan frequently, until they open. Discard any that remain closed and remove the others from their shells. Dry on paper towels.

Blend the turbot in a food processor, then mix in the salt and lemon juice followed by the egg whites. Pass through a sieve into a bowl placed over a bowl of ice, then gradually work in the cream. Add white pepper, cover and chill for 30 minutes.

Heat the oven to 300°F. Line the base of a terrine with buttered wax paper.

Divide the turbot mixture into two thirds and one third. Fold the green pepper into the larger portion and spread half of this in the base of the terrine. Cover with half the spinach leaves and lay half the mussels over them. Fold the shrimp into the remaining turbot mixture and carefully spread over the mussels. Place the remaining mussels on top, followed by the remaining spinach leaves. Spread the remaining green pepper mixture over the spinach leaves.

Cover with buttered wax paper and stand the terrine in a roasting or baking pan. Pour in boiling water to surround the terrine and place in the oven for 1 hour.

Purée the tomatoes, vinegar and oil for the sauce, then add the tomato paste, sugar and seasoning to taste and to adjust the color. Purée again and chill.

Leave the terrine to cool slightly before unmolding.

Cut the terrine into slices, place one on each plate and place a spoonful of the sauce to the side. Garnish with coriander leaves and tomato 'roses'.

Eggs with lettuce and sorrel and
champagne sauce
Recipe: page 96

OYSTER AND ZUCCHINI

CROUSTADES

INGREDIENTS (serves 4)
6 sheets of filo pastry (see p.81)
melted butter
8 oysters
½ cup dry white wine
1 tbsp finely chopped shallot
1 cup fish stock
2 tbsp dry vermouth
½ cup whipping cream
a few strands of saffron
4 tbsp butter, softened
sea salt and freshly ground white
*   pepper*
2 small zucchini, blanched and thinly
*   sliced*

FOR THE GARNISH
small sprigs of thyme
finely diced concassé tomatoes
or red and black roe and salmon eggs

Picture: page 103

Scallops may be substituted for oysters and should be prepared and served in the same way — poach the bodies for 1 minute, turn them over, add the corals and poach for another minute.

———————————

Heat the oven to 420°F.

Fold the sheets of filo in half and cut out a circle from each piece using a plain cutter. Line 4 cupcake or muffin pan cups with 3 circles, one on top of the other, brushing with melted butter in between.

Bake for about 8 minutes until crisp and golden.

Meanwhile, open the oysters, (see p.61), reserving the liquor, and cut into halves.

Heat the wine, add the shallots and reduce by half. Lower the heat, add the oysters and poach for 15 seconds.

Carefully transfer the oysters to a warmed dish with a slotted spoon. Cover.

Add the stock and vermouth to the poaching liquor and reduce to 2 tbsp. Stir in the oyster liquor, cream and saffron and simmer until slightly thickened.

Pass through a sieve. Reheat gently without boiling and gradually whisk in 3 tbsp of butter, making sure each piece is completely incorporated before adding the next. Season.

Heat the remaining butter. Carefully and briefly toss in the zucchini slices to warm through.

Put the oysters in the sauce for a few seconds to warm them, then place them in the center of the croustades. Arrange the zucchini slices around the sides, pour a little of the sauce over the oysters and garnish with the thyme and tomato dice or roe and salmon eggs.

ZUCCHINI AND TOMATO MOUSSES

INGREDIENTS (serves 6)

FOR THE TOMATO MOUSSE
2 tbsp butter, diced
2 shallots, finely chopped
½ carrot, finely chopped
flesh of 3 tomatoes, chopped
bouquet garni of a sprig of parsley, a
    sprig of thyme, 1 bay leaf, a small
    sprig of rosemary
scant 2 tsp gelatin
2 tbsp finely chopped mixed herbs
salt and freshly ground black pepper
½ cup whipping cream, lightly
    whipped

FOR THE ZUCCHINI MOUSSE
5 tbsp butter
¼ cup courgettes, diced in ¼ in pieces
salt and freshly ground black pepper
1 shallot, finely chopped
2 tbsp finely chopped mixed herbs
scant 2 tsp gelatin
½ cup whipping cream, lightly
    whipped
3 zucchini, finely chopped

FOR THE SALADS
1 tbsp olive oil
1 tsp red wine vinegar
1 tsp finely chopped chives
salt and freshly ground black pepper
1-2 leaves of curly endive

The salad in this recipe can be changed, and the mousse mixture made separately, perhaps to serve as a very light first course for 3 or 4 people.

Heat the butter for the tomato mousse, add the shallots and carrot and cook over a low heat, stirring frequently, until soft. Stir in the tomatoes and bouquet garni and simmer, stirring occasionally, for 25-30 minutes until reduced to 1 cup.

Dissolve the gelatin in 2 tbsp water in a bowl placed over a pan of hot water. Remove from the heat and leave to cool slightly.

Remove the bouquet garni from the tomato mixture, then purée the mixture. Add the herbs and seasoning.

Blend a little of the tomato mixture with the gelatin, then mix this back into the remaining tomato mixture. Leave until just approaching setting point, stirring frequently.

Meanwhile, for the zucchini mousse, heat 1 tbsp butter. Add the diced zucchini and cook over a moderate heat, stirring occasionally for about 2 minutes. Remove with a slotted spoon, drain on paper towels. Season.

Heat the remaining butter, add the shallot, cover and cook over a moderate heat, shaking the pan occasionally until the shallot is soft. Add the chopped zucchini and cook until the moisture has evaporated, stirring frequently. Purée — there should be 1 cup. If necessary, cook further to evaporate more moisture. Add the herbs and seasoning.

Dissolve the gelatin in 2 tbsp water in a bowl over a pan of hot water. Remove from the heat and cool slightly.

Blend a little of the zucchini purée with the gelatin, then mix back into the remaining purée. Leave until approaching setting point.

Lightly fold the cream into the thickening tomato mixture and divide between 6 oiled, decorative molds.

Lightly fold the cream and diced zucchini into the zucchini mixture. Spoon into the molds and stir through the two mixtures a few times to give a light marbled effect. Cover and leave to set.

Whisk the olive oil, vinegar, chives and seasoning together for the garnish. Arrange a little curly endive on the side of 6 cold plates. Spoon the dressing over. Unmold the mousses onto the plates.

ABOVE *Brawn of salmon*
Recipe: page 104
OPPOSITE *Oysters and zucchini croustades*
Recipe: page 100

103

ASPARAGUS GATEAUX

INGREDIENTS (serves 6)
1 lb green asparagus, trimmed
3 eggs
2 egg yolks
2 cups cereal cream
pinch of nutmeg
salt

FOR THE SAUCE
1 tbsp coriander seeds, crushed
1 cup dry white wine
½ cup dry vermouth
⅔ cup cereal cream
½ cup + 2 tbsp butter
salt and freshly ground black pepper

FOR THE GARNISH
36 asparagus tips, steamed
12 strips of blanched red pepper
sprigs of chervil

Picture: page 106

Steam the asparagus for about 8 minutes, until tender.

Heat the oven to 350°F.

Purée the asparagus, then pass through a fine sieve. Heat the purée, gently stirring to drive off any excess moisture.

Remove from the heat. Blend the eggs, egg yolk and cream together, then stir into the asparagus. Add a pinch of nutmeg and seasoning.

Divide between 6 buttered individual serving dishes. Place the dishes in a roasting or baking pan and surround with boiling water. Cover with wax paper.

Place in the oven for about 20 minutes until lightly set.

Meanwhile, lightly toast the coriander seeds in a dry nonstick pan for 2—3 minutes. Simmer with the wine and vermouth for 5 minutes, then reduce to about ¼ cup. Stir in the cream and simmer for 2—3 minutes, then pass through a sieve. Return to the rinsed pan and reheat, then reduce the heat to low. Dice the butter and gradually stir in, making sure that each piece is completely incorporated before adding the next. Season and keep warm, but do not allow to boil.

Remove the gâteaux from the heat and leave for a few minutes before unmolding onto 6 warmed plates. Spoon a circle of sauce around the gâteaux and garnish with the asparagus tips, red pepper and chervil.

BRAWN OF SALMON

INGREDIENTS (serves 4)
10 oysters
7 oz salmon fillet, cut into ¼ in wide
  strips
⅔ cup dry white wine
⅔ cup fish stock
1½ tbsp chopped parsley
salt and freshly ground black pepper
scant 1½ tbsp gelatin
½ tbsp chopped tarragon
½ tbsp chopped chervil
2 hard cooked eggs, yolks and white
  coarsely chopped
1½ lemons, rind cut into small squares
¼ cup red pepper, blanched and diced
2 heaped tsp green peppercorns

FOR THE GARNISH
slices of lime
coriander leaves
red pepper sauce (see p.93), for
  serving

Picture: page 102

Remove the oysters from their shells and marinade with the salmon in the wine, stock, parsley and seasoning for 1 hour in a shallow dish covered with plastic wrap.

Remove the salmon and oysters from the marinade with a slotted spoon and drain well. Strain the marinade.

Soften the gelatin in a little of the marinade. Gently warm the remaining marinade, then stir into the gelatin until dissolved. Cool quickly, then chill until syrupy.

Pour a thin layer of the syrupy gelatin over the base of a terrine and sprinkle some of the tarragon, chervil, egg, lemon rind, red pepper and peppercorns over. Arrange some of the salmon strips lengthways on top. Cover and chill.

Repeat the layering, adding the oysters when half the ingredients have been used.

Cover and chill for 24 hours.

Unmold onto a chilled plate and carefully cut into slices. Place the slices on cold plates and garnish with slices of lime and coriander leaves. Serve with a little red pepper sauce.

T R I P L E   V E G E T A B L E   T I M B A L E S

INGREDIENTS (serves 4)

FOR THE CARROTS
1½ cups young carrots, chopped
a pinch of sugar
salt
3 tbsp whipping cream
1 tbsp butter
white pepper
1½ small egg whites, lightly whisked

FOR THE TURNIPS
2 cups baby turnips, peeled and
    chopped
salt
¼ cup whipping cream
freshly ground white pepper
a pinch of cayenne
1½ small egg whites, lightly whisked

FOR THE BROCCOLI
3 cups broccoli flowerets
salt
¼ cup whipping cream
freshly ground black pepper
grated nutmeg
1½ small egg whites, lightly whisked

FOR THE SAUCE
lemon sauce (see p.108)

FOR THE GARNISH
broccoli flowerets
julienned carrot
baby turnips, turned

All the vegetables can be cooked and puréed in advance and all the other ingredients weighed out so that there is little to do to complete this first course.

Heat the oven to 350°F.

Cook the carrots with the sugar in simmering salted water until soft. Drain well, purée, then mix in the cream and butter. Add white pepper and fold in the egg whites. Spoon into 4 buttered molds.

Cook the turnips in simmering salted water until tender. Drain well, purée, then mix in the cream, freshly ground white pepper, and a pinch of cayenne pepper. Fold in the egg whites and spoon into 4 small buttered molds.

Cook the broccoli in simmering salted water until just tender. Drain well, purée, then mix in the cream, pepper and nutmeg. Fold in the egg whites and spoon the mixture into 4 small buttered molds.

Place all the molds in a roasting or baking pan. Surround with boiling water, cover the molds with buttered wax paper and place the pan in the oven for about 20 minutes until the custards are just set.

Meanwhile, prepare the lemon sauce and blanch, refresh and drain the vegetables for the garnish.

Remove the molds from the heat and leave to cool slightly before unmolding onto 4 warmed plates. Spoon the sauce to one side of the molds and decorate the other side of the plates with the vegetables.

C H I C K E N   L I V E R   C U S T A R D S

INGREDIENTS (serves 6)
1¼ cups whipping cream
10 oz chicken livers, trimmed
3 eggs
2 egg yolks
pinch of freshly grated nutmeg
salt and freshly ground black pepper
2 cups French beans

FOR THE GARNISH
fresh tomato paste (see p.302)
broccoli flowerets

Picture: page 107

Heat the oven to 350°F.

Slowly bring the cream to simmering point.

In a food processor or blender, purée the chicken livers (approx 1¼ cups), eggs, egg yolks, nutmeg and seasoning, then, with the motor running, slowly pour in the cream. Pass through a fine sieve, then pour into 6 individual buttered serving dishes or molds. Place the dishes or molds in a roasting or baking pan, pour boiling water around them, cover and place in the oven for 35—40 minutes.

Blanch the beans and the broccoli flowerets for the garnish separately. Refresh and drain well. Gently warm the paste.

Leave the custards to stand for a few minutes before turning them out onto warmed plates. Spoon a very small amount of the paste on top of each custard. Arrange the beans with a little more of the paste and serve the remaining paste separately. Garnish with broccoli flowerets.

ABOVE *Asparagus gâteaux*
Recipe: page 104
OPPOSITE *Chicken liver custards*
Recipe: page 105

OMELET GATEAU

INGREDIENTS (serves 6)
2½ tbsp olive oil
¾ cup very ripe, but not squashy,
  tomatoes, chopped
½ red pepper, blanched and chopped
½ tsp chopped thyme
1 tsp tomato paste
⅔ cup spinach
¼ cup watercress leaves
5 eggs, beaten
5½ tbsp crème fraîche
salt and freshly ground black pepper
a pinch of grated nutmeg
6 tbsp Comté cheese, finely grated
a small pinch of mustard powder
red pepper sauce (see p.93)

FOR THE GARNISH
slices of cucumber, carrot and radish

Picture: page 111

Heat the oven to 265°F.

Heat 1 tbsp olive oil, add the tomatoes, red pepper and thyme and cook until most of the moisture from the tomatoes has evaporated. Drain through a sieve, then mix the flesh in the sieve with the tomato paste.

In a clean pan, heat 1½ tbsp oil, add the spinach and watercress leaves and cook, stirring, until the moisture has evaporated. Turn into a sieve and press out any remaining moisture, then chop the spinach mixture and leave to cool.

Divide the eggs evenly between 3 bowls. Mix the tomatoes, 1½ tbsp crème fraîche and seasoning into one bowl; the spinach, 1½ tbsp crème fraîche, nutmeg and a little salt into another and the remaining crème fraîche, cheese, mustard and seasoning into the third.

Pour the tomato mixture into an aluminum foil loaf pan, place in a roasting or baking pan and surround with boiling water. Place in the oven for 20 minutes. Cover the other two bowls.

Carefully pour the cheese mixture onto the tomato when it is set and return to the oven for about 20 minutes.

Carefully pour the spinach mixture onto the cheese when it is set and return to the oven for about 20—25 minutes.

Remove from the heat and leave in a warm place for 10—15 minutes before turning out onto a warmed plate. Cut into slices. Serve warm with the sauce and garnish with the slices of cucumber, carrot and radish.

DUO OF BROCCOLI WITH

LEMON SAUCE

INGREDIENTS (serves 6)
2 lb broccoli
1 egg, separated
salt and freshly ground white pepper
¼ cup crème fraîche, lightly whipped

FOR THE SAUCE
1 tbsp lemon juice
1 tbsp whipping cream
1 cup cold butter

This light, fresh tasting dish serves 6 for a starter but larger portions could be served as a main course for vegetarians. The purée can be prepared in advance.

Trim the flowerets from the stems of the broccoli. Slice the stems.

Cook, refresh and drain the stems and flowerets separately. Reserve some of the flowerets for the garnish and purée the remaining broccoli until very smooth.

Heat the oven to 350°F.

Gently warm the purée, stirring frequently to drive off the excess moisture. When the purée is dry, remove it from the heat and beat in the egg yolk and seasoning.

Whisk the egg white until stiff but not dry and fold into the purée with the crème fraîche.

Divide the broccoli mixture between 6 lightly oiled decorative ovenproof molds. Place the molds in a roasting or baking pan, surround with boiling water, cover the molds and place in the oven for about 20—30 minutes until just set. Remove from the heat and leave to stand for a minute or two before unmolding.

For the sauce, boil the lemon juice until syrupy. Reduce the heat to very low, and whisk in the cream. Dice the butter and gradually whisk in, making sure each piece is fully incorporated before adding the next. Season.

Turn the molds out onto 6 warmed plates and arrange the flowerets around. Trickle some of the sauce over and around the base of the molds and spoon a little around the flowerets. Serve any remaining sauce separately.

A T R I O O F M O U S S E S W I T H

A T R I O O F S A U C E S

INGREDIENTS *(serves 6)*
FOR THE SCALLOP MOUSSES
9 large scallops
2 tbsp dry vermouth
salt
1 whole egg
1 egg white
1¼ cups whipping cream, chilled
freshly ground white pepper

FOR THE SPINACH MOUSSE
1½ lb spinach
4 tbsp butter
2 shallots, finely chopped
salt and freshly ground black pepper
1 whole egg beaten with 1 yolk
¼ cup whipping cream

FOR THE SALMON MOUSSES
7 oz salmon fillet
salt and lemon juice
1 small egg white
1 cup whipping cream, chilled
freshly ground white pepper
1 spinach leaf

FOR THE SAUCES
white wine sauce (see p.180)
½ quantity of red shellfish sauce (see p.176)

FOR THE GARNISH
salmon eggs
watercress leaves

For the scallop mousses, purée the scallops with the vermouth then add salt, followed by the whole egg, then the egg white. Pass through a sieve into a bowl placed over a bowl of ice. Very gradually work in the cream. Season, cover and chill for at least 30 minutes.

For the spinach mousses, blanch the spinach and drain very well, pressing down well on the leaves to extract as much liquid as possible. Heat the butter, add the shallots, cover and cook over a low heat, shaking the pan occasionally, until the shallots are soft. Stir in the spinach and seasoning then beat in the egg, egg yolk and cream. Purée, then pass through a fine sieve.

For the salmon mousses, purée the salmon then add the salt and lemon juice followed by the egg white. Pass through a sieve into a bowl over a bowl of ice. Gradually beat in the cream. Season. Cover and chill for at least 30 minutes.

Blanch the spinach leaf and drain very well. Purée with half the white wine sauce.

Warm the white wine sauce, the pale green colored white wine sauce and the red shellfish sauce separately.

Bring a sauteuse or large frying pan of salted water to the boil. Lower the heat so the water barely moves. With the help of two spoons, form each mixture into 6 quenelle shapes. Gently lower them into the water and poach for 3 minutes each side. Remove with a slotted spoon and drain on a cloth.

Cover a third of 6 warmed plates with white wine sauce, a third with green colored white wine sauce and the remaining third with the red shellfish sauce.

Place the spinach mousses on the white sauce, scallop mousses on the red shellfish sauce and the salmon mousses on the green sauce. Place salmon eggs in the center and garnish with watercress leaves.

Omelet gâteau
Recipe: page 108

TERRINE OF CRAB AND

SMOKED SALMON

INGREDIENTS *(serves 6—8)*
2 lb live crab
1 lb pike, skinned and filleted
3 egg whites
4 tbsp butter
salt and lemon juice
3 egg yolks
1¼ cups whipping cream, chilled
freshly ground white pepper
cayenne pepper
1 lb medium size spinach leaves,
 trimmed
5 oz smoked salmon slices, chilled

FOR THE GARNISH
carrot 'roses' (see p.70)
sprigs of fresh herbs

Picture: page 110

This attractive terrine is a good choice for a meal in which the main course requires a fair amount of last minute attention, as it has to be left overnight after cooking and before unmolding. For the choice of crab see p. 43.

———————————

Kill the crab (see p.61) and cook in boiling water for 3 minutes then refresh it in iced water.

Remove and crack the claws and remove the white meat.

Place the crab's body on a chopping board on its back and split it in half. Remove the brown meat, mix it in a liquidizer for 2 minutes, then pass it through a very fine sieve.

Combine the pike and white crab meat to make a total weight of 1¼ lb. Purée in a food processor or blender with the egg whites, butter, salt and lemon juice. Pass through a fine sieve.

Put the mixture into a bowl over a bowl of ice, then gradually beat in the egg yolks. Remove and reserve a quarter of the mixture. Gradually beat the cream into the remaining mixture while it is still on ice. Season with white pepper.

Slowly beat the brown crab meat into the reserved mixture. Check that the mixture does not become too runny by regularly dropping a teaspoonful into boiling water to see that the consistency is firm, but not rubbery. Season with a little cayenne pepper.

Blanch the spinach leaves, then refresh and drain well. Line a terrine with leaves allowing sufficient overlap to fold over the top of the terrine.

Fill a pastry bag with the white mixture and pipe it to a depth of about 1 inch on the bottom of the terrine and ½ inch thick up the sides. Put the terrine in the refrigerator.

Cover a large tray with plastic wrap. Form a large rectangle with the smoked salmon and spread the brown mixture over. Put the tray into the freezer for about 15 minutes, until it is very cold but not frozen.

Remove the tray from the freezer and, with the help of the plastic wrap, roll the mixture up like a jelly roll, then carefully place the roll in the center of the terrine. Fill in the sides and cover the top with the white mixture.

Heat the oven to 350°F. Cover with the overlapping spinach leaves. Cover with well buttered foil, wrapping the edges under the rim of the terrine to seal in the steam. Place the terrine in a roasting or baking pan, surround it with boiling water and place in the oven for 1 hour.

Cool and leave overnight before unmolding. Serve garnished with carrot 'roses' and sprigs of fresh herbs.

QUENELLES OF SWEETBREADS

INGREDIENTS (serves 4)
8 oz sweetbreads
¼ cup cognac
¼ cup dry white wine
a sprig of thyme
4 basil leaves
salt and lemon juice
1 egg white
1¼ cups whipping cream, chilled
freshly ground white pepper
chicken stock and dry white wine for
    poaching

FOR THE SAUCE
1 tbsp butter
2 tbsp shallot, finely chopped
5 tbsp dry vermouth
flesh of 3 large ripe tomatoes,
    chopped
2 tbsp tarragon vinegar
4 tbsp butter
salt and freshly ground white pepper

FOR THE GARNISH
artichoke bottoms, sliced
tarragon leaves
coriander leaves

Picture: page 114

Lay the sweetbreads in a shallow dish. Mix the cognac, wine, thyme and basil together and pour over the sweetbreads. Cover and leave in a cool place for 4 hours.

Remove the sweetbreads, drain and dry well, then purée in a food processor or blender. Add salt and lemon juice, then the egg white. Pass through a sieve into a bowl over a bowl of ice, then gradually beat in the cream. Add the white pepper, cover and chill for at least 30 minutes.

For the sauce, heat the butter, add the shallot, cover and cook over a moderate heat, shaking the pan occasionally, until soft. Stir in half the vermouth and the tomato flesh and simmer for about 10 minutes until most of the liquid has evaporated — if necessary, boil to evaporate the liquid. Pass through a fine sieve and measure off about ⅓ cup.

Boil the remaining vermouth and the vinegar until reduced to 1 tsp. Stir in the tomato mixture, bring to the boil, then reduce the heat to very low and gradually whisk in the butter, making sure that each piece is completely incorporated before adding the next. Season and keep warm, but do not allow to boil.

Heat a sauteuse or a large frying pan containing a mixture of chicken stock and dry white wine to just below simmering point. With the help of 2 spoons, form the sweetbread mixture into 8 oval shapes and gently lower them into the chicken stock/wine. Poach for about 3 minutes each side. Remove with a slotted spoon and drain on a cloth.

Arrange the quenelles on 4 warmed plates, add a little of the sauce and garnish with sliced artichoke bottoms, tarragon and coriander leaves.

SASHIMI OF TROUT

INGREDIENTS (serves 6)
3 trout, 6 oz each, chilled
juice of 1 orange
1 tsp finely grated orange rind
finely grated rind and juice of 1 lemon
1 tbsp olive oil
1 shallot, finely chopped
3 tbsp pink peppercorns
salt

FOR THE GARNISH
fine slices of orange and lemon
slices of cucumber

Picture: page 115

Do make sure the trout have a good true flavor. Chilling them well makes them easier to skin and slice thinly and neatly. Adjust the garnish according to your own degree of skill.

———————————

Skin the trout, then, with an extremely sharp, flexible knife, cut the flesh into wafer thin slices.

Lay the slices in a shallow dish, sprinkle the fruit juices and rinds, the oil, shallot, peppercorns and salt over and leave for 1 hour.

Carefully lift the trout slices from the marinade and arrange on 6 cold plates. Spoon a little of the marinade, including the peppercorns, over. Garnish with the orange, lemon and cucumber slices.

ABOVE *Quenelles of sweetbreads*
Recipe: page 113
OPPOSITE *Sashimi of trout*
Recipe: page 113

SEAFOOD SAUSAGE 'EN L'AIR'

INGREDIENTS (serves 6)
*Use apples with skin that has a
positive color, whether red or green,
to add brightness to the dish.*

14 oz whitefish, skinned and boned
salt and lemon juice
2 egg whites
½ tbsp chopped parsley
½ tbsp chopped chives
freshly ground white pepper
2½ cups whipping cream, chilled
6 Iceberg lettuce leaves
1¼ oz smoked salmon, diced
court bouillon, for poaching
⅔ cup fish stock
⅔ cup dry cider
1¼ cups whipping cream, lightly
   whipped
lemon juice
4 tbsp clarified butter
2 crisp apples

FOR THE GARNISH
sprigs of chervil

Picture: page 118

The inspiration for this dish comes from the traditional French way of serving boudins blancs (white sausages).

Purée the fish in a food processor or blender, then mix in the salt and lemon juice followed by the egg whites, herbs and pepper. Transfer to a bowl placed over a bowl of ice and very gradually beat in the cream. Cover and chill for at least 30 minutes.

Blanch the lettuce leaves, refresh and dry very well. Spread out.

Fold the smoked salmon into the whitefish mixture, divide it into 6 and place almost along the length of the base of the lettuce leaves. Fold the sides of the lettuce leaves over the mixture and roll each one up into a neat sausage shape.

Bring the court bouillon just to simmering point and poach the 'sausages', with the loose end on the bottom of the pan, for 7—10 minutes. Drain well and keep warm.

Reduce the stock and cider by a half, then stir in the cream and reduce by one third. Season and add a little lemon juice to taste. Keep warm, but do not allow to boil.

Meanwhile, heat the clarified butter. Core and slice, but do not peel the apples, and cook in the clarified butter for 1—2 minutes each side.

Slice the sausages, reform, cover and keep warm.

Spoon the sauce over 6 warmed plates. Arrange the sausage slices almost completely overlapping on the sauce and add the apple slices. Garnish with sprigs of chervil.

OYSTERS WITH WATERCRESS

INGREDIENTS (serves 2)
12 oysters
lemon juice
3 shallots, very finely chopped
1 tsp white wine vinegar
½ cup + 2 tbsp butter
freshly ground white pepper and sea
   salt
1½ tsp butter
¼ cup spinach, sliced
¼ cup watercress leaves
12 small spinach leaves

FOR THE GARNISH
julienned cucumber
chopped chives
radicchio leaves
mint leaves

Picture: page 119

Six oysters per person is quite a generous portion. For 4 people you may find it more practical to reduce the number to 4 for each serving, making a total of 16. The other ingredients can then be increased by half as much again.

Open the oysters (see p.61) and strain the juices into a pan. Add a squeeze of lemon juice and bring to just below simmering point. Add the oysters and heat for about 45 seconds. Transfer to a lightly warmed plate with a slotted spoon. Cover. Wash the oyster shells and put in a low oven.

Simmer the shallots in the vinegar and half the oyster cooking juices until nearly all the liquid has evaporated. Reduce the heat to very low. Dice the butter and gradually whisk in ½ cup + 2 tbsp, making sure each piece is fully incorporated before adding the next. Season with white pepper and a little juice if necessary.

Meanwhile heat the 1½ tsp butter in a small pan, add the spinach and watercress and cook until soft. Increase the heat to drive off the excess moisture. Purée, then season, adding a squeeze of lemon juice if necessary. Keep warm over a low heat.

Place the small spinach leaves and cucumber julienne in the top half of a steamer or a colander. Bring a pan of salted water to the boil. Cover with the top half of the steamer or the colander, cover and steam for 30 seconds.

Line the oyster shells with the spinach leaves, add the watercress and spinach purée, then the sauce and finally the oysters. Garnish with cucumber julienne and chives. Arrange the radicchio and mint leaves around.

SASHIMI OF SCALLOPS

INGREDIENTS (serves 4)
8 scallops
4 tbsp lime juice
a few strands of saffron
sea salt
4 tbsp dry white wine
6 tbsp mayonnaise
2 tbsp finely chopped chives
4 wakame (seaweed) soaked in
   cold water for 10 minutes

FOR THE GARNISH
sprigs of chervil

The technique of 'cooking' delicate flesh by the action of an acid, in this case lime juice, has been borrowed from the Japanese.

Remove the scallops from their shells (see p.61). Remove and reserve the corals. Carefully cut the scallop bodies into slices horizontally.

Mix the lime juice, saffron and a little sea salt together and lightly toss with the scallop slices. Cover and chill for 30—40 minutes.

Bring the wine to the boil with 4 tbsp water, pour over the corals, drain immediately, cover and chill the corals.

Remove the scallop slices from the marinade with a slotted spoon and dry on paper towels. Strain the marinade into the mayonnaise and add the chives.

Strain the seaweed and divide between the centers of 4 plates, spreading it out to form a circle. Place the slices of scallop and the corals on the circles of seaweed so that some of the seaweed shows.

Spoon a very small amount of the mayonnaise onto the slices of scallops and serve the rest separately. Garnish with sprigs of chervil.

OPPOSITE *Seafood sausage 'en l'air'*
Recipe: page 116
ABOVE *Oysters with watercress*
Recipe: page 116

VEGETABLE TERRINE

INGREDIENTS (serves 8)
6 long, slim leeks
4 young carrots
10 French beans, trimmed
3 artichoke bottoms
2 mint leaves
juice of 1 lemon
9 oz smoked chicken breast, diced
1 egg white
¾ cup olive oil
salt and freshly ground white pepper

FOR THE DRESSING
⅓ cup walnut oil
⅓ cup olive oil
3 tbsp lemon juice
3 tbsp sherry vinegar
salt and freshly ground white pepper

FOR THE GARNISH
slices of cucumber
concassé tomatoes
sprigs of parsley

Picture: page 122

The vegetables can be varied as long as the appearance and flavor of the dish are always considered. Strips of blanched red pepper could replace the carrot, and petits pois the French beans. Remember that the vegetables will receive further cooking in the oven.

Heat the oven to 350°F.

Cook the leeks, carrots, beans and artichoke bottoms separately in simmering, salted water, adding the mint leaves to the carrots and half the lemon juice to the artichokes, until just tender. Drain, refresh and dry well separately. Thinly slice the leeks, carrots and artichoke bottoms then wrap the vegetables separately in a cloth to make sure they are completely dry, especially the leeks.

Purée the chicken in a food processor then add the remaining lemon juice followed by the egg white. With the motor running slowly, pour in the oil in a thin stream. Season.

Line the bottom and sides of a terrine with a layer of the smoked chicken mixture. Lay one third of the leeks over the mixture. Mix the carrots, beans and artichoke bottoms with three quarters of the remaining smoked chicken mixture, then cover the leeks with half of this mixture. Cover with one third of the leeks, the remaining vegetable/smoked chicken mixture followed by the last of the leeks. Finish with the remaining plain smoked chicken mixture.

Place the terrine in a roasting pan and surround with boiling water. Cover the terrine with buttered wax paper and place in the oven for about 40 minutes.

Remove from the heat and leave to cool completely, then cut into slices and place a slice on each of 8 cold plates. Shake all the ingredients for the dressing together and trickle over the terrine. Garnish with slices of cucumber, concassé tomatoes and sprigs of parsley.

TROUT MOUSSE IN LEEK PARCELS

INGREDIENTS (serves 6)
3-4 very large leeks
salt
1½ lb boneless, skinless trout fillets,
    chopped
2 egg whites
1 cup crème fraîche, chilled
⅔ cup fish stock (see p.75)
olive oil for brushing the leeks

FOR THE SAUCE
2 tbsp finely chopped shallots
2 tbsp dry vermouth

If 3 'parcels' are served per person, this dish would provide a light luncheon main course for 4 people. The mousseline mixture can be prepared in advance. The remaining parts of the leeks can be used for Turbot with leek and mushroom mélange or Rack of lamb with leek purée.

Cut the roots and green parts from the leeks and make a lengthwise split in each one as deep as the center. Separate off 12 outer leaves about 9 inches long. Rinse well, if necessary. Use the remaining leeks in another dish.

2 tbsp white wine vinegar
1 cup cold butter
salt and freshly ground white pepper

FOR THE GARNISH
12 strips of red pepper, blanched
sprigs of parsley
strips of tomato

Picture: page 123

Cook the 12 leaves in boiling salted water for 2 minutes. Refresh, drain and dry well.

Purée the trout with a little salt in a food processor, then add the egg whites and mix until the mixture stiffens. Pass through a sieve.

Transfer the trout mixture to a bowl placed over ice and very gradually beat in the crème fraîche, beating the mixture well after each addition. Cover and chill for at least 30 minutes.

Heat the oven to 400°F.

Spread out the leek leaves and place about 3 tbsp of the trout mixture on the base of each. Roll up across the grain to make a neat parcel.

Place the parcels, seamside down, in a baking pan. Boil the stock and pour around the leeks. Place in the oven for 10-15 minutes.

Remove the parcels with a slotted spoon (reserve the liquid) and brush with a little olive oil to make them shiny. Cover and keep warm.

For the sauce, boil the shallot in the reserved cooking liquid, the vermouth, vinegar and 2 tbsp water until nearly all the liquid has evaporated. Reduce the heat to very low and gradually whisk in the butter, whisking well after each addition, to make a smooth, creamy sauce. Season.

Spoon the sauce onto 6 warmed plates, arrange 2 parcels on each plate and lay a strip of red pepper across the centre of each one. Garnish with parsley and tomato.

PARCELS OF SMOKED SALMON

INGREDIENTS *(serves 4)*
12 oz smoked salmon, very thinly
*   sliced*
2 tsp fresh tomato paste (see p.302)
a pinch of cayenne pepper
1 tbsp salmon eggs, optional
¾ cup crème fraîche, chilled and
*   whipped*
flesh of 1 lb tomatoes (approx 1½ cups)
2 tbsp olive oil
1 tbsp tarragon vinegar
salt and pepper
a pinch of sugar

FOR THE GARNISH
salmon eggs
sprigs of chervil

Line 4 lightly oiled individual serving dishes with about half the smoked salmon.

Pass the remaining smoked salmon through a sieve into a bowl over a bowl of ice. Beat in half the fresh tomato paste, cayenne pepper and salmon eggs, then gradually beat in three quarters of the crème fraîche. Fold in the remaining crème fraîche. Spoon the mixture into the individual dishes. Cover and chill for 2—3 hours.

Purée the tomatoes, then pass through a fine sieve. Gradually beat in the oil, then the vinegar and remaining fresh tomato paste. Season, adding a pinch of sugar if necessary, then cover and chill.

Invert the molds onto 4 plates. Spoon the sauce around and garnish with salmon eggs and sprigs of chervil.

ABOVE *Vegetable terrine*
Recipe: page 120
OPPOSITE *Trout mousse in leek parcels*
Recipe: page 120

CAULIFLOWER AND BROCCOLI

FEUILLETE

INGREDIENTS *(serves 4)*
6 oz puff pastry (see p.79)
1 beaten egg
*Approx 1½ cups even size cauliflower
  flowerets*
*Approx 1½ cups even size broccoli
  flowerets*
¼ cup vegetable stock
¼ cup full bodied dry white wine
a sprig of fennel
2 tbsp whipping cream
½ cup butter
1 tbsp lemon juice
1 tsp chopped parsley
salt and freshly ground white pepper

FOR THE GARNISH
lemon julienne

This is an attractive first course ideal for vegetarians. The feuilleté can be made from filo pastry with each layer comprised of 2 small sheets stacked together with melted butter or oil brushed between them.

Roll the pastry out to a circle about ¼ inch thick and, with a ¾ inch fluted cutter, cut 4 circles. With the point of a sharp knife score a line about ¼ inch all the way around from the edge. Transfer to a baking tray, cover and leave in a cool place for at least 30 minutes.

Heat the oven to 425°F.

Brush the tops of the pastries with beaten egg, taking care not to let any drip over the cut edges, then bake for about 8 minutes until golden brown and well risen.

Meanwhile, steam the cauliflower and broccoli flowerets until just tender.

Bring the stock, wine and fennel to the boil and reduce to 2 tbsp. Add the cream and boil for 1 minute. Dice the butter and gradually add, making sure each piece is fully incorporated before adding the next. Remove the fennel, add the lemon juice, parsley and seasoning. Keep warm but do not allow to boil.

Leave the pastries to cool very slightly on a wire rack, then carefully ease off the inner 'lids'. With the point of a sharp knife, carefully scoop out any soft pastry from the centers.

Reserve a few of the flowerets for the garnish and divide the remainder between the pastry cases. Spoon the sauce over and place the 'lids' on top. Garnish with the reserved flowerets and lemon julienne.

INDIVIDUAL SALMON, SOLE AND

WATERCRESS TERRINES

INGREDIENTS *(serves 4)*
8 oz salmon fillets
salt and freshly ground white pepper
5 tbsp full bodied dry white wine
½ cup + 2 tbsp butter, softened
1 tbsp finely chopped shallot
8 oz sole fillets, chopped (1 cup)
a squeeze of lemon juice
2 small egg whites
*1 small bunch watercress, trimmed
  and chopped*

This would be a good choice for a first course when the main course requires some last minute preparation.

Lightly season the salmon, pour the wine over, cover and leave in a cool place for about an hour.

Heat 1 tbsp butter, add the shallot, cover and cook over a moderate heat, shaking the pan occasionally until softened.

Mix the shallot with the sole in a food processor or blender until very smooth, then add salt and lemon juice, followed by the egg whites, then the remaining butter.

Blanch the watercress for 1 minute. Refresh and drain well.

Remove two thirds of the sole mixture, then put the watercress into the food processor and blend with the remaining sole mixture. Cover both mixtures and chill for 1 hour.

Heat the oven to 325°F.

Trim the salmon fillets so that they will fit into 4 individual dishes.

Lightly oil the dishes and cover the bases with the white sole mixture. Cover with the salmon, then add the green mixture.

Place the dishes in a roasting or baking pan, surround with boiling water, cover and place in the oven for 30—40 minutes until the terrines are lightly set.

Allow to cool slightly, then chill overnight. Unmold about half an hour before serving and leave at room temperature.

CHICKEN BREAST TERRINE

INGREDIENTS (serves 8)
1 lb chicken breasts, skinned
⅔ cup dry white wine
salt and freshly ground white pepper

FOR THE TOMATO ASPIC
2½ tsp gelatin
1½ cups clarified chicken stock
⅓ cup dry white wine
1 tbsp lemon juice
½ cup tomato juice
2 tbsp finely chopped chives
2 tbsp finely chopped tarragon
2 tbsp finely chopped chervil
¼ cup pistachio nuts, chopped
1¼ cups aspic, made with the strained chicken liquor

Poach the chicken breasts in the wine with salt and pepper for about 10 minutes until tender.

Remove the breasts with a slotted spoon. Strain the liquor and use in the making of the aspic. Allow the breasts to cool and then cut into slices. Leave to cool completely.

Dissolve the gelatin for the tomato aspic in a little of the clarified stock in a bowl placed over a pan of hot water. Leave to cool slightly.

Warm the remaining stock, the wine, lemon juice and tomato juice and season lightly. Stir in the dissolved gelatin.

Pour half into a cold loaf pan to form a layer over the base. Chill until set. Keep the remaining liquor just off setting point.

Sprinkle some of the herbs over the bottom of the terrine then add layers of chicken slices and pistachio nuts.

Have the aspic just on the point of setting and spoon it over the chicken, moving the meat slightly with the point of a knife to make sure the aspic flows right through. Leave in a cool place until just on the point of setting.

Sprinkle the remaining herbs over the top of the terrine and leave to set completely.

Cover with the remaining tomato aspic and leave for 3—4 hours.

Serve in slices on cold plates.

SOUPS

The soups of Cuisine Vivante have little in common with the thick and chunky varieties that are often more than an adequate meal in themselves. Cuisine Vivante soups are more appetite refreshers, providing a relaxing respite between courses. Delicately flavored servings of light liquids, often with a supplementary ingredient suspended as if by magic in the center giving off tantalizing and titillating aromas provide an enticing prelude to the dishes to come and create an air of anticipation in the diner.

MUSHROOM SOUP

INGREDIENTS (serves 4)
1 tbsp butter
2 tbsp olive oil
2 shallots, sliced
4 cups wild mushrooms, sliced
1 heaped tsp mixed finely chopped
    sage, rosemary and thyme
salt and freshly ground black pepper
2½ cups water
a squeeze of lemon juice

FOR THE GARNISH
4 pieces of chanterelle
1½ tsp butter
finely chopped chervil

Heat the butter with the oil, add the shallots, cover and cook over a very low heat, shaking the pan occasionally, until they are soft. Stir in the mushrooms and herbs, cover and cook gently for about 5 minutes.

Stir in 2½ cups water and simmer very gently for about 20 minutes. Season, adding a squeeze of lemon juice to taste. Pass through a sieve lined with cheesecloth then reheat in a clean saucepan.

Heat the butter for the garnish, add the chanterelles and cook for 2 minutes. Remove with a slotted spoon and drain on paper towels.

Pour the soup into 4 warmed bowls. Garnish with the chanterelles and sprinkle over the chervil.

SEAFOOD AND SAFFRON CONSOMME

INGREDIENTS (serves 4)
4 mussels
4 tbsp full bodied dry white wine
a few strands of saffron
1 fillet of turbot, cut into 4 strips
4 clams
8 crescent shapes of thinly sliced
    carrot
8 cooked shrimp, shelled
chervil leaves

FOR THE CONSOMME
5 cups fish stock (see p.75)
½ cup lemon sole, finely chopped
2 shallots, finely chopped
1 carrot, finely chopped
1 leek, finely chopped
4 mushroom stems, finely chopped
4 stalks of parsley
1 bay leaf
4 sprigs of chervil
8 white peppercorns, crushed
½ tsp tomato paste
3 tbsp lemon juice
a long strip of lemon peel
2 egg whites
2 egg shells, crushed
sea salt

Picture: page 130

For the consommé, bring the stock to the boil. Mix all the remaining ingredients together in a large pan, then gradually whisk in the stock. Return to the boil, whisking continuously. Stop whisking, reduce the heat to very low and simmer for 5 minutes.

Remove the pan from the heat, cover and leave for 10 minutes.

Carefully skim the scum from the surface and ladle the stock into a cheesecloth lined sieve. Leave to cool, then remove any fat from the surface.

Poach the mussels in a little water in a coverd pan over a moderate heat, shaking the pan frequently until the mussels open. Remove them from their shells. Discard any closed mussels.

Gradually bring the wine and saffron to just below simmering point. Add the fish and poach for 1—2 minutes until opaque. Remove with a slotted spoon.

Open the clams (see p.43) and poach them in the wine until just opaque. Remove with a slotted spoon.

Blanch the carrot crescents. Refresh and drain well.

Add the wine to the consommé and bring to the boil.

Meanwhile, divide the fish and carrot crescents between 4 warmed bowls. Pour the consommé over and garnish with sprigs of chervil.

CHILLED BEET CONSOMME

INGREDIENTS *(serves 6)*
7½ cups jellied chicken stock
2 beets, each approximately 6 oz
3 shallots, finely chopped
2 leeks, chopped
2 stalks of celery, chopped
2 carrots, chopped
2 egg whites
shells of 2 eggs, crushed
4 tbsp fresh orange juice, strained

FOR THE GARNISH
6 tbsp crème fraîche or sour cream
orange peel julienne
sprigs of chervil
sprigs of chervil

Picture: page 131

There is a flavor of Russian Borscht here but this recipe is more delicate than the traditional version, the good jellied chicken stock replacing the beef stock of the original.

Bring the stock to the boil in a large pan, add the beets, shallot, leek, celery and carrot, then stir in the egg whites and shells and return to the boil, whisking continuously. Simmer gently for 1 hour.

Very carefully remove the scum from the surface of the liquid, then strain the liquid through a cheesecloth sieve. Leave to cool completely and remove all the fat from the surface. Stir in the orange juice and chill in the refrigerator.

Spoon into 6 cold bowls and garnish with a spoonful of crème fraîche or sour cream, orange and chervil.

GREEN PEA SOUP

INGREDIENTS *(serves 6)*
3 lb peas in the pod or 1 lb shelled
peas
1 tbsp butter
4 scallions, chopped
½ head of round lettuce
2 tbsp mixed chopped chervil, parsley
and tarragon
½ cup chicken stock
½ cup whipping cream
salt and freshly ground white pepper

FOR THE GARNISH
julienned cucumber
flower shapes cut from very thin slices
of carrot and turnip

Shell the peas, reserving a few of the best looking pods and setting some peas aside for the garnish.

Heat the butter and add the scallions, lettuce and herbs. Cover and cook over a moderate heat, shaking the pan occasionally, until the onions are soft. Stir in the peas, reserved pods and chicken stock, then simmer until the peas are just tender.

Strain off and reserve the liquor. Pass the peas through a sieve.

Blend the purée with the liquor and heat through gently. Stir in the cream and heat just long enough to warm it. Season.

Meanwhile, blanch, refresh and drain the cucumber, carrot, turnip and reserved peas for the garnish.

Divide the soup between 6 warmed soup bowls then very carefully slide the garnish on to the surface of the soup so that it floats. Serve immediately.

ABOVE *Quail*
consommé
Recipe: page 132

LEFT *Mussel soup*
Recipe: page 132

◆
ABOVE
*Clear vegetable
and scallop soup
Recipe: page 133*

◆
LEFT
*Chilled beet
consommé
Recipe: page 129*

QUAIL CONSOMME

INGREDIENTS (serves 4)
2 quails
1 tbsp butter
½ veal knuckle bone, chopped
½ small onion
1 clove
½ bay leaf
1 young carrot
½ small leek
1 stalk of celery
3 oz chicken breast meat (½ cup)
2 egg whites
2 egg shells, crushed
1 small tomato, chopped
6 parsley stalks
4 tarragon stalks
½ cup full bodied dry white wine
salt and pepper

FOR THE GARNISH
4 quails eggs
julienned celery
julienned leek
julienned carrot
sprigs of watercress

Picture: page 130

Carefully skin the quails and remove the flesh from the carcasses.

Heat the butter, add the quail skin and carcasses and the knuckle bone and cook, stirring occasionally, until lightly browned. Pour out the excess fat, add 5 cups water and bring to the boil. Remove the scum from the surface and simmer for 45 minutes.

Stud the onion with the clove and add to the pan with the bay leaf, carrot, leek and celery and simmer for 30 minutes. Pass through a conical sieve, pressing down well on the bones and vegetables to extract as much liquid as possible. Leave to cool then remove the fat from the surface.

Chop the quail flesh and chicken breast coarsely and put into a pan with the egg whites, shells, tomato, herbs, wine and the prepared stock. Bring to the boil, stirring constantly, then simmer for 20 minutes. Season.

Boil the quails eggs for 2½ minutes, then carefully remove the shells.

Blanch, refresh and drain the vegetables.

Pass the soup through a cheesecloth lined sieve and remove the fat from the surface. Reheat gently then pour into 4 warmed soup bowls. Garnish with the quails eggs, julienned vegetables and sprigs of watercress.

MUSSEL SOUP

INGREDIENTS (serves 4)
2 lb 3 oz mussels, cleaned
¾ cup full bodied dry white wine
1½ tbsp butter
1 shallot, finely chopped
½ cup celery, chopped
½ cup carrot, chopped
2½ cups fish stock (p.75)
a sprig of thyme
1 small bay leaf
5 tbsp whipping cream
salt and freshly ground white pepper
a pinch of saffron threads soaked in a
    little dry vermouth

FOR THE QUENELLES
4 oz skinned fillet of sole (½ cup)
a very small pinch of grated nutmeg
salt and lemon juice
½ egg white
5 tbsp whipping cream, chilled
freshly ground white pepper

Cook the mussels in the wine in a covered, heavy based pan over a high heat for about 5 minutes, shaking the pan frequently, until they open. Discard any mussels that remain closed and remove the rest from their shells. Place the mussels in a covered bowl and strain the cooking liquor.

Heat the butter, add the shallot, celery and carrot, cover the pan and cook over a low heat, shaking the pan frequently until the vegetables have softened. Stir in the cooking liquor, stock and herbs, bring to the boil then reduce the heat and simmer for 40 minutes.

Meanwhile, purée the sole in a food processor or blender with the nutmeg. Add the salt and lemon juice followed by the egg white. Pass through a fine sieve into a bowl placed over a bowl of ice, then gradually work in the cream. Add the white pepper, cover and chill for at least 30 minutes.

Pour the soup through a sieve lined with cheesecloth, return to the rinsed pan and bring to the boil. Stir in the cream and saffron with its soaking liquor, return to the boil then reduce the heat to very low. Adjust the seasoning.

Bring a wide shallow pan of salted, acidulated water to simmering point. Using 2 teaspoons, shape the sole mixture into 8 quenelles. Carefully lower them into the water and

FOR THE GARNISH
julienned carrot and celery
sprigs of dill

Picture: page 130

poach for about 2 minutes until just firm. Remove with a slotted spoon and drain on a cloth. Blanch the carrot and celery for the garnish.

Divide the mussels between 4 warmed soup bowls, pour the soup over, add the carrot and celery and carefully float the quenelles on the surface. Finish with a sprig of dill on each plate.

CLEAR VEGETABLE AND

SCALLOP SOUP

INGREDIENTS (serves 5)
¼ cup very fine julienned carrot
¼ cup very fine julienned celery
½ cup button mushroom caps, finely
* sliced*
⅔ cup dry white wine
salt and freshly ground white pepper
9 scallops
2 tbsp gin

FOR THE STOCK
2 egg whites, lightly whisked
3 lb white fish bones and heads,
* cleaned and chopped*
2 leeks, sliced
stalk of celery, chopped
9 parsley stalks
4 sprigs of chervil
4 tbsp lemon juice
1¼ cups dry white wine
⅔ cup water

FOR THE GARNISH
1 small red pepper, blanched, skinned
* and cut into julienne strips*
sprigs of chervil

Picture: page 131

This is a very light, elegant soup. The stock can be prepared in advance up to the point of reheating.

For the stock, put all ingredients except the wine into a large saucepan, cover with about ⅔ cup water and gradually bring to the boil, whisking. Lower the heat and simmer without whisking for 30 minutes. Remove the scum from the surface.

Pass through a sieve lined with a double thickness of cheesecloth and leave to cool.

Carefully ladle off 6 cups of the stock, taking care to avoid the sediment and heat gently with the carrot, celery and mushrooms to just below simmering point.

Gently heat the wine with the seasoning.

Open the scallops (see p.61) and slice into three, leaving the corals whole. Poach the scallops for 30 seconds in the wine until just opaque.

Remove with a slotted spoon. Add the gin to the poaching wine and reduce to 1½ tbsp. Strain into the stock. Add to the scallops and season.

Ladle the vegetables, scallops and the liquor into 5 warmed bowls and garnish with red pepper and sprigs of chervil.

SALADS

Cuisine Vivante salads can be served either as a first course or as a light main course. In the latter case it may be necessary to increase the quantity of one or two of the main ingredients. However, it is important that the overall balance of the ingredients is not disturbed — striking the correct balance between the various ingredients is part of the art of creating a successful salad. Always select ingredients that compliment each other in terms of taste, texture and color, and remember that the dressing should be treated as one of the integral ingredients.

ENDIVE, TOMATO AND QUAILS EGGS

SALAD

INGREDIENTS *(serves 4)*
flesh from 1 lb tomatoes, diced
   (1½ cups)
salt
4 quails eggs
2 tbsp sherry vinegar
1½ tsp Dijon mustard
6 tbsp olive oil
scant ¼ cup finely chopped watercress
   leaves
freshly ground black pepper
12 endive leaves

To serve individual portions choose small plates and use enough endive leaves to give a balanced appearance.

_____

Place the tomatoes in a sieve, sprinkle with salt and leave to drain for 30 minutes.

Cook the quails eggs in gently boiling water for 2 minutes. Cool under running water, then peel.

Blend the vinegar, mustard and a pinch of salt together, then gradually whisk in the oil. Mix in the watercress and the pepper.

Dry the tomatoes on paper towels and mix into the dressing.

Arrange 6 endive leaves in a circle around 2 cold plates. With a slotted spoon lift some of the tomatoes and watercress from the dressing and place a little in the bases of the endive leaves. Quarter the quails eggs and arrange in front of the endive. Lift the remaining tomato and watercress from the dressing and place in the center of the plates. Trickle a little of the dressing over the tomatoes and watercress and the endive. Serve any remaining dressing separately. Serve 1 plate of salad between 2 people.

SMOKED CHICKEN SALAD

WITH FIGS

INGREDIENTS *(serves 4)*
½ ripe avocado
lemon juice
curly endive
sprigs of watercress
12 oz smoked chicken breast, thinly
   sliced (2 cups)
4 fresh figs, sliced
¼ cup hazelnuts, chopped
julienned orange rind

FOR THE DRESSING
3 tbsp olive oil
1 tbsp lemon juice
salt and freshly ground black pepper
a pinch of sugar

Picture: page 138

Peel the avocado, remove the stone and cut the flesh into slices. Brush with lemon juice.

Arrange the curly endive, watercress, chicken, figs and avocado on 4 cold plates. Sprinkle with hazelnuts. Shake the ingredients for the dressing together and spoon a little over each salad. Finish with julienned orange peel.

SALAD TAHITIENNE

INGREDIENTS (serves 4)
1 lb mixed fish and shellfish
juice of 2 limes
1 small shallot, finely chopped
1 small coconut
1 small pink grapefruit
1 orange
1 tomato, peeled and chopped
½ green pepper, blanched, skinned
    and diced
1 small shallot, finely diced

FOR THE GARNISH
slices of lime
capers
cubes of pineapple
salmon eggs

Picture: page 139

Mix the fish with the lime juice and shallot. Cover and leave in a cool place for 2-4 hours, turning occasionally.

Pierce 2 of the 3 eyes in the coconut and strain out and reserve the milk. Crack the shell open, prize out the flesh and remove any dark skin with a small sharp knife. Chop the flesh finely in a blender or food processor. Remove half the flesh. Add the coconut milk to the blender or food processor and mix briefly. Turn into a cheesecloth lined sieve and leave to drain. Press down firmly to extract as much liquid as possible.

Strain the liquid from the fish and mix with the coconut liquor. Season.

Peel the grapefruit and orange, adding any juice that comes out to the coconut liquid. Divide into segments, making sure that all the skin and membrane are removed.

Lightly toss the fish, reserved coconut flesh, grapefruit, orange and tomato together with the coconut liquor.

Spoon into 4 halves of coconut shell, if available.

Garnish with the slices of lime, capers, pineapple and salmon eggs.

WARM SALAD OF BROCCOLI, AVOCADO AND SOLE WITH ORANGE DRESSING

INGREDIENTS (serves 4)
1 shallot, finely chopped
1 tbsp orange peel julienne
⅓ cup orange juice
salt and freshly ground white pepper
3 sole fillets, skinned and cut into
    strips
¼ cup fish stock
¼ cup dry white wine
a sprig of thyme
about 2½ cups broccoli flowerets
½ cup butter
1 avocado
a squeeze of lemon juice
finely chopped chives

Simmer the shallot and orange rind in the orange juice until the liquid is reduced to 1 tbsp.

Season the sole.

Heat the stock and wine with the thyme to simmering point. Add the sole, cover with buttered paper and poach for about 2 minutes until the flesh is just opaque. Remove with a slotted spoon. Cover and keep warm.

Meanwhile, cook the broccoli in boiling salted water for about 5 minutes until just tender. Refresh, drain and dry well.

Gradually whisk the butter into the reduced orange juice over a very low heat to make a thickened, fluffy sauce. Season.

Peel then thinly slice the avocado. Cut the slices in half and brush with lemon juice.

Arrange the broccoli flowerets, avocado and sole on 4 warm plates, then spoon the dressing over. Sprinkle chopped chives over the dressing on the sole and avocado.

ABOVE *Smoked chicken salad with figs*
Recipe: page 136
OPPOSITE *Salad Tahitienne*
Recipe: page 137

WARM BUNDLES OF FRENCH BEANS

WITH SHRIMPS

INGREDIENTS (serves 4)
3 cups slim French beans, trimmed
   to equal lengths
salt
1 cup cooked, peeled shrimps
court bouillon (see p.76)
1 small red pepper, skinned and cut
   into fine julienne

FOR THE DRESSING
2 tbsp softened butter
2 tbsp hazelnut oil
2 tbsp tarragon vinegar
a pinch of cayenne pepper
salt and freshly ground white pepper

FOR THE GARNISH
small sprigs of chervil
peeled shrimps
concassé tomatoes

This very neat salad makes a light first course — for a more substantial portion, serve the beans and shrimps on a bed of lettuce.

Cook the beans in simmering salted water until just tender. Refresh and drain well. Cut the beans in half if they are long.

Place the shrimps in a single layer in the top half of a steamer and place over the bottom half of a steamer containing a little simmering court bouillon for 2-3 minutes, to warm through gently.

Divide the beans into 20 small bundles and tie a strip of red pepper around each bundle leaving the ends of the pepper loose. Keep the bundles just warm.

Gently heat the ingredients for the dressing, whisking them together.

Arrange the bundles of beans on 4 plates, then arrange the shrimps in the centers. Spoon a little of the warm dressing over the shrimps and trickle a small amount on the beans. Garnish with sprigs of chervil, peeled shrimps and concassé tomatoes.

NEW POTATO, PEA AND SOFT

CHEESE SALAD

INGREDIENTS (serves 4)
16 small new potatoes
salt
¾ quantity pea and mint purée
   (see p.300)
¾ cup soft cheese, chilled
vinaigrette dresssing, lightly warmed
   (see p.76)
1 head radicchio
finely chopped chervil

In the summer months a good quality soft goats cheese is an excellent choice, because at that time of the year, when the goats are feeding on young grass, the flavor of the cheese is at its best.

Put the potatoes into a pan of boiling salted water and boil gently for 12-15 minutes until tender.

Prepare and warm the pea and mint purée.

Form the cheese into small balls using a melon baller or teaspoon. Keep them cool.

Drain the potatoes very well. Cut them in half horizontally and carefully scoop out the centers with a teaspoon, taking care not to pierce the sides, to make potato cups. If necessary cut a small slice from the bottom of the cups so that they will stand straight.

Spoon or pipe pea and mint purée into the cups. Keep warm.

Gently warm the dressing in a bowl over a pan of hot water, whisking. Arrange the radicchio on 4 plates. Place the potatoes in the center, spoon the dressing over the radicchio then place the balls of cheese on top. Sprinkle the cheese with chervil.

LOBSTER SALAD WITH RED PEPPER MOUSSE

INGREDIENTS (serves 6)
flesh from 2 cooked lobsters
concassé tomatoes
julienned zucchini
lamb's lettuce

FOR THE MOUSSE
⅓ cup red wine vinegar
2 tbsp raspberry vinegar
1¼ cups red pepper, skinned and diced
1 red pimento
salt and freshly ground white pepper
1 tsp gelatin
½ cup whipping cream, lightly
    whipped

FOR THE DRESSING
¼ tsp Dijon mustard
4 tbsp olive oil
2 tbsp white wine vinegar
salt and freshly ground white pepper
a squeeze of lemon juice
finely chopped chives

FOR THE GARNISH
basil leaves
strips of cucumber
ends of lobster tails

Picture: page 142

For choosing lobster see p.43. The mousse should not be prepared more than 2 or 3 hours in advance. It also goes very well with crayfish, Dublin Bay shrimp and sole.

Reduce the vinegars for the mousse by two thirds, then add the red pepper and simmer until thick. Purée with the pimento and seasoning, then pass through a fine sieve. Dissolve the gelatin in 2 tbsp water in a small bowl placed over a pan of hot water. Remove from the heat, leave to cool, then blend in the red pepper mixture. Gently fold in the cream, cover and chill until set.

Use 2 spoons to form 12 oval shapes from the mousse and place 2 on 6 cold plates. Arrange the lobster, tomatoes, zucchini and lettuce attractively.

Mix the mustard, oil and vinegar together, then season with salt, pepper, lemon juice and chives. Spoon a little over the salad. Garnish with basil leaves, strips of cucumber and ends of lobster tails.

◆

OPPOSITE *Lobster salad with red pepper*
mousse
Recipe: page 141
ABOVE *Warm chicken liver with*
pistachio salad
Recipe: page 144

WARM CHICKEN LIVER AND

PISTACHIO SALAD

INGREDIENTS *(serves 4)*
12 oz whole chicken livers, trimmed
4 tbsp olive oil
4 tbsp raspberry vinegar
3 tbsp pistachio nuts, skinned and
*   roughly chopped*
salt and freshly ground black pepper
1 head radicchio lettuce
1 small head curly endive

FOR THE GARNISH
4 tbsp raspberries
a little white wine

Picture: page 143

Serve this salad as a first course or a light main course — to increase the size of each portion add about 1¾ cups lightly cooked mushrooms. Raspberry vinegar makes a delightful complementary dressing.

——————————

Heat the oil, add the livers and cook over a moderate heat for 2-3 minutes — they should remain pink inside.

Remove the livers with a slotted spoon and stir the vinegar, nuts and seasoning into the pan. Bring to the boil and remove from the heat.

Arrange the radicchio and curly endive on 4 plates.

Gently heat the raspberries for the garnish in the wine.

Cut the livers into lengthways strips, place on the salad leaves and spoon the vinegar and nuts over the liver. Remove the raspberries from the wine with a slotted spoon and arrange around the livers.

SALAD OF QUAIL WITH GRAPES

INGREDIENTS *(serves 4)*
4 plump quail
salt and freshly ground black pepper
8 juniper berries, crushed
4 slices of smoked bacon
a heart of Romaine lettuce
1 head of oak leaf lettuce
1½ tbsp butter
1 generous cup seedless green grapes,
*   peeled and halved*
½ cup walnut halves
3 tbsp red wine vinegar
⅓ cup walnut oil
¼ cup olive oil
1 tsp Dijon mustard
2 tbsp finely chopped chervil

Heat the oven to 450°F.

Season the quail inside and out. Place 2 juniper berries in the cavity of each bird and tie a slice of bacon over the breasts. Place on a rack in a roasting pan and roast for 8 minutes. Remove the bacon and return the quail to the oven for 5 minutes.

Just before the quail are cooked divide the lettuces between 4 plates.

Heat the butter, add the grapes and nuts and cook, stirring occasionally, for 2-3 minutes until warmed through. Remove the quails from the roasting pan, stir the vinegar into the cooking juices and simmer briefly, stirring up the sediment. Pour into a bowl and immediately whisk in the oils and mustard. Cover to keep warm.

Remove the grapes and nuts with a slotted spoon and keep warm.

Skin the quails and quickly remove the flesh from the breasts. Divide the quail meat, grapes and nuts between the plates of lettuce. Stir the dressing, adjust the seasoning and spoon over the salads. Finish with the chervil.

CRAB-PASTA SALAD

INGREDIENTS (serves 6)
1½ tsp butter
1 tbsp finely chopped shallot
½ cup crab meat
salt and lemon juice
½ egg white
½ cup whipping cream, chilled
freshly ground white pepper
½ quantity of red pepper pasta (see p.78)

FOR THE SAUCE
⅔ cup fish stock (see p.75)
5 tbsp whipping cream
5 tbsp hazelnut oil
salt and freshly ground white pepper
lemon juice

FOR THE SALAD
2 heads of radicchio lettuce
2 tbsp finely chopped basil

Heat the butter in a small saucepan, add the shallot, cover and cook over a moderate heat, shaking the pan occasionally, until the shallot is soft.

Purée the crab in a food processor or blender with the shallot, then add salt and a squeeze of lemon juice. Mix in the egg white, then, with the motor still running, gradually pour in the cream. Season, cover and chill for an hour.

Prepare the red pepper pasta and leave to relax under an inverted bowl for 1 hour.

Divide the pasta dough in half. Keep one half covered by the bowl and roll the other half out very thinly. Cut out 18 circles with a plain cutter. Divide the crab mixture between the circles, placing a small mound on each one. Roll out the other piece of pasta dough very thinly and cut out another 18 circles. Dampen the edges of the first set of circles and carefully cover each one with a circle from the second set. Line up the top and bottom edges and press them together.

Bring a pan of salted water to boiling point, add the pasta in batches and cook for 5 - 7 minutes. Remove with a slotted spoon and drain on a cloth.

Meanwhile, reserve a little of the stock for the sauce and boil the remainder until reduced to a slightly syrupy glaze. Stir in the cream and bring just to the boil. Pour into a blender, then, with the motor still running, slowly pour in the oil. Season with salt, pepper and a squeeze of lemon juice. If the sauce is too thick add a little of the reserved stock.

Divide the radicchio between 6 plates. Place 3 pasta parcels on each plate, pour the sauce over and sprinkle with basil.

FENNEL AND FRENCH BEAN SALAD

INGREDIENTS (serves 4)
2 tsp tarragon vinegar
½ cup fromage blanc
1 tbsp green peppercorns, crushed
salt
¾ cup French beans, cut into strips
1 head of fennel, julienned
1 small zucchini, julienned
leaves from ½ bunch of watercress
½ green pepper, blanched, peeled and
    cut into diamond shapes
1½ tbsp finely chopped tarragon

FOR THE GARNISH
fennel leaves

A green salad with a difference. Serve it as a first course or to accompany simply cooked meats or fish. Fromage blanc is a soft, low fat cheese that is available from good delicatessens and supermarkets.

___

Beat the vinegar into the fromage blanc, then stir in the peppercorns and salt. Chill lightly.

Cut the strips of French beans in half, lightly toss together with the fennel, zucchini, watercress, green pepper and tarragon.

Arrange the vegetables to make 4 salads. Pour the green peppercorn dressing to one side. Garnish the dressing with fennel leaves.

FISH AND SHELLFISH

Fish and shellfish feature strongly in Cuisine Vivante recipes, and for obvious reasons. Largely delicate creatures they demand a great deal of precision and careful judgement when cooking if the most is to be made of their subtle flesh and absolute freshness. The abundant variety of flavors, textures and styles provides immense scope for innovative sauce combinations that exentuate the nuances and subtleties of the flesh, be it sole, scallops, turbot or lobster.

T R O U T   W I T H   C H A M P A G N E   S A U C E

INGREDIENTS (serves 4—6)
1 trout, approximately 2¼ lb, with
    head, cleaned
1¾ cups champagne or good quality
    sparkling dry white wine
1 cup fish stock
1 sprig of tarragon
1 sprig of dill
5 green peppercorns
sea salt
1¼ cups whipping cream

FOR THE GARNISH
salmon eggs
sprigs of dill

Picture: page 150

The cucumber and tomato for the garnish can be prepared by any of the methods described on p.70-73.

Heat the oven to 375°F.

Place the fish in a fish kettle or a large casserole, pour the champagne or sparkling wine and fish stock over, add the herbs, peppercorns and sea salt, cover closely with buttered wax paper, then bring just to the boil over a low heat. Transfer to the oven and cook for 20 minutes or until the flesh flakes easily.

Carefully transfer the fish to a warmed plate, cover and keep warm.

Boil the champagne liquor until reduced by about three quarters.

Strain the liquor and reheat, stirring in the cream. Simmer until thick enough to coat the back of a spoon. Season.

Carefully remove the fillets from the fish, discard the skin and place on 4 warmed plates. Spoon a very little of the sauce over the fish. Spoon the rest around the fish. Scatter the salmon eggs over the trout and lay the sprigs of dill on the sauce.

S A L M O N   W I T H   L E M O N

B U T T E R   S A U C E

INGREDIENTS (serves 4)
16 slim asparagus spears, trimmed
salt and freshly ground white pepper
4 salmon escalopes
1 tbsp finely chopped shallot
⅔ cup dry white wine
⅔ cup fish stock
2 tbsp lemon juice
1 cup butter, cold

FOR THE GARNISH
salmon eggs
strips of lemon peel

Picture: page 151

Steam the asparagus for 12 — 15 minutes until tender. Blanch the strips of lemon peel for the garnish, refresh and drain and dry well.

Meanwhile, season the salmon and poach with the shallots in the wine and stock in a large, buttered frying pan for about 8-10 minutes, until the flesh flakes easily.

Transfer the salmon to a warmed plate using a fish slice. Cover and keep warm.

Reduce the poaching liquor with the lemon juice to 1 tbsp. Reduce the heat to very low. Dice the butter and gradually whisk in, making sure that each piece is completely incorporated before adding the next. Season.

Divide the sauce between 4 warmed plates. Place the salmon on top and place the salmon eggs on the salmon. Arrange the asparagus spears attractively on the sauce and garnish with lemon.

SLICES OF SALMON WITH DILL

INGREDIENTS (serves 6)
1 lb salmon fillet, chilled
3 tbsp lemon juice
salt and freshly ground white pepper
3 tbsp butter
2 shallots, finely chopped
¾ cup fish stock
1 tbsp finely chopped celery leaves
3 stalks of parsley, chopped
4 tbsp finely chopped dill
1 cup full bodied dry white wine
2 egg yolks
¼ cup whipping cream

FOR THE GARNISH
diamond shapes of red and green
    pepper
julienned lemon rind

At least 8 hours before serving, slice the salmon very thinly, lay the slices in a large shallow, non-metal dish, sprinkle with lemon juice and seasoning, cover and leave in a cool place.

Heat the butter and add the shallots. Cover and cook over a moderate heat, shaking the pan occasionally, until the shallots are soft. Stir in the stock and reduce to a syrupy glaze. Stir in the celery leaves, parsley stalks, 3 tbsp dill and the wine, cover and simmer for 15 minutes. Reduce to ¾ cup. Pass through a sieve. Leave to cool, then remove the fat from the surface.

Just before serving, dry the salmon slices on paper towels. Place 6 plates in a very low oven to warm.

Bring the reduced liquid to the boil.

Blend the egg yolks and cream together. Stir in a little of the hot liquid then stir this mixture into the remaining liquid and cook over a very low heat, stirring constantly, until the sauce coats the back of a spoon. Remove from the heat, season and stir in the remaining dill.

Spoon most of the sauce over the plates. Place the salmon slices on top and trickle the remaining sauce over it. Garnish with the red and green pepper diamonds and lemon julienne.

SMALL SALMON LOAVES

INGREDIENTS (serves 4)
10 oz fillet of salmon, skinned, chilled
2 eggs, separated
2 tbsp whipping cream, chilled and
    lightly whipped
salt and freshly ground white pepper
½ cup Swiss chard leaves, green part
    only
4 pigs caul
white wine sauce (see p.180)

Chop half the salmon, then mix in a food processor with the egg yolks to make a smooth purée. With the motor running, add the cream and seasoning and mix to a smooth light mixture. Chill for at least 30 minutes.

Heat the oven to 350°F.

Blanch the chard leaves, refresh, drain and dry on paper towels.

Slice the remaining salmon into 8 small thin circles.

Place 4 of the salmon circles on the work surface. Use half the chard to cover the salmon, add a layer of the salmon mousse and cover with the remaining chard. Finally, top with the remaining circles of salmon.

Wrap each pile in caul. Beat the egg whites lightly and use to seal the caul.

Place the loaves in the oven for about 10 minutes.

Prepare the sauce.

Remove the loaves from the oven and leave to stand for a few minutes.

Spoon the sauce over 4 warmed plates. Cut the loaves in half and place on the sauce.

Trout with champagne sauce
Recipe: page 148

Salmon with lemon butter sauce
Recipe: page 148

BRAIDED CROWN OF SALMON AND TURBOT

INGREDIENTS (serves 6)
1 lb turbot fillets, cut lengthwise into
*   9 thin strips*
1 lb salmon fillets, cut lengthwise,
*   into 9 thin strips*
salt and freshly ground white pepper
1 cup cold butter
1 red pepper, skinned and chopped
2 tbsp white wine vinegar
1 tbsp lemon juice
3 tbsp medium bodied, fruity dry
*   white wine*
3 tbsp finely chopped shallot

FOR THE GARNISH
cucumber, turned, with the skin on
diamond shapes of skinned red pepper
sprigs of fennel

Make 3 braids of 1 strip of turbot and 2 strips of salmon and 3 braids of 2 strips of turbot and 1 of salmon. Form the braids into rings and hold in place with wooden toothpicks. Season.

Heat 1 tbsp butter in a large nonstick frying pan over a low heat. Add the fish, cover closely with buttered wax paper and cook for 5—8 minutes, turning carefully once, until the flesh is just opaque.

Steam the cucumber for the garnish for 3—4 minutes until just tender.

Meanwhile, purée the red pepper. Boil the vinegar, lemon juice, wine and shallot until nearly all the liquid has evaporated. Remove from the heat and whisk in 1 tbsp butter. Place over a very low heat. Dice the butter and very gradually whisk in the remaining, making sure each piece is fully incorporated before adding the next. When all the butter has been incorporated, whisk in the red pepper purée. Season.

Divide the sauce between 6 plates. Place the rings on the sauce. Place the cucumber in the center of the rings. Arrange the red pepper in the cucumber. Place sprigs of fennel on the sauce.

SALMON AND SCALLOPS WITH SEAWEED AND CHAMPAGNE SAUCE

INGREDIENTS (serves 4)
4 scallops
2½ cups fish stock
1 lb salmon, cut into strips
1 tbsp finely chopped parsley
1 tbsp finely chopped chives
1 stalk of celery, julienned
1 leek, julienned
3 inch piece of cucumber, seeded and
*   julienned*
⅔ cup champagne or other good quality
*   sparkling dry white wine*
6 tbsp whipping cream
salt and freshly ground white pepper
1 sheet of nori (Japanese dried
*   seaweed)*
4 tbsp concassé tomato

Picture: page 154

Nori is available in Oriental food shops and some health food shops. If it is not available, another type of Japanese seaweed could be substituted — prepare it according to the instructions on the package or ask the advice of the store clerk.

Remove the scallops from their shells (see p.61). Reserve the liquor. Cut the scallop bodies in half. Season.

Boil the stock and reduce by one third. Add the scallop liquor and reduce the heat so the stock just simmers.

Add the salmon, parsley and chives and poach for about 5 minutes. Add the scallop slices and corals and cook for 2—3 minutes, turning them once, until just opaque.

Meanwhile, steam the celery and leek for about 3 minutes, then add the cucumber and steam for 30 seconds.

Remove the fish with a slotted spoon and keep warm.

Stir the champagne or sparkling wine into the poaching liquor, then stir in the cream and simmer until slightly thickened. Season and keep warm without boiling.

Place the nori under a hot broiler for a few moments, then julienne.

Spoon the sauce over 4 warmed plates. Arrange the fish, then arrange the vegetable julienne, nori and tomato concassé around.

STRIPS OF SALMON WITH
MUSHROOMS AND QUAILS EGGS

INGREDIENTS (serves 4)
4 tbsp butter
1¼ lb salmon, cut into strips
salt and freshly ground white pepper
3½ cups wild mushrooms
4 quails eggs
2 tbsp finely chopped chervil,
   tarragon, chives, and parsley,
   mixed

FOR THE SAUCE
1½ cups light, fruity red wine, eg red
   Loire or Beaujolais Villages
3 tbsp chopped shallots
a sprig of thyme
1 bay leaf
1 tbsp fish glaze (see p.75)
2 tbsp whipping cream
¾ cup butter

For the sauce, simmer the wine, shallots, thyme and bay leaf until syrupy, then stir in the fish glaze and cream. Pass through a sieve, return to the rinsed pan and reheat gently over a very low heat. Dice the butter and gradually stir in, making sure that each piece is fully incorporated before adding the next. Season and keep warm but do not allow to boil.

Heat 1½ tbsp butter. Season the salmon lightly, add to the pan for 2—3 minutes, turning the strips so they cook evenly. Remove with a slotted spoon and drain on paper towels.

Add the remaining butter to the pan, then add the mushrooms and cook for 2—3 minutes, depending on the type. Remove with a slotted spoon and drain on paper towels. Sprinkle with seasoning.

Meanwhile, cook the quails eggs in gently boiling water for 2 minutes. Peel then cut into quarters.

Arrange the salmon and mushrooms in the center of 4 warmed plates. Pour the sauce over and arrange the eggs. Sprinkle with the herbs.

Salmon and scallops with seaweed
and champagne sauce
Recipe: page 152

154

Turbot with leeks and mushroom
mélange
Recipe: page 157

T U R B O T   A N D   P R A W N   T I M B A L E S

INGREDIENTS (serves 4—6)
8 oz skinless turbot fillets
salt and lemon juice
1 egg white
1¼ cups whipping cream, chilled
a few strands of saffron
freshly ground white pepper
½ cup peeled cooked shrimp
1½ tbsp chopped pistachio nuts

FOR THE SAUCE
1 shallot, finely chopped
a small pinch of finely chopped
    tarragon
½ tbsp butter
6 tbsp dry white wine
6 tbsp champagne or good
    quality sparkling dry white wine
1¼ cups whipping cream

FOR THE GARNISH
cooked shrimp, some in their shells,
    some shelled
sprigs of fennel
slices of cucumber

Picture: page 158

Purée the turbot in a food processor or blender, then mix in the salt and lemon juice followed by the egg white.

Pass through a sieve into a bowl placed over a bowl of ice. Reserve 2 tbsp of the cream and very gradually beat the remainder into the fish with the saffron and pepper. Cover and chill for at least 30 minutes.

Heat the oven to 325°F. Line the bottom of 4 or 6 molds with buttered wax paper.

Mix the shrimp with the reserved cream, pistachio nuts and seasoning.

Line the base and sides of the molds with most of the turbot mixture, then spoon the shrimp mixture into the centers and cover with the remaining turbot mixture. Tap the molds firmly to get rid of the air bubbles, then place them in a roasting or baking pan and surround with boiling water. Cover the tops of the molds with buttered wax paper and place in the oven for about 20 minutes.

For the sauce, add the shallot and tarragon to the butter, cover and cook over a moderate heat, shaking the pan occasionally until soft. Stir in the wines and reduce to 2 tbsp. Stir in the cream and simmer until the sauce coats the back of a spoon. Pass through a fine sieve, season and keep warm.

Remove the timbales from the heat and allow to stand for a few minutes before unmolding onto warm plates. Spoon the sauce around and garnish with the shrimp, fennel and slices of cucumber.

P A R C E L S   O F   T U R B O T   W I T H

S C A L L O P S

INGREDIENTS (serves 4)
4 fillets of turbot, thinly sliced, each
    approximately 4 oz
salt and freshly ground white pepper
4 scallops
4 large spinach leaves
1¼ cups medium bodied dry white
    wine
1 cup whipping cream
a few strands of saffron soaked in
    2 tbsp medium bodied dry white
    wine
2 egg yolks

Season the turbot fillets.

Open the scallops and separate the bodies from the corals (see p.61). Slice the bodies into 3 horizontally, then place along half the length of the fillets. Put the corals in the center. Fold the remaining lengths of the fillets over the filling.

Blanch, refresh, drain and dry the spinach leaves then wrap around the turbot fillets to form neat parcels. Place in the top part of a steamer and cover with buttered wax paper.

Bring some seasoned water to simmering point in the bottom part of the steamer. Put the top part in place and cover. Cook the fish to 5—6 minutes until the fish is just opaque throughout.

Meanwhile, boil the wine until reduced to about ½ cup. Stir in the cream and reduce again to ½ cup. Stir in the saffron liquor.

Blend the egg yolks together in a small bowl then whisk in

the hot liquid. Place the bowl over a pan of hot water and whisk until the mixture coats the back of the spoon. Remove from the heat and season.

Carefully cut each parcel from end to end, about two thirds of the way down.

Spoon the sauce over 4 warmed plates and place the parcels, partially opened to show the fish, in the center of the plates.

TURBOT WITH LEEKS AND MUSHROOM MELANGE

INGREDIENTS (serves 6)
12 young leeks, white parts only
salt and freshly ground white pepper
6 turbot fillets, each approximately
*   5 oz*
3 tbsp lemon juice
1 cup butter
2 shallots, finely chopped
1¼ cups fruity dry white wine
2 cups button mushrooms, finely
*   chopped*
3⅔ cups chanterelles, morels or
*   mousserons*
2 tbsp truffle juice (optional)
2 tbsp sercial madeira (or 4 tbsp if
*   truffle juice is not used)*
2 tbsp whipping cream
¾ cup butter
1 tbsp finely chopped chives

Picture: page 155

Choose dishes that do not require much last minute preparation to serve before and after this dish. Just a simple vegetable is all that is needed to accompany it.

Heat the oven to 400°F.

Blanch the leeks for 3—4 minutes. Refresh, drain well, then cut into ½ inch slices.

Season the turbot and sprinkle with some of the lemon juice.

Heat 1 tbsp butter in a sauteuse or frying pan large enough enough to hold the turbot fillets in one layer. Add the shallots and cook over a moderate heat until soft. Stir in the wine and boil for 1 minute. Add the button mushrooms and place the turbot on top. Place a piece of buttered wax paper on the fish, put on the lid and put in the oven for 3 minutes.

Meanwhile, melt 1 tbsp butter, add the wild mushrooms and cook for 2—3 minutes. Add a squeeze of lemon juice and the truffle juice (if using), and cook for 1 minute. Remove the mushrooms with a slotted spoon, cover and keep warm.

Stir the madeira into the mushroom juices and reduce until syrupy. Reduce the heat to very low and gradually whisk in 1 tbsp butter.

Gently warm the slices of leek in 1 tbsp butter and a very little water in a small covered pan.

Lift the turbot from the sauteuse, cover and keep warm. Pass the juices through a fine sieve, pressing hard to extract as much flavor as possible, then boil until reduced by one third. Stir in the cream, bring to the boil and gradually whisk in the remaining butter at a full boil. Add the chives, seasoning and lemon juice to taste. Keep warm, but do not boil.

Place a turbot fillet in the center of each warmed plate and arrange small mounds of leeks and small circles of dark sauce alternately around the fish. Place small mounds of mushrooms on the sauce. Pour the white wine sauce over the fish.

LEFT *Turbot and shrimp timbales*
Recipe: page 156
ABOVE *Pike quenelles with white wine*
sauce
Recipe: page 180

TURBOT WITH TOMATOES AND

MUSHROOMS

INGREDIENTS (serves 4)
⅔ cup good quality sparkling dry
   white wine
⅔ cup sercial madeira
1 cup fish stock
2 tbsp very finely chopped shallots
flesh of 3 tomatoes, chopped
4 cups button mushrooms, sliced
4 fillets of turbot, each approximately
   6 oz
salt and freshly ground black pepper
1 cup whipping cream
2 tbsp finely chopped parsley

Heat the sparkling wine, madeira and stock in a saucepan or flameproof dish that is large enough to hold the fish in a single layer, to simmering point. Add the shallots, tomatoes and mushrooms, reduce the heat so the liquid is just moving, then lay the fillets on the vegetables. Season, cover the fish with buttered wax paper and poach for 4 minutes.

Carefully transfer the fish to a warmed plate, cover and keep warm.

Boil the liquor until reduced to about ⅓ cup. Stir in the cream and any juices that have come out of the fish and boil until the sauce is slightly thickened, stirring frequently.

Divide the sauce between 4 warmed plates and arrange a bed of vegetables on one half of each plate. Sprinkle the parsley over the borders of the 'beds' and the surrounding sauce then place the fillets on the 'beds'.

FILLETS OF TURBOT WITH

CUCUMBERS

INGREDIENTS (serves 4)
1½ tbsp finely chopped shallot
salt and freshly ground white pepper
4 turbot fillets, approximately 6 oz
   each cut into 3
⅔ cup dry white wine
⅓ cup fish stock
½ large firm straight cucumber
¼ cup dry vermouth
⅔ cup whipping cream
3 tbsp butter, diced
a squeeze of lemon juice
½ tsp finely chopped tarragon

FOR THE GARNISH
small sprigs of tarragon
lemon

Scatter the shallots over a large buttered flameproof dish. Season the turbot and lay the slices side by side on the shallots. Heat the wine and stock and pour over the turbot. Cover with buttered foil. Bring just to the boil, lower the heat and poach for 5 minutes.

Cut the cucumber in half lengthways, scoop out the seeds and 'turn' the flesh (see p.65) so that each piece is backed by green skin. Blanch, refresh and drain well.

Carefully transfer the fish to a warmed plate, cover and keep warm.

Add the vermouth to the poaching liquor and reduce by a quarter. Stir in the cream and boil until slightly thickened. Pass through a sieve and reheat gently. Gradually swirl in 2 tbsp butter, making sure each piece is fully incorporated before adding the next. Season and add a squeeze of lemon juice. Keep warm but do not boil.

Heat the remaining 1 tbsp butter, stir in the tarragon, add the cucumber and heat through gently, shaking the pan frequently. Carefully remove with a slotted spoon.

Spoon the sauce over 4 warmed plates, carefully arrange the fish on top, add the cucumber and garnish with the sprigs of tarragon and lemon.

TROUT WITH GREEN SAUCE

INGREDIENTS *(serves 4)*
½ cup medium bodied dry white wine
1 shallot, chopped
1 small stalk of celery, with leaves,
    chopped
½ carrot, chopped
1 small bay leaf
a sprig of thyme
salt and freshly ground black pepper
4 trout
approx 2 lettuce leaves
2 egg yolks
1 tsp lime juice
½ cup clarified butter, melted
⅓ scallion, very finely chopped

FOR THE GARNISH
turned cucumber
sprigs of dill
salmon eggs

Heat the oven to 350°F.

Put the wine, vegetables, herbs and seasoning into a greased flameproof dish large enough to hold the fish. Bring to the boil, add the trout, cover with buttered wax paper and put in the oven for about 15 minutes until the flesh is just opaque.

Blanch the lettuce leaves for 2 minutes. Refresh, drain well and dry on paper towels.

Carefully remove the skin from the trout, then gently lift the fillets off the bones. Place on a warmed plate, cover and keep warm.

Steam the cucumber for 2 minutes.

Boil the cooking juices until reduced to 1 tbsp.

Combine the lettuce, egg yolks, lime juice and cooking juices in a food processor. With the motor still running, pour in the hot butter in a slow stream. Add the scallion and taste for seasoning.

Place the trout on 4 warmed plates. Spoon the sauce to the side. Garnish with cucumber, sprigs of dill and a few salmon eggs.

TROUT WITH CUCUMBER SAUCE

INGREDIENTS *(serves 4)*
3 tbsp butter, chopped
1 shallot, finely chopped
4 trout, filleted and skinned
salt and freshly ground white pepper
½ cup dry white vermouth
1¼ cups fish stock
½ large, firm cucumber, peeled, seeded
    and chopped
a sprig of thyme
⅓ cup good quality sparkling dry
    white wine
½ cup whipping cream

FOR THE GARNISH
baby new potatoes
small balls of pea or pea and mint
    purée (see p.300)
concassé tomatoes

This light main course fish dish, which needs no other accompaniment except wine, is an ideal choice for a summer luncheon.

Heat 1 tbsp butter, add the shallot and cook gently for 2—3 minutes.

Cut each trout fillet into 3 strips lengthwise. Lay them on top of the shallots. Season. Pour the vermouth over. Cover with buttered wax paper and cook over a low heat for about 2 minutes until the flesh is just opaque. Transfer to a warmed dish, cover and keep warm.

Add the stock, cucumber and thyme and reduce by three quarters. Remove the thyme, purée the sauce then pass through a sieve. Add the sparkling wine and cream and simmer for about 3 minutes. Gradually swirl in the remaining butter over a low heat.

Meanwhile, cook the baby new potatoes in a steamer and warm the balls of purée on a piece of foil on top of it.

Coat 4 warmed plates with the sauce. Arrange the strips of trout on the sauce and arrange the potatoes and purée around. Finish with the tomato.

Scallops with dill
Recipe: page 164

Scallops with saffron sauce
Recipe: page 165

SCALLOPS WITH MUSSEL PARCELS

INGREDIENTS *(serves 4)*
½ *cup dry white wine*
16 mussels
16 spinach leaves
spinach mousseline (see p.308)
(optional)
salt and freshly ground white pepper
28 small scallops

FOR THE SAUCE
6 tbsp butter, diced
2 lb shells from cooked shrimp,
crushed
1-1½ cups mixed chopped carrots and
leeks and diced celery
1 tsp tomato paste
2 tbsp cognac
1 cup dry white wine
2 cups fish stock
⅔ *cup whipping cream*
salt and freshly ground white pepper

Picture: page 166

For the sauce, heat the butter and add the shrimp shells and vegetables and cook over a low heat for about 5 minutes, stirring occasionally. Stir in the purée and cognac and ignite with a taper. Stir in the wine and boil until nearly all the liquid has evaporated. Stir in the stock and reduce until syrupy. Stir in the cream and seasoning and simmer for about 3 minutes. Pass through a conical strainer, pressing down well to extract as much liquid as possible. Keep warm over a low heat.

Heat the wine, add the mussels and steam for a few seconds until they have only just opened. Remove them from their shells and drain well.

Blanch and refresh the spinach leaves and drain well, then spread them out and place a mussel and a spoonful of spinach mousseline in the center of each. Fold the leaves over to make neat parcels, but leave one end open so part of the mussel shows. Place over a steamer to keep warm.

Reheat the wine with a little seasoning to just below simmering point. Remove the scallops from their shells (see p.61), add to the wine and poach for about 45 seconds each side.

Coat 4 warmed plates with sauce, arrange 4 spinach-wrapped mussels in the center of each one and arrange 7 scallops around.

SCALLOPS WITH DILL

INGREDIENTS *(serves 4)*
12 scallops
4 tbsp butter
2 small leeks, julienned
2 small carrots, julienned
1 zucchini, cut into fine batons
⅔ *cup fish stock*
⅔ *cup dry white wine*
5 tbsp whipping cream
sea salt and freshly ground white
pepper
2 tbsp chopped dill

FOR THE GARNISH
snow peas, julienned or
sprigs of dill

Picture: page 162

Remove the scallops from their shells. Reserve their liquor. Separate the corals and cut the bodies in half horizontally.

Heat half the butter in a large heavy pan, add the vegetables and cook, covered, over a low heat for about 4 minutes, shaking the pan occasionally. Do not allow them to brown. Stir in the stock, scallop liquor, and wine and bring to the boil. Reduce to about 5 tbsp, then stir in the cream and simmer for a few minutes until the sauce thickens slightly. Season lightly.

Heat the remaining butter, add the scallops, a little salt and most of the dill. Cook gently for 1 minute, turn them over, add the corals and cook for a further minute — do not allow them to brown or toughen.

Tip a little of the scallop cooking liquor into the sauce and stir briefly to mix.

Meanwhile, blanch, refresh and drain the julienned snow peas, if using.

Divide the sauce and vegetables between 4 warmed dishes and arrange the scallops and corals on top. Sprinkle with the remaining dill and garnish with julienned snow peas or sprigs of dill.

SCALLOPS WITH SMOKED SALMON

AND BASIL

INGREDIENTS (serves 4)
16 scallops
2 tbsp butter
2 shallots, finely chopped
4 thin slices of smoked salmon, cut
    into thin strips
2½ tbsp finely chopped basil
¼ cup full bodied dry white wine
¾ cup whipping cream
salt and freshly ground black pepper
1 cup noodles (see p.78)
1 tbsp oil
⅓ cup hazelnuts, toasted and coarsely
    chopped

FOR THE GARNISH
asparagus tips

Use 2 or 3 different colors of noodles to produce a delightful harlequin effect.

Open the scallops (see p.61), separate the corals from the bodies and slice the bodies horizontally into 3.

Heat the butter, add the shallots, cover and cook over a moderate heat, shaking the pan occasionally until the shallots are soft. Stir in half the smoked salmon and the basil and cook for 2 minutes. Stir in the wine and cream and reduce by a quarter. Season.

Cook the noodles with the oil in plenty of salted water until just tender. Steam the asparagus tips for the garnish.

Meanwhile, add the scallops to the sauce and cook with the sauce just below simmering point for about 1 minute. Add the corals and cook for a further minute until the scallops are just opaque. Season.

Drain the noodles well and toss with freshly ground black pepper and the hazelnuts.

Spoon the scallops and sauce onto 4 warmed plates and arrange the noodles around in small mounds. Garnish with asparagus tips.

SCALLOPS WITH SAFFRON SAUCE

INGREDIENTS (serves 4)
16 large scallops
1½ tbsp butter
2 tbsp finely chopped shallots
salt and freshly ground pepper
⅔ cup medium bodied fruity dry white
    wine
1 cup fish stock
1 cup whipping cream
several strands of saffron dissolved
    in a little of the white wine

FOR THE GARNISH
sprigs of dill
concassé tomatoes

Picture: page 163

Open the scallops (see p.61). Separate the corals from the bodies and cut the bodies in half horizontally. Place on a cloth.

Heat the butter, add the shallots, cover and cook over a low heat, shaking the pan occasionally, until soft.

Season the scallops, add the bodies to the pan, then cook over a low heat for 1 minute. Add the corals and cook for a further minute.

Remove the scallops with a slotted spoon, cover and keep warm.

Stir the wine into the pan and reduce to 2 tbsp. Stir in the stock and reduce to ¼ cup. Stir in the cream and dissolved saffron, and simmer until slightly thickened. Season.

Divide the sauce between the warmed plates. Arrange the scallop bodies and corals on top. Garnish with sprigs of dill and concassé tomatoes.

LEFT *Scallops with mussel parcels*
Recipe: page 164
ABOVE *Lobster medallions with chive sauce*
Recipe: page 177

R O L L S   O F   S O L E   W I T H   S O R R E L   S A U C E

INGREDIENTS (serves 4)
8 oz turbot
salt and lemon juice
1 large egg white
1 cup whipping cream, chilled
1 tbsp cognac
approximately 2 tbsp well drained
    puréed watercress
freshly ground white pepper
8 sole fillets, skinned
court bouillon

FOR THE SAUCE
1 cup fish stock
¾ cup dry white wine
¾ cup dry vermouth
1 shallot, finely chopped
1 cup crème fraîche
¼ cup sorrel, thinly sliced
salt
lemon juice

FOR THE GARNISH
carrot shapes (see p.70)
long lozenges of tomato
sprigs of dill

Picture: page 171

Purée the turbot in a food processor or blender. Mix in the salt and lemon juice, followed by the egg white. Pass through a sieve into a bowl in a bowl of ice. Gradually beat in the cream. Add the cognac and enough puréed watercress to give a good green color. Add the pepper. Cover and chill for at least 30 minutes.

Lightly score the skinned side of the sole fillets. Season lightly, then spread the turbot mixture over. Roll up the fillets.

Pack the fillets into a well buttered sauteuse or frying pan which they should just fit. Gently pour in sufficient court bouillon to come almost up the sides of the sole. Cover the rolls with buttered wax paper and poach for about 12 minutes.

For the sauce, boil the stock, wine, vermouth and shallot until reduced to ¼ cup. Whisk in the crème fraîche and simmer until slightly thickened. Add the sorrel and simmer for 30 seconds. Season and add lemon juice to taste.

Remove the fish rolls with a slotted spoon and place on 4 warmed plates. Spoon the sauce around and garnish with carrot, tomato and dill.

S O L E   W I T H   O Y S T E R   P A R C E L S

INGREDIENTS (serves 4)
1 tbsp finely chopped shallot
⅔ cup fish stock
5 tbsp dry vermouth
6 fillets of sole, skinned and cut into
    strips
salt and freshly ground pepper
12 oysters
12 lettuce leaves
a small sprig of fresh thyme
½ cup + 2 tbsp whipping cream
1½ tsp white wine vinegar
1 tbsp butter
1 tsp finely chopped chervil

FOR THE GARNISH
12 diamond shapes of tomato flesh

Simmer the shallot in the stock and vermouth for 3-4 minutes in a small covered pan. Pour into a sauteuse or frying pan that will hold the sole in a single layer. Lay the sole strips in the pan, season, cover with wax paper and poach for about 1½ minutes until just opaque.

Carefully transfer to a warmed dish with a slotted spoon, cover and keep warm.

Meanwhile open the oysters. Blanch the lettuce leaves, drain well and dry on paper towels.

Add the oysters to the poaching liquor and poach for 30 seconds. Remove with a slotted spoon and wrap each oyster into a lettuce leaf, folding the leaf over to make a neat parcel.

Meanwhile, add the thyme to the liquor and reduce to ¼ cup. Pour into a small saucepan, stir in the cream and simmer for 5 minutes. Pass through a sieve. Return to the heat, stir in the vinegar and reheat gently. Dice the butter and gradually whisk in over a low heat, making sure each piece is fully incorporated before adding the next. Stir in the chervil.

Spoon the sauce over 4 warmed plates. Arrange the strips of sole and the oyster parcels in the sauce. Place a diamond of tomato on each parcel.

ROULADE OF SOLE

INGREDIENTS (serves 4)
6 poached crayfish, shelled
3 tbsp whipping cream
salt and freshly ground white pepper
4 fillets of sole, skinned
court bouillon

FOR THE WHITE SAUCE
$\frac{1}{4}$ cup fish stock
1 cup full bodied dry white wine
6 tbsp butter
salt and freshly ground white pepper

FOR THE RED SAUCE
$\frac{1}{3}$ cup red shellfish glaze (see Lobster
    gâteaux in lobster sauce p.176)
6 tbsp butter

Peel the crayfish and remove the veins running down the back. Chop the flesh coarsely, then process briefly in a food processor. Add the cream and seasoning and mix briefly. Pass through a fine sieve.

Lightly season the skinned side of the sole then spread the crayfish mixture in a line down the center. Fold the sides of the sole over the filling. Place with the join underneath in the top half of a steamer. Put the lid on.

Heat some court bouillon in the bottom half of the steamer to simmering point. Put the top half in place and cook the fish for about 5 minutes until just opaque.

Meanwhile, reduce the fish stock and wine for the white sauce to $\frac{1}{4}$ cup. Reduce the heat to very low. Dice the butter and gradually stir in, making sure that each piece is fully incorporated before adding the next. Season and keep warm but do not allow to boil.

Remove the fish from the heat but keep warm.

Heat the shellfish glaze to simmering point, then reduce the heat to very low. Dice the butter and gradually stir in, making sure each piece is fully incorporated before adding the next. Season and keep warm but do not allow to boil.

Trim the ends from the fillets, then cut each fillet into 6 slices and arrange around the center of 4 warmed plates.

Spoon some of the red sauce into the centers of the plates. Spoon the white sauce around the edge and streak the remaining red sauce from the center onto the white sauce.

SOLE WITH SNOW PEAS

INGREDIENTS (serves 4)
1$\frac{1}{2}$ cups snow peas
2 small carrots, julienned
salt and freshly ground white pepper
8 fillets of sole, cut in half lengthwise
16 very thin slices of fresh ginger
    root, cut into strips
8 scallions, cut in half lengthwise
2 tsp olive oil
rind of 2 oranges, cut into short
    julienned pieces
1 tbsp finely chopped ginger root
2 tbsp soy sauce
6 tbsp fino sherry
a squeeze of lemon juice

Picture: page 170

Arrange the snow peas and carrots in a large steamer or 2 small ones. Sprinkle with salt and freshly ground white pepper. Season the skin side of the pieces of sole, then roll them up loosely, seasoned side innermost, starting from the narrow end. Place a little way apart on the vegetables. Place a piece of ginger and a scallion half on each piece of fish.

Place the steamer over a pan of simmering water and steam for about 8 minutes until the sole is just opaque all the way through.

Meanwhile, heat the oil, add the orange julienne and cook until just beginning to curl. Stir in the chopped ginger and cook for about 30 seconds, then stir in the soy sauce, sherry, lemon juice and 4 tbsp water. Bring to the boil, then reduce the heat and simmer for 5 minutes.

Spoon the sauce onto parts of 4 warmed plates. Carefully place the rolls of sole on the sauce. Scatter the orange julienne on the rolls and garnish the plates with the vegetables.

ABOVE *Sole with snow peas*
Recipe: page 169
OPPOSITE *Rolls of sole with sorrel sauce*
Recipe: page 168

SOLE AND DUBLIN BAY SHRIMP

WITH RED PEPPER CREAM

INGREDIENTS (serves 4)
4 tbsp butter
1 lb red peppers, diced
1 tbsp sugar
1 tbsp cider vinegar
$\frac{1}{2}$ tsp paprika
salt
4 scallops
1 tbsp finely chopped shallot
freshly ground white pepper
1 cup medium bodied dry white wine
3 fillets of sole, cut into cubes
12-16 cooked Dublin Bay or other
    large shrimp, peeled
$\frac{1}{4}$ cup medium dry sherry
1 cup whipping cream

FOR THE GARNISH
$\frac{1}{2}$ large cucumber, peeled, cut into 12
    slices, $\frac{1}{2}$ inch thick, centers
    removed, sprinkled with salt, left to
    drain for 3 minutes
flesh of 1 tomato, finely diced
sprigs of dill

Heat half the butter in a small heavy saucepan, stir in the peppers, sugar, vinegar, paprika and salt, cover and cook for about 5 minutes or until the peppers are very soft, stirring occasionally. Uncover, increase the heat to medium and cook to a thick purée and until all the liquid has evaporated, stirring frequently. Pass through a sieve.

Open the scallops, reserve the liquor and separate the bodies from the corals (see p.61).

Heat the remaining butter in a sauteuse or large frying pan, stir in the shallots, seasoning and half the wine and simmer for 2-3 minutes. Add the sole, reduce the heat and poach the sole for 1$\frac{1}{4}$ minutes. Turn it over, add the shrimp and cook for a further minute until the sole is just opaque. Transfer to a warmed dish with a slotted spoon and cover.

Add the remaining wine and the sherry to the pan and reduce to $\frac{1}{4}$ cup. Whisk in the cream and boil until the sauce is slightly thickened, stirring occasionally.

Whisk the red pepper purée into the sauce and warm through but do not allow to boil. Season.

Place a sheet of foil on the bottom of the top part of a steamer. Place the cucumber rings on the foil. Divide the tomato amongst the cucumber rings, then steam for 2 minutes. Divide the sauce between 4 warmed plates. Arrange the sole, shrimp, scallop bodies and corals, then garnish with 3 tomato-topped cucumber rings per plate and sprigs of dill.

FILLETS OF SOLE WITH LIGHT

TOMATO FILLING

INGREDIENTS (serves 4)
flesh of 4 tomatoes, chopped
salt and pepper
3 small egg whites, lightly whisked
4 large fillets of sole, skinned
2 tbsp finely chopped shallot
2 tbsp chopped basil
$\frac{3}{4}$ cup fish stock
$\frac{2}{3}$ cup full bodied dry white wine
$\frac{1}{3}$ cup whipping cream
2 tbsp butter

FOR THE GARNISH
4 diamond shapes of puff pastry
caviar

Cook the tomatoes over a very low heat, stirring frequently until nearly all the moisture has evaporated and the mixture is very thick. Season, leave to cool then turn into a bowl over a bowl of crushed ice and leave to chill.

Gradually beat the egg whites into the tomato pulp.

Season the skinned side of the sole then spread the tomato mixture over the widest half of the length of each fillet. Fold the other half over the mousse and place in the top half of a steamer. Cover with buttered wax paper.

Heat the shallots and basil in the stock and wine in the bottom half of the steamer to simmering point. Put the top half of the steamer in place and cook the sole for about 10 minutes until the flesh is opaque.

Warm the puff pastry diamonds.

Transfer the sole to a warmed plate, cover and keep warm.

Reduce the cooking liquor to $\frac{1}{2}$ cup then stir in the cream and reduce until thick enough to coat the back of a spoon. Pass through a sieve then reheat in a clean saucepan. Dice the butter and over a very low heat, gradually stir in, making sure each piece is completely incorporated before adding the next. Season.

Spoon the sauce over 4 warmed plates. Place the sole on the sauce. Split the puff pastry diamonds in half lengthwise, place some caviar on the bottom half and replace the top at an angle. Place on the plates.

CROWN OF LOBSTER AND SCALLOPS

WITH ASPARAGUS

INGREDIENTS (serves 4)
a sprig of thyme
1 shallot, chopped
$\frac{3}{4}$ cup pink champagne or other good quality dry sparkling rosé wine
$1\frac{1}{4}$ cups fish stock
$\frac{1}{2}$ cup whipping cream
4 tbsp butter
1 tbsp champagne vinegar
salt and freshly ground white pepper
12 scallops
$\frac{1}{2}$ cup fruity dry white wine
flesh from 2 cooked lobster tails, sliced
12 green asparagus spears, sliced on the diagonal

FOR THE GARNISH
crayfish tails
slices of truffle

This is a very elegant looking and tasting dish that is not at all complicated. It is ideal for a summer dinner.

Bring the thyme, shallot, champagne and stock to the boil and reduce by three quarters. Pass through a fine sieve, return to the rinsed pan, stir in the cream and simmer for 5 minutes. Dice the butter, reduce the heat to very low, and gradually whisk in 2 tbsp butter, making sure that each piece is completely incorporated before adding the next. Stir in the vinegar. Season and keep warm, but do not allow to boil.

Remove the scallops from their shells (see p.61) and separate the corals from the bodies. Slice the bodies in half horizontally.

Heat the wine, season lightly, add the scallop bodies and slices of lobster tail and poach for about 1 minute. Turn them over, add the corals and poach for a further minute.

Meanwhile, steam the slices of asparagus for about 5 minutes.

Spoon the sauce over 4 warmed plates. Remove the fish from the wine with a slotted spoon and arrange on the sauce in a circle like a crown. Arrange the asparagus in the centres and garnish with crayfish tails and slices of truffle.

ABOVE *Lobster gâteaux with lobster sauce*
Recipe: page 176
OPPOSITE *Crayfish and mushroom ragoût*
Recipe: page 177

LOBSTER GATEAUX WITH

LOBSTER SAUCE

INGREDIENTS (serves 4)
2 tbsp olive oil
½ lobster shell, crushed and pounded
2 shallots, finely chopped
1 carrot, finely chopped
2 parsley stalks
10 red peppercorns
1 bay leaf, broken
2 tbsp cognac
1 cup fish stock
½ cup dry white wine
salt and white pepper
1 cup butter

FOR THE GATEAUX
7 oz turbot fillets
¼ cup lobster tail meat
¼ cup lobster coral, sieved
salt and lemon juice
1 large egg white
1¼ cups whipping cream, chilled
a small pinch of cayenne pepper

FOR THE GARNISH
sprigs of chervil
crayfish claws

Picture: page 174

The base for the sauce and the lobster gâteaux mixture can be prepared in advance. Other ways of glazing apart from the cobweb pattern in the photograph, include a halo around the gâteaux or teardrop shapes in the sauce.

Heat the oil, add the lobster shell and cook for 5 minutes, stirring occasionally. Stir in the shallots, carrot, parsley, peppercorns and bayleaf and cook, stirring occasionally, until the shallots are transparent. Pour the cognac over and ignite with a taper. When the flames have subsided, stir in the stock, wine, and seasoning. Cover and simmer for 10 minutes.

Pass through a conical strainer, pressing down well onto the vegetables and shell to extract as much liquid as possible. There should be about ¾ cup — if it is not reduced sufficiently, boil down further.

For the gâteaux, mix the turbot, lobster meat and coral in a food processor, then add the salt and lemon juice, followed by the egg white. Pass through a sieve into a bowl placed over a bowl of ice, then gradually beat in the cream. Season with cayenne pepper. Cover and chill for at least 30 minutes.

Heat the oven to 370°F.

Divide the lobster mixture between 4 individual serving dishes or molds, place in a roasting or baking pan, surround with boiling water and cover the tops of the molds with buttered wax paper. Place in the oven for 20 minutes.

Bring ½ cup of the lobster liquor to the boil. Dice the butter, reduce the heat to very low, then gradually whisk in the butter, making sure each piece is completely incorporated before adding the next. Season and keep warm but do not allow to boil.

Meanwhile, boil the remaining liquor to a light syrupy glaze.

Remove the gâteaux from the heat and allow to stand for a few minutes before turning out onto 4 warmed plates. Place a sprig of chervil on each one. Spoon the sauce around. Make a pattern in the sauce with the lobster glaze and garnish with chervil and crayfish claws.

L O B S T E R   M E D A L L I O N S   W I T H

C H I V E   S A U C E

INGREDIENTS (serves 4)
8 slices blanched lobster meat from
    the tail
8 slices of blanched lobster meat from
    the large claw
2 tbsp sweet butter

FOR THE SAUCE
1 shallot, finely chopped
½ cup dry white wine
½ cup fish stock (see p.75)
½ cup whipping cream
6 tbsp sweet butter
1 tsp puréed chives
salt and freshly ground black pepper

FOR THE GARNISH
cucumber shapes (see p.70)
tomato shapes

Picture: page 167

The cucumber and tomato for the garnish can be prepared in advance, or a less complicated garnish can be prepared at the last minute.

Gently cook the lobster slices in the butter for 30 seconds each side. Remove with a slotted spoon, cover with plastic wrap and keep warm.

For the sauce, cook the shallot in the pan in which the lobster was cooked over a moderate heat until soft. Stir in the wine, stock and cream and boil until slightly syrupy.

Dice the butter and gradually whisk in a piece at a time, making sure that each piece is incorporated before adding the next. Add the chives and seasonings.

Pour the sauce over 4 warmed plates and arrange 2 slices of lobster tail meat and 2 slices of lobster claw meat on each one. Garnish with cucumber and tomato.

C R A Y F I S H   A N D   M U S H R O O M   R A G O U T

INGREDIENTS (serves 4)
16 fresh crayfish
court bouillon (see p.76)
1 tbsp butter
2 oz ceps, sliced
½ tbsp finely chopped shallots
¼ tsp finely chopped thyme
½ clove of garlic, finely chopped
salt and freshly ground white pepper
1 tbsp Pernod
⅓ cup dry white wine
1¼ cups whipping cream

FOR THE GARNISH
sprigs of chervil
slices of truffle
crayfish

Picture: page 175

Poach the crayfish in the court bouillon for about 10 minutes until bright red. Remove and keep warm. Keep the court bouillon warm.

Heat the butter, add the shallots, thyme, garlic and seasoning and cook for 2—3 minutes. Stir in the Pernod and wine and reduce by half. Stir in the cream. Season.

Remove the crayfish from their shells. Bring the court bouillon to just below simmering point. Add the crayfish and heat for 30 seconds.

Transfer the crayfish to 4 warmed plates with a slotted spoon and pour the sauce over. Garnish with sprigs of chervil and slices of truffle. Arrange the crayfish around the edge of the plates.

ABOVE *Fillets of turbot with tomatoes and
vermouth sauce*
Recipe: page 180
OPPOSITE *Gougons of turbot with
red currant dressing*
Recipe: page 181

FILLETS OF TURBOT WITH TOMATOES

AND VERMOUTH SAUCE

INGREDIENTS *(serves 4)*
2 tbsp butter, diced
6 fillets of turbot, each 5—6oz
salt and freshly ground black pepper
2 shallots, sliced
2 tbsp chopped chives
flesh of 4 tomatoes, chopped
⅔ cup dry vermouth
2 cups fish stock
1 cup whipping cream

FOR THE GARNISH
saffron rice timbales (see p.301)
tomato concassé
sprigs of chervil

Picture: page 178

Prepare the saffron rice timbales.

Heat the butter. Season the turbot and the butter and cook gently until the flesh is just opaque — do not allow it to color. Remove carefully, cover and keep warm.

Add the shallots to the pan, cover and cook over a moderate heat, shaking the pan occasionally, until soft. Stir in the chives, tomatoes, vermouth and stock and simmer until reduced to about ½—¾ cup. Stir in the cream and simmer until slightly thickened. Purée, season and reheat gently.

Spoon the sauce over 4 warmed plates. Unmold the saffron rice timbales, place the fish on the sauce and garnish with tomato concassé and chervil.

PIKE QUENELLES WITH

WHITE WINE SAUCE

INGREDIENTS *(serves 4)*
9 oz skinless pike, chopped and chilled
salt and white pepper
a squeeze of lemon juice
1 egg white
1 cup whipping cream, chilled
½ tsp tomato paste
*4½ cups fish stock (see p.75), for
    poaching*
1 tbsp butter
1 tbsp finely chopped shallot
½ cup blanched spinach, well drained

FOR THE SAUCE
5 tbsp butter
1½ tbsp finely chopped shallot
1 cup fish stock
½ cup full bodied dry white wine
2 tbsp dry vermouth
½ cup whipping cream
salt and freshly ground white pepper

Mix the pike in a food processor until it is puréed , add the salt and lemon juice then mix in the egg white until smooth.

Pass through a fine sieve into a bowl placed over a bowl of ice, then gradually beat in the cream. Add the pepper, then divide the mixture in half and add sufficient tomato paste to one half to color it a delicate pink. Cover both mixtures and chill for at least 30 minutes.

Fill a sauteuse or large frying pan with fish stock and bring to just simmering point.

Using 2 spoons, form each of the pike mixtures into 4 quenelles, gently lower them into the stock and poach for about 3 minutes each side.

For the sauce, heat 1 tbsp butter, add the shallot and cook over a moderate heat in a covered pan, shaking the pan occasionally, until soft. Stir in the stock, wine and vermouth and reduce to 1 tbsp. Stir in the cream and simmer for 2 minutes. Pass through a sieve, place over a very low heat and whisk in the remaining butter. Do not allow it to boil. Season and keep warm.

Heat the butter, add the shallot and cook over a moderate heat in a covered pan, shaking the pan occasionally until soft. Stir in the spinach and cook for about 3 minutes, stirring frequently.

Remove the quenelles from the poaching liquor with a

FOR THE GARNISH
8 slices of truffle (or strips of blanched yellow and red pepper)

Picture: page 159

slotted spoon and drain on a cloth. With a sharp knife, cut each quenelle diagonally across to form halves.

Divide the spinach between 4 warmed plates. Place half a pink quenelle and half a white one on each plate with the edges touching so that they form one complete quenelle. Spoon the sauce around. Place a strip of truffle or yellow and red pepper on the join in each quenelle.

WHITEFISH WITH BASIL

INGREDIENTS (serves 6)
1 cup fish stock
1 cup full bodied dry white wine
2 tbsp finely chopped shallots
3 tbsp finely chopped basil
salt and pepper
1½ lb piece of filleted whitefish, cut into 16 slices
¼ cup champagne vinegar or white wine vinegar
½ cup butter

FOR THE GARNISH
concassé tomatoes

In a sauteuse or frying pan large enough to hold the fish in a single layer, heat the stock, wine, shallots, 1 tbsp basil and salt and pepper to simmering point. Add the fish and poach until the flesh is just opaque.

Transfer the fish to a warmed plate, cover and keep warm.

Boil the poaching liquor until reduced to ¾ cup. Pass through a sieve into a clean saucepan, stir in the vinegar and simmer for a minute or two, then reduce the heat to very low. Dice the butter and gradually whisk in, making sure each piece is fully incorporated before adding the next. Season. Add the remaining basil, season and spoon over 4 warmed plates.

Arrange the slices of whitefish on the sauce and garnish with concassé tomatoes.

GOUJONS OF TURBOT WITH

RED CURRANT DRESSING

INGREDIENTS (serves 4)
4 fillets of turbot, each approximately 6 oz, skinned and cut into strips
oak leaf lettuce

FOR THE DRESSING
3 tbsp champagne vinegar
9 tbsp olive oil
3 tbsp red currant juice
1½ tbsp finely chopped shallot
½ tbsp finely chopped chives
1¾ cups red currants
salt and freshly ground black pepper

FOR THE GARNISH
red currants
sprigs of chervil

Picture: page 179

Shake all the ingredients together for the dressing.

Steam the turbot for about 5 minutes until just opaque — take care not to overcook. Remove the turbot from the heat, cover and keep warm.

Gently warm the dressing.

Meanwhile, arrange the lettuce on 4 large cold plates.

Arrange the turbot in the center of the plates and spoon the dressing over. Garnish with red currants and sprigs of chervil.

Grouper with lemon and fennel
sauce
Recipe: page 184

Mussels on a spinach bed
Recipe: page 185

MEDITERRANEAN GROUPER WITH LEMON AND FENNEL SAUCE

INGREDIENTS (serves 4)
1½ lemons
3 tbsp white wine vinegar
1 tsp fennel seeds
2 tbsp butter
1 tbsp olive oil
4 fillets of grouper, approximately
*   6 oz, skinned and cut into 3 strips*
1 cup fish stock
½ cup full bodied dry white wine
2 tbsp dry vermouth
1 tbsp crème fraîche
1—2 tbsp finely chopped dill
salt and freshly ground white pepper

FOR THE GARNISH
sprigs of broccoli
slices of lemon
sprigs of chervil

Picture: page 182

The day before the dish is required, pare the rind of half a lemon finely, squeeze 1 tsp of juice, and strain. Mix the rind and juice with the vinegar and fennel seeds, cover and leave in a cool place.

The next day thinly pare the rind from the remaining lemon, cut into fine julienne pieces, then blanch for 2 minutes. Refresh and drain well.

Heat the butter and oil, add the grouper and cook gently for 2-3 minutes until just opaque. Remove with a slotted spoon, drain on paper towels, then cover and keep warm.

Meanwhile, boil the stock until reduced by half.

Tip the excess fat and oil from the pan. Stir in the wine, vermouth and stock. Remove the lemon rind from the vinegar and add the vinegar to the pan. Boil until slightly thickened.

Meanwhile, blanch the broccoli for the garnish, refresh and drain well.

Reduce the heat beneath the pan with the sauce and stir in the crème fraîche, dill and lemon julienne. Season.

Arrange the fish on 4 warmed plates. Spoon the sauce over and garnish with sprigs of broccoli, lemon slices and chervil.

MUSSELS WITH SAFFRON AND GINGER SAUCE AND POTATO BASKETS OF VEGETABLES

INGREDIENTS (serves 4)
1 shallot, finely chopped
3 parsley stalks
½ cup dry white wine
4½ cups mussels
3 tsp finely chopped fresh root ginger
a pinch of freshly grated nutmeg
1¼ cups fish stock
⅔ cup whipping cream
several strands of saffron soaked in a
*   little warm dry white vermouth*
butter
salt and freshly ground white pepper
a squeeze of lemon juice
4 potato baskets (see p.302)
macédoine of colorful vegetables —
*   petit pois, finely diced carrots,*
*   turnips, zucchini, small cauliflower*
*   flowerets or asparagus*
sprigs of dill

Put the shallot, parsley and wine into a pan. Add the mussels, cover and put over a moderately high heat for about 5 minutes, shaking the pan frequently, until the shells open. Remove them as they are ready. Remove the mussels from their shells and keep warm. Discard any that remain closed.

Add 2 tsp ginger, the nutmeg and stock to the pan and reduce by three quarters. Pass through a sieve. Simmer with the cream and saffron in a clean saucepan for about 3 minutes. Add the remaining ginger. Reduce the heat to very low and gradually swirl in the butter. Season with salt and pepper and a squeeze of lemon juice.

In the meantime, prepare and cook the potato baskets and steam the vegetables.

Divide the vegetables between the baskets and place either in the center or to one side of 4 warmed plates. Spoon the sauce around. Arrange the mussels in the sauce. Finish with sprigs of dill.

MUSSELS ON A SPINACH BED

INGREDIENTS (serves 4)
8 sheets of filo pastry
melted butter
2½ cups fish stock
1 cup dry white wine
16 mussels
¼ cup zucchini, julienned
¼ cup red pepper, skinned, and
    julienned
¼ cup celery, julienned
1 cup butter
salt and freshly ground white pepper
1 cup spinach purée, well drained
    (see p.62)
¼ cup whipping cream

Picture: page 183

Very thinly rolled puff pastry (see p.79) could be used instead of filo pastry. The scallop shells should be lined in advance, covered and kept in a cool place.

———————

Heat the oven to 425°F.

Fold the sheets of filo in half and use half of them to line 4 buttered scallop shells. Brush with melted butter and cover with the remaining sheets. Brush the edges with melted butter. Bake for about 8-10 minutes until crisp and a light golden brown.

Gently heat the fish stock and wine, add the mussels and cook until they open. Reserve the liquor. Remove the mussels from their shells.

Blanch the vegetables in the liquor until they are just tender. Remove them with a slotted spoon, drain well and keep warm.

Reduce the liquor to ½ cup. Reduce the heat to very low. Dice the butter and then gradually whisk in, making sure that each piece is completely incorporated before adding the next. Season and keep warm, but do not allow to boil.

Gently heat the spinach purée, then beat in the cream and seasoning. Divide between the pastry shells. Arrange the mussels on top. Spoon a little of the sauce over and scatter the vegetables over.

◆

LEFT *Seafood
cassolette*
Recipe: page 188
ABOVE *Seafood with
a rainbow of
noodles*
Recipe: page 188

◆

LEFT *Panaché of
seafood*
Recipe: page 189

SEAFOOD CASSOLETTE

INGREDIENTS (serves 4)
2 tbsp butter
¼ cup shallots, finely chopped
4 cooked crayfish, shelled
4 scallops
4 oz sole fillets, cut into strips
½ cup cooked shrimp, shelled
12 fresh basil leaves, thinly sliced
¾ cup dry white wine
¾ cup fish stock
½ cup whipping cream
2 tbsp red shellfish butter (see p.77)
salt and freshly ground white pepper

FOR THE GARNISH
tomato concassé
crayfish
sprigs of dill

Picture: page 186

Cuisine Vivante transforms a traditional cassoulet, with its long slow cooking and hearty ingredients, into a light quickly cooked cassolette.

———————

Heat the butter, add the shallots, cover and cook over a moderate heat, shaking the pan occasionally, until soft. Add the crayfish and cook for 2 minutes.

Remove the scallops from their shells (see p.61), separate the bodies from the corals and cut the bodies in half. Add to the pan with the sole, shrimp, basil, wine and stock and cook gently for 2 minutes. Remove the fish with a slotted spoon and keep warm.

Reduce the liquor by three quarters, then stir in the cream and simmer until slightly thickened. Reduce the heat to very low. Dice the red shellfish butter and gradually whisk in, making sure that each piece is completely incorporated before adding the next. Season.

Divide the fish between 4 warmed plates, arranging them attractively, then spoon the sauce over. Garnish with the concassé tomatoes, crayfish and sprigs of dill.

SEAFOOD WITH A RAINBOW OF NOODLES

INGREDIENTS (serves 4)
4 oz salmon fillets, cut into strips
4 peeled large shrimp
8 clams out of their shells
8 mussels out of their shells
2 tbsp lemon juice
salt and freshly ground white pepper
1 tbsp each of chopped parsley, basil
   and thyme
½ cup fresh pink noodles (see p.78)
½ cup fresh green noodles (see p.78)
½ cup fresh white noodles (see p.78)
1 tbsp oil
1 tbsp butter
1 tbsp finely chopped shallot
1 tbsp cognac
1 cup full bodied dry white wine
1¼ cups whipping cream
3 tbsp red shellfish butter (see p.77)

Providing the amounts are kept fairly constant, and bearing in mind the appearance of the dish, the type of fish can be altered. Eight scallops, their bodies separated from the corals, could be used instead of mussels and clams, and crayfish in place of large shrimp.

———————

Put the fish and shellfish into a shallow dish, keeping the varieties separate. Spoon the lemon juice over and sprinkle with seasoning and herbs. Cover and leave in a cool place for 30 minutes.

Cook the noodles together with the oil, in boiling salted water until just tender.

Meanwhile, heat the butter, add the shallot, cover and cook over a moderate heat, shaking the pan occasionally until soft.

Remove the fish from the marinade with a slotted spoon, strain the marinade and reserve. Add the salmon and large shrimp to the shallots, pour in the cognac and ignite with a taper. Cook gently for 2 minutes.

Add the clams, mussels and the wine and cook for 2 minutes.

FOR THE GARNISH
large shrimp
sprigs of parsley
julienned truffle

Picture: page 187

Remove the fish with a slotted spoon and keep warm. Reduce the liquor by two thirds, then stir in the cream and simmer until slightly thickened. Reduce the heat to very low, dice the red shellfish butter and gradually stir in, making sure that each piece is completely incorporated before adding the next. Add the fish to the sauce. Season and add a little of the marinade.

Drain the noodles (if necessary, they can be kept warm in a steamer) and arrange them on 4 warmed plates, forming a slight well in the center. Divide the fish and sauce between them and garnish with the shrimp, the sprigs of parsley and the truffle.

PANACHE OF SEAFOOD

INGREDIENTS *(serves 4)*
4 oz skinned, boned salmon
salt
½ tsp egg white
⅔ cup whipping cream, chilled
cayenne pepper
a few strands of saffron
1 cup fish stock
½ cup dry white wine
1½ tsp lemon juice
freshly ground white pepper
4 scallops
12 oz sole fillets
8 oz sea bass fillets
8 oz whitefish fillets

FOR THE GARNISH
sprigs of coriander and chervil

Picture: page 187

Start to cook the sea bass and whitefish before adding the sole and then the scallops to the steamer, as the more delicate fish will become too tough if cooked for the same length of time as the firmer ones.

———

Purée the salmon in a food processor or blender, add the salt then the egg white. Pass through a sieve into a bowl over a bowl of ice, then gradually beat in the chilled cream. Add a little cayenne pepper, cover and chill for 30 minutes.

Pipe the salmon mixture into 4 small decorative molds, pushing it well into the sides. Place the molds in a shallow pan, surround with hot water, place over a low heat and poach for 10 minutes. Leave to stand off the heat for 2 minutes.

Meanwhile, stir the saffron into a little of the stock. Bring the remaining stock, the wine and lemon juice to the boil and reduce by three quarters. Stir in the cream and saffron liquor and simmer for 2 minutes. Season and add a little more lemon juice if necessary.

Open the scallops (see p.61) and cut the other fish into 4 pieces each. Season all the fish lightly and steam for 3-5 minutes until just opaque.

Unmold the salmon molds onto the center of 4 warmed plates. Spoon the sauce around and arrange the fish on top. Garnish with sprigs of coriander and chervil.

MEAT

DISHES

The portions of meat in Cuisine Vivante recipes are generally kept to a size that will not defeat the appetite, overload the stomach or overwhelm the digestive system but they can, of course, be adjusted to accommodate individual requirements. In a meal of five, six or even seven courses just 3-4oz of meat per person should provide the right balance, whereas 4-6oz would be more acceptable for a hearty eater of a short menu. Recommendations for quantities in the following recipes are intended as guidelines only and amounts can easily be changed.

VEAL WITH SALSIFY

INGREDIENTS (serves 4)
2 cups veal stock
4 inch piece of white of leek, sliced in'
half lengthwise
a long strip of lemon peel
4 parsley sprigs
1¼ lbs salsify
lemon juice
4 tbsp butter
salt and freshly ground black pepper
4 tournedos of veal, approximately
5-6 oz
1 cup dry white wine
½ cup dry vermouth
½ cup whipping cream
freshly ground white pepper

FOR THE GARNISH
French beans cut into 1½ inch lengths
diamond shapes of blanched red
pepper

Picture: page 194

Either salsify or scorzonera can be used — see p.31. The base for the sauce can be prepared in advance.

Simmer the stock with the leek, lemon peel and parsley for 30 minutes, then boil until reduced to about 1 cup. Strain.

Meanwhile, peel the salsify with a potato peeler and cut into 1½ inch pieces — as each one is prepared, put it into water acidulated with lemon juice to prevent discoloration.

Simmer the salsify in acidulated water for about 45 minutes until tender. Drain well.

Meanwhile, heat half the butter. Season the veal and cook in the butter for 3—4 minutes each side. Transfer to a warmed plate with a slotted spoon, cover and keep warm.

Stir the wine and the vermouth into the pan and reduce to 3 tbsp. Stir in the stock and simmer for 2—3 minutes. Stir in the cream and simmer until slightly thickened. Reduce the heat to very low and swirl in the remaining butter. Season and keep warm, but do not boil.

Blanch the beans for the garnish, refresh and drain.

Place the tournedos on 4 warmed plates and spoon the sauce around. Arrange the diamonds of red pepper around the plate and place the French beans on the tournedos.

ROLLED ESCALOPES OF VEAL WITH LIGHT PISTACHIO SAUCE

INGREDIENTS (serves 4)
4 escalopes of veal
1 cup or ½ lb spinach leaves
salt and freshly ground black pepper
⅔ cup medium bodied dry white wine
1 cup veal stock
a sprig of marjoram
½ cup pistachio nuts
¼ cup armagnac or cognac
½ cup whipping cream

FOR THE GARNISH
white wine sauce (see p.180)
skinned pistachio nuts

The pistachios can be prepared in advance. Put the escalopes of veal between 2 sheets of plastic wrap to flatten them but take care not to break holes in the flesh.

Prepare the white wine sauce for the garnish. Cover the surface with wax paper or plastic wrap and keep warm in a bowl over a pan of hot water.

Blanch the spinach leaves, refresh, drain and dry very well on paper towels. Lay the spinach leaves over the veal and roll each escalope up like a jelly roll. Season and place seam side down in the top of a steamer. Put the lid on.

Bring the wine, ¼ cup of stock and the marjoram to the boil in the bottom part of the steamer. Cover with the top part. Reduce the heat to simmering and cook the veal for about 3 minutes.

Meanwhile, bring a saucepan of water to the boil, add the pistachios and return to the boil. Drain the pistachios and remove the skins. Place the nuts in a food processor or blender and mix to a smooth paste.

Transfer the veal to a warmed plate, cover and keep warm.

Ignite the armagnac or cognac, pour into the wine and remaining stock then reduce to $\frac{1}{4}$ cup.

Remove the marjoram, stir in the cream and simmer for 2—3 minutes. Reduce the heat to very low and gradually whisk in the pistachio paste, making sure each piece is incorporated before adding the next. Season and keep warm but do not allow to boil.

Trim the ends from the veal rolls then cut the rolls into thin slices. Reform and keep warm.

Divide the pistachio sauce between 4 warmed plates. Arrange the veal slices on top. Carefully pour on some of the white wine sauce around the edge of the pistachio sauce then swirl the rest of the white wine sauce at intervals into the pistachio sauce. Garnish with pistachio nuts.

POACHED VEAL WITH TOMATO

SAUCE

INGREDIENTS (serves 4)
$2\frac{1}{2}$ cups veal stock
12 parsley sprigs chopped
a strip of lemon peel
6 black peppercorns, crushed
4 medallions of veal about 5-6oz each
2 tbsp butter
2 tbsp finely chopped shallot
$1\frac{1}{2}$ cups (1 lb) tomatoes, diced
$\frac{2}{3}$ cup whipping cream
2 tbsp sweet vermouth
salt and freshly ground black pepper

FOR THE GARNISH
1 tbsp butter
a squeeze of lemon juice
chervil leaves
8 button mushrooms
baby carrots

Picture: page 198

Be sure to use fleshy, sun ripened tomatoes for this delicate, light and fresh tasting dish.

Bring the stock, parsley sprigs, lemon peel and peppercorns to the boil, add the veal, reduce the heat to just simmering and poach the veal for about 6 minutes.

Meanwhile, heat the butter, add the shallots, cover and cook over a moderate heat, shaking the pan occasionally, until just soft. Stir in the tomatoes and simmer for 10 minutes, then pass through a sieve. Return to the rinsed pan and boil rapidly to thicken, if necessary. Stir in the cream and vermouth and boil for 2 minutes. Season and keep warm without boiling.

Heat the butter for the garnish, add the lemon juice and mushrooms and cook for 3—4 minutes. Remove with a slotted spoon and drain on paper towels. Slice into fans.

Meanwhile, blanch, refresh and drain the carrots for the garnish and keep warm in a steamer.

Remove the veal and dry on paper towels. Season lightly.

Spoon the sauce over 4 warmed plates, place the veal on top and sprinkle the chervil over the sauce. Garnish with the mushrooms and baby carrots.

ABOVE *Veal with salsify*
Recipe: page 192
OPPOSITE *Croustade of a mélange of veal*
Recipe: page 197

VEAL WITH ZUCCHINI AND GRAPEFRUIT

INGREDIENTS (serves 4)
1 lb loin of veal, very thinly sliced
salt and freshly ground black pepper
4 tbsp butter
4 large zucchini, thinly sliced
½ cup veal stock
juice of 1 grapefruit
1 grapefruit, peeled, all skin and pith
    removed, thinly sliced
a few strands of saffron dissolved in
    ⅔ cup dry vermouth

FOR THE GARNISH
sprigs of chervil

Season the veal.

Heat the 3 tbsp butter in a sauteuse or large frying pan, add the veal and cook for 1 minute each side.

Meanwhile, place the slices of zucchini in the top half of a steamer or a colander. Heat some salted water in the bottom half of the steamer to simmering point, cover with the top half of the colander, cover and cook for about 2 minutes until just tender.

Transfer the veal to a warmed plate, cover and keep warm. Pour nearly all the fat from the pan.

Stir the stock, grapefruit juice and the saffron/vermouth liquid into the pan and reduce to 6 tbsp. Reduce the heat to very low, dice the butter and gradually swirl in, making sure each piece is fully incorporated before adding the next. Add the slices of grapefruit and heat through gently and briefly. Season, then spoon over 4 warmed plates.

Arrange the slices of veal and slices of grapefruit and zucchini on the sauce and garnish with sprigs of chervil.

POCKET OF VEAL WITH VEGETABLES AND LEMON SAUCE

INGREDIENTS (serves 4)
5 tbsp butter
¼ cup leek, diced
¼ cup zucchini, diced
½ cup button mushroom caps, diced
¼ cup skinned red pepper, diced
a pinch of chopped thyme
salt and freshly ground black pepper
approximately 1 lb 6 oz loin of veal,
    trimmed

FOR THE SAUCE
1 tbsp finely chopped shallot
½ cup dry white wine
2 tbsp dry vermouth
⅔ cup veal stock
2 tbsp lemon juice
1 cup butter
salt and freshly ground black pepper

Picture: page 199

Heat 1½ tbsp butter, add the leeks, cover and cook over a low heat for about 3 minutes, stirring occasionally, until softened. Stir in the zucchini and cook for 2 minutes, then add the mushrooms and red pepper and cook for 2 minutes. Stir in the thyme and seasoning and leave to cool.

Cut the veal into 4 tournedos and partially cut through each one horizontally to form a pocket. Season the pocket.

Divide the vegetables between the pockets, then season the outside of the tournedos.

Heat the remaining butter in an ovenproof casserole that the veal will just fit. Add the veal and cook for 3—4 minutes each side. Transfer to a warmed plate, cover and keep warm.

For the sauce, reduce the shallots, wine, vermouth, stock and lemon juice to 1 tbsp. Reduce the heat to very low, dice the butter and gradually whisk in, making sure each piece is completely incorporated before adding the next. Season.

Transfer the veal pockets to warmed plates, spoon the sauce around.

CROUSTADE OF A MELANGE

OF VEAL

INGREDIENTS *(serves 4)*
1 lb calves sweetbreads, soaked in several changes of cold water until the water is clear
salt
12 sheets of filo pastry
melted butter
1 lb fillet of veal, trimmed
1 lb calves kidneys, trimmed
freshly ground black pepper
3 tbsp butter
½ cup veal stock
⅓ cup full bodied dry white wine
6 tbsp butter
1 tbsp Meaux mustard
1 tbsp green peppercorns
2 tbsp whipping cream, whipped

FOR THE GARNISH
concassé tomatoes

Picture: page 195

If you wish to prepare some of the dish in advance you can bake the croustade cases and warm them through about 4 minutes before required. Or use very thinly rolled puff pastry, cover with plastic wrap and chill ready to put in a pre-heated oven about 6 minutes before serving.

Heat the oven to 420°F.

Cook the sweetbreads in simmering, salted, acidulated water for 5 minutes. Drain well, then trim and remove the skin. Place in a cloth and press under a lightly weighted board.

Line 4 individual well buttered ovenproof dishes with 4 of the sheets of filo pastry. Brush with melted butter, cover with another sheet, brush with melted butter and cover with the remaining sheets. Brush once more with butter and bake for about 12 minutes.

Cut the sweetbreads, veal and kidneys into ½ inch cubes. Season.

Heat 2 tbsp butter, add the sweetbreads and cook over a low heat for 5—6 minutes. In a separate pan, heat 1 tbsp butter, add the veal and cook for 2 minutes, stirring occasionally. Remove with a slotted spoon, drain on paper towels, cover and keep warm.

Add the kidneys to the pan in which the veal was cooked and cook, stirring occasionally, for 2—3 minutes. Remove with a slotted spoon, drain on paper towels, cover and keep warm.

Stir the stock and wine into the pan, dislodging any sediment and reduce by half. Reduce the heat to very low, dice the butter then gradually whisk in, along with the mustard, making sure that each piece is completely incorporated before adding the next. Lightly stir in the peppercorns and cream. Season.

Drain the sweetbreads on paper towels when they are cooked. Cover and keep warm.

Lightly mix the veal, kidneys and sweetbreads into the sauce and divide between the croustades. Garnish with concassé tomatoes.

FILLET OF VEAL WITH SHELLFISH AND SHERRY SAUCES

INGREDIENTS *(serves 4)*
1 fillet of veal
1 whole, cooked lobster tail
salt and freshly ground black pepper
2 tbsp butter

FOR THE SHERRY SAUCE
$\frac{1}{4}$ cup shallots, finely chopped
1 tsp meat glaze (see p.74)
$\frac{2}{3}$ cup fino sherry
2 tbsp whipping cream
1 cup butter
salt and freshly ground black pepper

FOR THE SHELLFISH SAUCE
2 tbsp butter
$\frac{1}{4}$ cup shallots, finely chopped
$\frac{1}{4}$ cup celery, finely chopped
$\frac{1}{4}$ cup leeks, finely chopped
$\frac{1}{4}$ cup fennel bulb, finely chopped
1 lb lobster or shellfish shells, crushed
2 tbsp cognac
1 tsp finely chopped mixed herbs
$\frac{2}{3}$ cup dry vermouth
1 tsp tomato paste
2 tbsp whipping cream
salt and freshly ground white pepper

FOR THE GARNISH
Sprigs of chervil

Picture: page 202

For a well balanced meal serve simple, light dishes before and after this luxurious main course.

Heat the oven to 425°F.

For the sherry sauce, boil the shallots, meat glaze and $\frac{1}{2}$ cup sherry until reduced to 1 tbsp. Stir in the cream. Reduce the heat to very low, dice the butter and gradually whisk in, making sure that each piece is completely incorporated before adding the next. Pass through a fine sieve then stir in a little more sherry to give a smooth sauce. Season and keep warm but do not boil.

Trim the veal to a neat shape, then cut a slit along the fillet and carefully insert the lobster tail. Tie the veal into a good shape and season lightly.

Heat the butter in an ovenproof casserole that the veal will just fit, add the veal and sear evenly all over. Place in the oven for about 15 minutes. The veal will be pink and moist inside. Transfer to a warmed plate, cover and keep warm.

For the shellfish sauce, heat the butter, add the vegetables, lobster or shellfish shells and cook for 2—3 minutes, stirring frequently. Stir in the cognac and ignite with a taper. When the flames have died down stir in the herbs, vermouth, tomato paste and cream and simmer, still stirring, until slightly thickened. Pass through a conical sieve, pressing down well to extract as much flavor as possible. Season and heat very gently but do not allow to boil.

Slice the veal, reform into one piece, cover and keep warm.

Spoon some of the shellfish sauce onto the center of 4 warmed plates. Arrange the veal slices on top and spoon the sherry sauce around. Streak the shellfish sauce into the sherry sauce. Garnish with sprigs of chervil.

MEDALLIONS OF VEAL WITH

RHUBARB

INGREDIENTS (serves 4)
1 lb tender, young pink rhubarb
approximately ¼ cup sugar
6 tbsp butter
1 cup full bodied, fruity dry white
*   wine*
⅔ cup whipping cream
4 medallions of veal about 5oz each
salt and freshly ground white pepper

FOR THE GARNISH
4 red currants (or cranberries)
2 apples
approximately ¼ cup full bodied fruity
*   dry white wine*
4 sprigs of mint

Picture: page 203

Gently cook the rhubarb with the sugar and half the butter in a covered pan until it softens. Reduce to a very smooth pureé, then pass through a sieve.

Boil the wine until reduced to ¼ cup. Stir in the rhubarb juice and simmer together for 2-3 minutes.

Stir in the cream and bring to the boil.

Meanwhile, heat 2 tbsp butter, add the veal and cook for about 3 minutes each side.

As soon as the sauce comes to the boil, reduce the heat and swirl in the remaining butter. Season. Keep the sauce warm over a low heat.

Poach the red currants or cranberries in the wine until tender. Remove with a slotted spoon and keep warm.

Peel and core the apples then slice very thinly. Gently poach in the wine until just tender. Carefully remove with a slotted spoon.

Spoon the sauce over 4 warmed plates. Place a veal medallion in the center of each. Arrange the slices of apple around the veal and place a red currant or cranberry on top. Add a sprig of mint.

*Fillet of veal with shellfish and sherry
sauces
Recipe: page 200*

Medallions of veal with rhubarb
Recipe: page 201

MEDALLIONS OF VEAL WITH

ZUCCHINI AND LEMONS

INGREDIENTS *(serves 4)*
rind of 3 lemons, julienned
1 tbsp sugar
1½ lb veal fillet, trimmed
salt and freshly ground white pepper
1½ cups cold sweet butter
¾ cup dry white wine
4-6 medium zucchini, thinly sliced
*   lengthwise*

FOR THE GARNISH
mint leaves

Picture: page 207

The lemon julienne for this light summery dish can be prepared in advance.

———————————

Blanch and refresh the lemon julienne.

Dissolve the sugar in 6 tbsp water, add the lemon julienne and boil until the water has just evaporated. Remove from the heat immediately, as the lemon must not brown.

Slice the veal into 12 equal medallions, flatten slightly and season on both sides.

Heat ½ cup butter and cook the medallions for 3-4 minutes each side. Remove with a slotted spoon, cover and keep warm.

Pour the butter out of the pan, then place the pan over a high heat and stir in the wine, dislodging the sediment from the bottom. Boil until reduced to 6 tbsp. Remove from the heat.

Briefly cook the zucchini slices in 2 tbsp butter until only just tender. Remove from the pan carefully with a slotted spoon and keep warm.

Reheat the reduced wine, dice the remaining butter then gradually whisk in, making sure that each piece is completely incorporated before adding the next, to make a smooth sauce. Season.

Arrange 3 medallions on each of 4 warmed plates, spoon the sauce around and add the zucchini slices. Sprinkle the lemon julienne on the medallions and garnish the zucchini slices with mint leaves.

L A M B   P R O V E N Ç A L

INGREDIENTS (serves 4)
8 slices of eggplant, about ¼ inch thick
   and 2½ inches wide
salt
5 tbsp butter
2 tbsp shallot, finely chopped
3 ripe tomatoes, peeled, seeded and
   finely chopped
½ red pepper, skinned and finely
   chopped
1 small sprig of thyme
¼ bay leaf
1 cup (½ lb) spinach, washed and
   trimmed
2 fillets of lamb
2 sprigs of thyme
1 small sprig of rosemary
2 cups veal stock (see p.75)
freshly ground black pepper
2 tsp parsley, finely chopped
4 tbsp meat glaze (see p.74)

FOR THE GARNISH
3 tbsp concassé tomatoes (see p.64)
4 small basil leaves

This recipe is not as complicated as it may seem at first sight — it is merely a series of simple steps. The vegetable molds (tians) may be prepared in advance and heated in a warm oven while the lamb is 'resting'.

Heat the oven to 425°F.

Place the eggplant slices in a colander, sprinkle with salt and leave to drain for 30 minutes. Rinse in cold water then dry well with paper towels.

Heat 1 tbsp butter, add the shallot, cover and cook over a low heat, shaking the pan occasionally, until softened. Stir in the tomatoes, red pepper, small sprig of thyme and the bay leaf and simmer for about 15 minutes until the excess moisture has evaporated.

Cook the spinach over a moderately high heat, stirring constantly until the excess moisture has evaporated. Season.

Remove the thyme and bay leaf from the tomato mixture. Season. Heat 1 tbsp butter in a sauteuse or large frying pan, add the lamb and cook for about 2 minutes, turning each fillet so that it is evenly browned. Place in the oven for 6-8 minutes until pink and still moist in the center.

Transfer the fillets to a warmed plate, cover and keep warm. Turn the oven off. Add the 2 sprigs of thyme and the rosemary to the stock and reduce to ⅔ cup.

Meanwhile, heat 1 tbsp butter in a large sauteuse or frying pan, add the eggplant slices in a single layer and cook for 1 minute on each side. Remove with a slotted spoon and drain on paper towels. Sprinkle with pepper and parsley. Place a slice of eggplant in the bottom of 4 lightly oiled individual serving dishes of a slightly larger diameter than the eggplant. Cover with a layer of spinach and then the tomato mixture. Finish with a slice of eggplant. Place in the oven to warm. Place the concassé tomatoes for the garnish in the oven as well.

Remove the herbs from the stock and stir in the meat glaze. Keep warm over a low heat.

Cut the lamb into thick slices. Cover and keep warm. Unmold the vegetables onto 4 warmed plates and place a little concassé tomato and a basil leaf on each mound. Divide the sauce between the plates then place the slices of lamb around the vegetable mounds.

*Medallions of veal with zucchini and
lemons
Recipe: page 204*

NOISETTES OF LAMB WITH

TARRAGON

INGREDIENTS (serves 4)
3 tbsp walnut oil
4 tbsp butter
12 noisettes of lamb, seasoned
6 tbsp sercial madeira
2 tbsp coarsely chopped tarragon
4 tbsp whipping cream
salt and freshly ground black pepper

FOR THE GARNISH
tarragon leaves

Picture: page 210

In a sauteuse or large frying pan, heat the oil and half the butter. Add the noisettes and cook for about 3 minutes on each side until they are pink in the center and still moist.

Remove with a slotted spoon, cover and keep warm.

Tip off the excess oil from the pan then melt the remaining butter in it. Stir in the madeira, dislodging the sediment, then stir in the tarragon and cream. Boil until slightly thickened then pass through a sieve. Season and divide between 4 warmed plates. Place 3 noisettes on each plate and garnish with tarragon leaves.

RACK OF LAMB

WITH MANGOS AND MINT

INGREDIENTS (serves 4)
2 racks of lamb with 6 bones each,
    trimmed
1 clove of garlic
salt and freshly ground black pepper
1 large ripe mango, peeled, puréed
    and sieved
⅔ cup full bodied dry white wine
½ cup butter
a squeeze of lime juice
⅔ cup red wine
2½ cups brown veal stock (see p.74)
1 tsp finely chopped fresh mint

FOR THE GARNISH
slices of lime
or *slices of mango*
strips of red pepper, blanched
slices of cucumber

Picture: page 211

Heat the oven to 425°F.

Rub the racks with garlic then season with salt and pepper. Cover the tips of the bones with foil and place in the oven for about 30 minutes — the meat should remain pink and moist. Cover the racks loosely and leave in a warm place.

Boil the mango flesh with the white wine until reduced to a fairly thick consistency. Reduce the heat to very low and gradually whisk in the butter — do not allow the sauce to boil. Add the lime juice and season. Keep warm but do not allow to boil.

Boil the red wine and stock until reduced by half, then stir in the mint. Keep warm.

Divide the lamb into cutlets and arrange on 4 warmed plates. Add the mango purée and spoon the sauce around. Garnish with slices of lime, or mango, red pepper and cucumber.

LAMB WITH LIMA BEANS

INGREDIENTS *(serves 4)*
2 cups shelled lima beans
salt and freshly ground black pepper
4 sprigs of summer savory
3 tbsp butter
1¼ lb loin of lamb, cut into 12 slices
1 shallot, finely chopped
¾ cup full bodied dry white wine
1 cup chicken stock
1 cup whipping cream

To get the very best out of lima beans, you should remove the outer skin — inside there lies a heart of almost unbelievable tenderness and flavor.

Cook the lima beans in simmering salted water with the savory until tender. Drain well then squeeze the beans between a finger and thumb so that the tender centers pop out of the outer skin. Reserve some of the beans and purée the remainder. Season.

Heat 2 tbsp butter, season the slices of lamb and cook in the butter for 1-2 minutes. Remove with a slotted spoon, cover and keep warm.

Stir the shallot into the butter, cover and cook over a moderate heat, shaking the pan occasionally. Pour off the surplus fat then stir in ½ cup of the wine and reduce to 1 tbsp. Stir in ¾ cup stock and reduce to ¼ cup. Stir in the cream and simmer briefly. Pass through a sieve, return to the rinsed pan and reheat gently, then over a very low heat, gradually swirl in the remaining butter, making sure each piece is fully incorporated before adding the next. Season and keep warm.

Place the reserved beans in a steamer over a pan of simmering water to warm.

Spread about 1 tbsp lima bean purée over each of 4 slices of lamb. Cover with slices of lamb. Spread with another 1 tbsp lima bean purée and top with the remaining lamb slices, cover and keep warm.

Gently heat the remaining lima bean purée with the remaining wine and cream until bubbling gently.

Spoon the purée onto 4 warmed plates, place the lamb on top, spoon the other sauce around the purée and garnish with the lima beans and sprigs of savory.

Noisettes of lamb with tarragon
Recipe: page 208

Rack of lamb with mangos and mint
Recipe: page 208

STRIPS OF LAMB WITH ROSEMARY SAUCE

INGREDIENTS (serves 4)
2 cups green noodles (see p.78)
1 tbsp oil
salt and freshly ground black pepper
1 cup full bodied dry white wine
⅓ cup dry vermouth
1 tbsp finely chopped shallot
1½ cups chicken stock
1lb loin of lamb, cut into strips
3 tsp finely chopped rosemary
2 small spinach leaves
⅔ cup whipping cream

FOR THE GARNISH
small sprigs of rosemary, with flowers
    if possible
coriander leaves

Picture: page 215

The spinach leaves do not flavor the sauce, just tint it a delicate shade of green. If you are feeling adventurous, tie the noodles into knots.

Cook the noodles in boiling salted water with the oil until just tender.

Pour the wine, vermouth, shallot and ⅓ cup stock into the bottom of a steamer and bring to the boil.

Season the lamb and put into the top half of the steamer. Put this in place on the bottom part of the steamer and cook for about 5 minutes. The lamb will still be pink in the center.

Meanwhile, simmer the rosemary and spinach leaves in the remaining stock for about 4 minutes, then reduce to ½ cup.

Remove the lamb from the steamer, cover and keep warm. Add the rosemary, spinach and liquid to the bottom part of the steamer and reduce to ⅓ cup. Stir in the cream.

Process briefly in a blender, then pass through a sieve. Season and heat gently.

Drain the noodles and arrange them on 4 warmed plates. Put the lamb in the center and pour the sauce over the lamb. Arrange the sprigs of rosemary in the noodles and garnish with coriander leaves.

NOISETTES OF LAMB WITH ROSEMARY AND WALNUTS

INGREDIENTS (serves 4)
2 tbsp walnut oil
⅔ cup butter
salt and freshly ground black pepper
8 noisettes of lamb
1 tsp finely chopped shallots
⅔ cup red wine
2½ cups brown lamb stock
1 tsp finely chopped rosemary
12 walnuts, shelled or ½ cup chopped
    walnuts
½ cup tomato flesh, diced

FOR THE GARNISH
12 small zucchini 'turned' (see p.65)
8 small carrots, 'turned' (see p.65)
small sprigs of rosemary
walnut halves

Picture: page 214

Heat half the oil and 1 tbsp butter in a sauteuse or large frying pan. Season the noisettes, add to the pan and cook for 3-4 minutes on each side so they are still pink in the center. Remove with a slotted spoon, cover and keep warm.

Tip the excess fat from the pan, stir in the shallots, wine and stock and boil until reduced to a quarter. Add the rosemary. Reduce the heat to very low and gradually whisk in 4 tbsp butter. Season and keep warm but do not allow to boil.

Heat the remaining butter and oil, add the walnuts and tomatoes and cook for 2-3 minutes. Season.

Blanch, refresh and drain the zucchini and carrots.

Cut the noisettes in half and arrange on 4 warmed plates. Spoon the sauce around and divide the walnuts between the plates. Garnish with zucchini, carrots and rosemary.

CASSOLETTE OF SWEETBREADS AND KIDNEYS

INGREDIENTS (serves 4)

1lb calves sweetbreads, soaked in
    in several changes of cold water
    until the water is clear
1 tbsp lemon juice
½ cup butter
salt and freshly ground black pepper
2 crisp dessert apples, peeled, cored
    and chopped
2 shallots, finely chopped
1 lb veal kidneys, cut into 1 inch cubes
5 tbsp calvados
¼ cup dry vermouth
1½ cups veal stock
1 tbsp tarragon mustard

FOR THE GARNISH
julienned lemon peel and red apple
    skin tossed in lemon juice
tarragon leaves

This is another Cuisine Vivante adaptation of a traditional French dish.

————————————

Simmer the sweetbreads with the lemon juice and covered by 2 inches of salted water for 15 minutes. Refresh and drain well. Remove the membrane and any gristle, place in a cloth between 2 weighted boards and leave to cool.

Cut the sweetbreads into 1 inch cubes. Heat 2 tbsp butter in a sauteuse or large frying pan. Add the sweetbreads, apples, shallots and seasoning. Cover and cook over a low heat for 15 minutes.

Heat 2 tbsp butter in another sauteuse or large frying pan. Season the kidneys, add to the pan and cook for 2 minutes, stirring. Transfer to a warmed dish, cover and keep warm.

With a slotted spoon, transfer the sweetbreads, apples, shallots and kidneys to a warmed dish, cover and keep warm.

Pour the excess fat from the pan in which the sweetbreads were cooked, stir in the calvados and ignite with a taper. When the flames have died down, stir in the vermouth and reduce by half. Stir in the stock and reduce by half. Reduce the heat to very low, then gradually whisk in the mustard, dice the butter and whisk in, making sure that each piece is completely incorporated before adding the next. Season.

Meanwhile, blanch, refresh and drain the julienned lemon and apple.

Divide the sauce between 4 warmed plates. Arrange the sweetbreads and kidneys on the sauce and garnish with lemon and apple julienne and tarragon leaves.

*Noisettes of lamb with rosemary and
walnuts
Recipe: page 212*

Strips of lamb with rosemary sauce
Recipe: page 212

LAMBS LIVER IN RED WINE

INGREDIENTS (serves 4)
1 lb piece of lambs liver
1 tbsp chopped thyme
1 tbsp chopped basil
salt and freshly ground black pepper
1 cup chicken stock
1 cup red wine
1 stalk of celery, chopped
1 carrot, chopped
2 tbsp cereal cream
2 tbsp cognac
3 tbsp butter, diced

FOR THE GARNISH
'turned' mushrooms
sprigs of parsley
red pepper petals

Picture: page 218

Lambs liver is not as delicate as calves but it is quite suitable for this recipe where the liver is gently steamed and the accompanying sauce has quite a full flavor.

———————————

Remove any membrane from the liver and coat with the herbs and seasoning. Put into a steaming basket.

Pour the stock and the wine into the base of the steamer, add the celery and carrot and bring to the boil. Put the steamer over the base, cover tightly and steam for 15 minutes.

Transfer the liver to a warmed serving plate, cover and keep warm.

Boil the steaming liquor until reduced to 1 cup. Pass through a sieve and return to the pan. Reheat, then stir in the cream and cognac. Reduce the heat to very low, dice the butter and gradually stir in, making sure that each piece is completely incorporated before adding the next. Season and keep warm, but do not allow to boil.

Slice the liver thinly and arrange on 4 warmed plates. Spoon the sauce around and garnish with 'turned' mushrooms, sprigs of parsley and red pepper petals.

LAMBS TONGUES AND MORELS

FEUILLETES

INGREDIENTS (serves 4)

8 lambs tongues, soaked for 3-4 hours
   in several changes of cold water
1 carrot, chopped
½ stalk of celery, chopped
bouquet garni of 1 bay leaf, 4 parsley
   sprigs, sprig of thyme and 4 basil
   leaves
salt
6 oz puff pastry (see p 79)
beaten egg yolk
½ cup butter
2 shallots, finely chopped
1¾ cups morels or other wild
   mushrooms
1 cup red wine
1¼ cups lamb stock
½ cup skinned red pepper,
   blanched and cut into diamond
   shapes
1 tsp chopped sage
freshly ground black pepper

FOR THE GARNISH

diamond shapes of blanched red
   pepper
mint leaves

Picture: page 219

It may be necessary to order fresh lambs tongues from the butcher in advance — do not use frozen ones. Pickled, smoked or canned tongues are also unsuitable.

———

Cover the lambs tongues with water, add the carrot, celery, bouquet garni and salt and simmer very gently, removing any scum as necessary, for $1\frac{1}{4}$-$1\frac{1}{2}$ hours.

Allow the tongues to cool slightly, remove the skins, then cut the tongues into strips.

Roll the pastry out to a rectangle $\frac{1}{4}$ inch thick. Trim the edges with a large sharp knife, then cut into 4 rectangles. Transfer to a baking sheet, cover and leave in a cool place for at least 30 minutes.

Heat the oven to 425°F.

Meanwhile, heat half the butter, add the shallots and cook over a moderate heat, shaking the pan occasionally, until they are soft. Add the mushrooms and cook for 2-3 minutes. Stir in the wine and reduce by half, then stir in the stock and reduce until slightly thickened. Add the tongue and red pepper and heat gently for a few minutes. Add the sage, reduce the heat to very low, dice the remaining butter, and gradually stir in, making sure that each piece is completely incorporated before adding the next. Season and keep warm, but do not allow to boil.

Leave the pastries to cool very slightly on a wire rack, then carefully slit them in half horizontally. Carefully remove any very soft pastry. Return to the oven briefly.

Place the bottom halves of the feuilletés on 4 warmed plates. Spoon the filling over and cover with the tops. Garnish with diamonds of red pepper and mint leaves.

OPPOSITE *Lambs liver in red wine*
Recipe: page 216
ABOVE *Lambs tongues and morels*
feuilletés
Recipe: page 217

SLICES OF LAMB WITH ASPARAGUS

INGREDIENTS (serves 4)
4 tbsp butter, diced
2 shallots, chopped
½ carrot, chopped
2½ cups brown veal stock
bouquet garni of 5 parsley sprigs,
   1 bay leaf, a spring of thyme and a
   sprig of chervil
4 lamb steaks (½ inch thick),
   weighing 5-6 oz, cut from the top
   of the leg and cut in half if large
salt and freshly ground black pepper
¾ cup red wine
2 tsp finely chopped chives
2 tsp finely chopped parsley
16-20 asparagus tips

FOR THE GARNISH
sprigs of parsley

If each slice of lamb is cut in half, making a total of 8, cook them in 4 batches, as they must be cooked in a single layer and not crowded in the pan. If fat white asparagus is used, halve the number of spears and slice each one in half lengthwise just before it is served.

———————

Heat 1 tbsp butter, add the shallots and carrot, cover and cook over a moderate heat, shaking the pan occasionally, until the shallots are soft. Stir in the stock and bouquet garni, then simmer until reduced to 1 cup. Pass through a sieve

Place each piece of lamb between 2 sheets of plastic wrap and beat to a thickness of ¼ inch, retaining the oval shape. Season.

Heat 1 tbsp butter in a sauteuse or large frying pan. Add half the lamb and cook for 1 minute each side. Transfer to a warmed plate with a slotted spoon. Cover and keep warm. Cook the remaining lamb for 1 minute each side. Cover and keep warm. Lay the slices in a single layer — do not stack them.

Pour the excess fat from the pan, stir in the wine and reduce to ¼ cup. Stir in the reduced stock and reduce to ¾ cup. Pass through a sieve into a clean pan, add the chives and parsley and reheat gently over a very low heat. Dice the remaining butter and gradually swirl in, making sure each piece is fully incorporated before adding the next. Season.

Meanwhile, blanch, refresh and drain the asparagus tips.

Spoon the sauce over the plates. Lay the slices of lamb on the sauce. Arrange the asparagus tips on the lamb and garnish with sprigs of parsley around the edge of the lamb.

R A C K   O F   L A M B   W I T H   L E E K   P U R E E

INGREDIENTS (serves 4)
2 racks of lamb, with 6 bones,
    trimmed
4 cloves of garlic, crushed
1 lb untrimmed leeks
½ cup butter
2 tbsp chicken stock
2 tsp finely chopped parsley
salt and freshly ground black pepper
¾ cup shallots, chopped
¾ cup dry vermouth
2 cups veal stock
1 tsp chopped rosemary

FOR THE GARNISH
mint leaves
tomato 'flowers'

Picture: page 222

If this dish is prepared towards the end of the year or before the lambing season, when lambs are larger and more fatty, 2 cutlets per person will be sufficient. In the spring and early summer the cutlets will only have a fine layer of fat, and more will be needed.

———————————

Heat the oven to 425°F.

Rub the lamb with 2 of the garlic cloves, protect the ends of the bones with foil and roast for 30 minutes until pink and still moist.

Transfer the lamb to a warmed plate, cover and keep warm.

Trim the leeks, leaving on 5 cm/2 inches of the green part. Slice thinly.

Heat the butter, stir in the leeks, stock and parsley, season lightly, cover and cook gently until the liquid has almost completely evaporated and the leeks are tender, but do not allow them to color. Purée the leeks and keep warm.

Boil the shallots and remaining garlic in the vermouth until reduced by three quarters. Stir in the stock and reduce by one third. Add the rosemary and simmer gently for 5 minutes. Check the seasoning, keep warm.

Divide the lamb into cutlets.

Place the leek purée in the center of 4 warmed plates, arrange the cutlets on top and spoon the sauce around. Garnish with mint leaves and tomato 'flowers'.

N O I S E T T E S   O F   L A M B   W I T H   R E D ,

G R E E N   A N D   Y E L L O W   P E P P E R   S A U C E

INGREDIENTS (serves 4)
½ cup red peppers, skinned and diced
½ cup green peppers, skinned and diced
½ cup yellow peppers, skinned and diced
2½ cups vegetable stock (see p.74)
2 cups dry white wine
⅓ cup whipping cream
3 tbsp butter
12 noisettes of lamb
salt and freshly ground black pepper

FOR THE GARNISH
strips of red, green and yellow peppers, skinned and blanched

Picture: page 223

Simmer each of the peppers separately in a third of the stock for 2-3 minutes, then boil each until the liquid is reduced to 2 tbsp. Stir a third of the wine into each and reduce to ¼ cup. Stir a third of the cream into each, then simmer for 1-2 minutes. Pureé, then pass through a sieve.

Heat the butter, add the noisettes and cook for about 2 minutes. Turn them over and cook for a further 2 minutes.

Meanwhile, gently reheat the sauces separately. Season each one. Place a spoonful of each sauce on 4 warmed plates and place a noisette on each bed of sauce. Garnish with contrasting colors of peppers.

OPPOSITE *Rack of lamb with leek purée*
Recipe: page 221
ABOVE *Noisettes of lamb with red, green*
and yellow pepper sauce
Recipe: page 221

MEDALLIONS OF LAMB WITH LIGHT MUSTARD SAUCE

INGREDIENTS (serves 4)
4 tbsp butter
approx 7 cups (1 lb) wild mushrooms
1 cup veal stock
1 tsp mustard seeds
2 tsp whole grain mustard
¾ cup whipping cream
salt and freshly ground black pepper
a squeeze of lemon juice
16 medallions of lamb, about 1½ oz
    each

FOR THE GARNISH
5-6 long carrots cut into julienne of
    even lengths
20 chives
16 sprigs of chervil

Heat 1 tbsp butter, add the mushrooms and cook over a moderate heat, stirring occasionally, until all the moisture has evaporated. Transfer to a warmed plate with a slotted spoon, cover and keep warm.

Stir the stock and mustard seeds into the pan and reduce to about ¼ cup.

Stir in the mustard and cream and simmer until slightly thickened. Reduce the heat to very low and gradually whisk in 1 tbsp butter, making sure each piece is fully incorporated before adding the next. Season and add a squeeze of lemon juice to taste. Keep warm over a very low heat but do not allow to boil.

Meanwhile, blanch the carrot julienne for the garnish, refresh and drain well.

Season the medallions, heat the remaining butter in a sauteuse or large frying pan, add the medallions and cook for 2 minutes each side. They should still be pink and moist in the center. Transfer to a warmed plate, cover and keep warm.

Whilst the lamb is cooking, group the carrot julienne into 20 bundles and tie a chive around the center of each bundle.

Spoon the sauce over 4 warmed plates. Place the mushrooms in the center of the plates. Arrange the medallions around. Place a bundle of carrots in between the medallions and place a sprig of chervil on each medallion.

LAMB WITH ARTICHOKE SAUCE

INGREDIENTS (serves 4)
1 large or 2 small globe artichokes,
    trimmed
lime juice
1 tbsp crème fraîche
1¼ lb fillet of young lamb, sliced
a few sprigs of lemon balm
1 cup whipping cream
salt and freshly ground white pepper

FOR THE GARNISH
1-2 small zucchini
concassé tomatoes
parsley sprigs
slices of lime

Picture: page 226

This is really a dish for late spring or early summer, when the flavor of lamb is still delicate enough not to dominate the artichokes.

Place the artichoke in a pan of water, add a squeeze of lime juice and bring to the boil. Cover and cook for 35-45 minutes until tender.

Remove the artichoke from the pan and leave to drain upside down. When cool enough to handle, remove the leaves, scraping the edible flesh into a bowl. Discard the hairy choke. Purée the artichoke bottom, and the scrapings in a food processor or blender with the crème fraîche and 1 tsp lime juice.

Steam the lamb over a pan of water scented with lemon balm for 3-4 minutes or until the inside is pale pink. Remove from the heat and keep warm.

Boil the whipping cream until reduced by a quarter, then

whisk in the artichoke purée and season.

Blanch the zucchini for the garnish. Refresh and drain well and cut into fine slices.

Spoon the sauce over 4 warmed plates, add the lamb and garnish with the slices of zucchini, concassé tomatoes and parsley and slices of lime.

LOIN OF LAMB WITH SWEETBREADS AND BASIL

INGREDIENTS (serves 4)
1 bunch of basil
2 loin of lamb
2 cloves of garlic, crushed
bones from loin
2 shallots, chopped
1 carrot, chopped
1 stalk of celery, chopped
2 pigs cauls
8 oz lambs sweetbreads, soaked
    for 3-4 hours in frequent changes
    of cold water
salt and freshly ground black pepper
½ cup butter
16 button mushroom caps, turned (see
    p.65)
a squeeze of lemon juice
1 cup light red wine
flesh of 2 firm ripe tomatoes, cut into
    concassé

FOR THE GARNISH
thin strips of cucumber

Picture: page 230

Chop the stalks of the basil and scatter over and around the lamb with the garlic. Cover and leave for 3-4 hours.

Place the bones in a roasting pan and brown under a hot broiler, then tip into a saucepan, add the vegetables and garlic and basil stalks from the lamb. Place the roasting pan over the heat and stir in about $1\frac{1}{4}$ cups water, dislodging the sediment. Pour the water into the saucepan — add more if necessary to cover the bones. Bring to the boil, remove the scum from the surface, then simmer for about an hour.

Pass through a conical strainer, pressing down well on the vegetables to extract as much liquid as possible.

Heat the oven to 425°F.

Lay the pigs cauls out on a warm surface and place a piece of lamb at one end of each.

Drain, dry and slice the sweetbreads and place over the remaining area of caul. Finely chop the basil leaves (3-4 tbsp) and sprinkle over the sweetbreads with salt and pepper. Starting with the end on which the lamb is placed, roll up the cauls like a jelly roll. Tie the ends with string and loosely tie around the body in two places along its length.

Heat 1 tbsp butter in a roasting pan, add the lamb roll and sear evenly. Place in the oven for about 8 minutes, turning occasionally, to cook evenly.

Transfer to a warmed plate, cover and keep warm.

Heat 2 tbsp butter, add the mushrooms and a squeeze of lemon juice and cook until slightly softened but not colored.

Boil the stock and wine until reduced to $\frac{3}{4}$ cup, reduce the heat to very low, dice the remaining butter and gradually stir in, making sure that each piece is completely incorporated before adding the next. Add the tomato, check the seasoning and add more finely chopped basil, if necessary. Keep warm but do not allow to boil.

Cut off the end pieces from the rolls of lamb, then cut the rolls into 12 slices.

Spoon the sauce over 4 warmed plates and arrange the slices of lamb and the mushrooms. Place thin strips of cucumber around the rims of the plates.

ABOVE *Lamb with artichoke sauce*
Recipe: page 224
OPPOSITE *Sweetbreads with leek and*
spinach sauce
Recipe: page 228

SWEETBREADS WITH LEEK AND SPINACH SAUCE

INGREDIENTS (serves 4)
4 veal sweetbreads, approximately
    8oz each, soaked in several
    changes of cold water, until the
    water is clear
salt and freshly ground black pepper
1 tbsp butter
1 tbsp olive oil

FOR THE SAUCE
7 tbsp butter
4 leeks, white part only, chopped
1¼ cups chicken stock
¼ cup spinach
⅔ cup whipping cream
salt and freshly ground black pepper

FOR THE GARNISH
snow peas, trimmed
spinach leaves
slices of truffle

Picture: page 227

Bring the sweetbreads slowly to the boil in a large saucepan of salted, acidulated water, then simmer for 5-6 minutes. Refresh and drain them carefully, remove the membrane and any gristle and fat. Place between two cloths, then press under a lightly weighted board until cold.

For the sauce, heat 1 tbsp butter, add the leeks, cover and cook over a moderate heat, shaking the pan occasionally, for about 3 minutes. Stir in the stock and simmer until almost tender. Stir in the spinach and simmer for 2-3 minutes, then reduce the liquid by just over a half. Stir in the cream and simmer until slightly thickened. Purée, then reheat gently, dice the remaining butter and gradually whisk in, making sure that each piece is completely incorporated before adding the next. Season and keep warm but do not allow to boil.

Slice and season the sweetbreads.

Heat the butter and oil, add the sweetbreads and cook lightly for 2-3 minutes each side. Remove with a slotted spoon.

Meanwhile, separately blanch, refresh and drain the snow peas and spinach — this should be blanched very briefly and drained very well. Cut the spinach into julienne.

Place the sweetbreads on 4 warmed plates and spoon the sauce around. Arrange the snow peas and truffles in the center of the sweetbreads and scatter the spinach julienne on the sauce.

NOISETTES OF LAMB WITH MINT

INGREDIENTS *(serves 4)*
*16 noisettes of lamb (from the best
    ends), about 1 inch thick*
salt and freshly ground black pepper
4 tbsp butter
1 cup full bodied dry white wine
2 cups lamb stock
2 tbsp finely chopped mint

FOR THE GARNISH
2 tbsp butter
1 tbsp sugar
salt and freshly ground black pepper
*1 cucumber, 2-3 carrots and 2-3
    turnips, peeled and cut into inch
    batons of uniform thickness*
4 small zucchini, cut into slices
mint leaves

Picture: page 231

An old favorite that has been given an entirely new look. For the best effect, serve on really large plates. When preparing the garnish measure the batons against the plates you are to use to make sure they fit.

Season the noisettes.

Heat half the butter in a sauteuse, add the noisettes and cook for about 3 minutes each side. They will be pink in the center. Transfer to a warmed plate with a slotted spoon. Cover and keep warm.

Tip the excess fat from the sauteuse. Stir in the wine and reduce to about 3 tbsp. Stir in the stock and reduce to about $\frac{3}{4}$ cup.

Melt the butter and sugar for the garnish with the seasoning in 1 cup water, then bring to the boil and cook the vegetables separately in it until they are just tender but still crisp. Remove with a slotted spoon, refresh, drain and keep warm.

Pass the sauce through a sieve, reheat, then, over a very low heat, swirl in the remaining butter. Add the mint. Season.

Spoon the sauce over 4 warmed plates. Place the batons in the shape of a cross. Place the noisettes in the 4 corners and garnish with mint and zucchini slices.

STRIPS OF PORK WITH ORANGE AND GREEN PEPPERCORNS

INGREDIENTS *(serves 4)*
*finely grated rind and juice of 2
    oranges*
1 tsp ground ginger
salt and freshly ground black pepper
1¼ lb pork fillet, cut into strips
4 tbsp butter
2 tbsp cognac
⅔ cup veal stock
⅔ cup Gewürztraminer wine
*1 tbsp finely chopped peeled fresh
    ginger root*
1½ tbsp green peppercorns

FOR THE GARNISH
scallion tassels (see p.71)
small segments of tangerine or orange
julienned orange rind, blanched
julienned cucumber, blanched

An Oriental influence can be detected in the flavourings used in this dish.

Mix the orange rind, ground ginger and seasoning together.

Coat the pork in the orange mixture.

Heat half the butter, add the pork and cook for 2-3 minutes, stirring frequently. Remove with a slotted spoon, cover and keep warm.

Stir the cognac into the pan and ignite with a taper. When the flames die down, stir in the stock, wine, orange juice and ginger root. Reheat gently. Stir in the peppercorns, dice the remaining butter then gradually swirl in, making sure each piece is fully incorporated before adding the next. Season. Spoon the sauce over 4 warmed plates. Arrange the strips of pork on the sauce, then arrange the garnish.

BEEF WITH SHALLOTS

INGREDIENTS *(serves 4)*
2 tbsp oil
salt and freshly ground black pepper
1¼ lb fillet of beef, trimmed
2 tbsp butter
2 shallots, finely chopped

FOR THE SAUCE
4 tbsp butter
2 shallots, chopped
½ stalk of celery, chopped
1 sprig of thyme
1 small bay leaf
1 tomato, chopped
1 tsp tomato paste
1½ tbsp black peppercorns, crushed
1¼ cups full bodied red wine
2 tbsp red wine vinegar
1¼ cups brown veal stock
salt

FOR THE GARNISH
slices of carrot
small sprigs of parsley

Picture: page 234

Heat the oven to 420°F.

Heat half the butter for the sauce, add the shallots and celery, cover and cook over a moderate heat, shaking the pan occasionally, until softened. Stir in the herbs, tomato, tomato paste, peppercorns and wine and simmer until reduced to about 3—4 tbsp. Stir in the vinegar and stock and reduce by half.

Meanwhile, heat the oil, season the beef, add to the oil and sear evenly, then place in the oven for 15 minutes, so that it remains rare. Transfer to a warmed plate, cover and keep warm.

Pass the sauce through a fine sieve, reheat gently, dice the remaining butter and gradually stir in, making sure each piece is completely incorporated before adding the next. Add salt and keep warm, but do not allow to boil.

Cook the slices of carrot for the garnish, refresh and drain.

Heat the butter, add the shallots and cook over a moderate heat, stirring occasionally until just beginning to soften. Remove with a slotted spoon and drain on paper towels.

Cut the beef into 24 slices. Spoon the sauce over 4 warmed plates. Arrange the beef on top and scatter the shallots over the sauce. Garnish with the slices of carrot and the sprigs of parsley.

BEEF WITH SAGE

INGREDIENTS *(serves 4)*
2 tbsp butter
salt and freshly ground black pepper
4 fillet steaks

FOR THE SAUCE
4 tbsp butter
1 tbsp finely chopped shallot
16 sage leaves
½ cup sercial madeira
2 cups brown veal stock
salt and freshly ground black pepper

FOR THE GARNISH
Brussels sprout leaves
½ quantity cauliflower purée (see
  p.301)
sage leaves

Picture: page 235

The sage leaves are simmered with the sauce ingredients so they give out their delicate flavor, but they are then sieved out, as they can taste bitter when bitten into.

For the sauce, heat 1 tbsp butter, add the shallot, cover and cook over a moderate heat, shaking the pan occasionally, until just soft. Stir in the sage leaves and madeira, simmer for 10 minutes, then reduce to about 1 tbsp. Stir in the stock and reduce by half. Pass through a sieve, reheat, then, over a very low heat, stir in the remaining butter. Season and keep warm, but do not allow to boil.

Heat the butter, season the steaks, add to the pan and cook for 2—3 minutes on each side so that they are rare. Remove with a slotted spoon.

Meanwhile, for the garnish, blanch the Brussels sprout leaves, refresh and drain well. Warm the cauliflower mousseline in a bowl over a pan of hot water, stirring occasionally.

Spoon the sauce over 4 warmed plates. Place the steaks on top. Add the sage leaves and cauliflower purée wrapped in Brussels sprout leaves.

BEEF WITH HORSERADISH AND SHALLOTS

INGREDIENTS (serves 4)
approximately 1 lb 6 oz fillet
    of beef
salt and pepper
½ cup butter
12 firm, even sized shallots, unpeeled
    but roots and tops trimmed
1 carrot, chopped
½ onion, chopped
½ stalk of celery, chopped
¼ cup fresh horseradish root,
    peeled and shredded
2 tbsp cognac
2½ cups brown veal stock
half quantity turnip purée (see p.300)

FOR THE GARNISH
4 potato baskets (see p.302)

A very traditional combination of ingredients given a new look in the way it is cooked and presented. Fresh horseradish is not always easy to buy, but it *is* easy to grow — even a small piece of root will take shoot. But, be warned whilst preparing it — it produces strong fumes that can make the eyes and nose run.

―――――――――――――

Heat the oven to 425°F.

Season the beef. Heat 2 tbsp butter in a roasting pan, add the beef and sear evenly. Place in the oven and cook for about 15 minutes until rare, then transfer to a warmed plate, cover and keep warm.

Meanwhile, wrap the shallots in a parcel of foil, sealing the seam well. Spread ¼ inch salt in a heavy ovenproof dish and place the parcel of shallots on it. Place in the oven for 20-30 minutes until tender.

Heat butter in an ovenproof dish, add the 2 tbsp vegetables and horseradish and cook in the oven until browned, turning frequently.

Drain off the surplus fat, stir in the cognac and ignite with a taper. Stir in the stock and reduce by two thirds. Pass through a sieve and measure the liquid — there should be about ½ cup.

Pour into a clean saucepan, reheat, reducing further if necessary, dice the remaining butter and over a very low heat, gradually swirl in, making sure each piece is fully incorporated before adding the next. Season and keep warm but do not boil.

Warm the turnip purée and cook the potato baskets.

Cut the beef into 24 slices. Reform and keep warm. Cut the shallots into halves.

Spoon the sauce over 4 warmed plates. Lay the slices of beef on it, arrange the shallots and add the turnip purée and potato baskets.

◆

Beef with shallots
Recipe: page 232

◆

Beef with sage
Recipe: page 232

BEEF WITH GLAZED VEGETABLES

INGREDIENTS *(serves 4)*
½ *cup butter*
2 shallots, chopped
2 small carrots, chopped
2 stalks of celery, chopped
¾ *cup wild mushrooms*
salt and freshly ground black pepper
4 fillet steaks, approximately 5 oz
⅔ *cup ruby port*
2 cups brown veal stock
4 tsp chopped tarragon

FOR THE GARNISH
potato galettes (see p.303)
glazed 'turned' baby carrots (see p.63)
glazed 'turned' baby turnips (see p.63)
glazed chestnuts (see p.63)
sprigs of parsley

Picture: page 238

No extra vegetables are necessary with this dish as it is a complete meal in itself.

Heat 2 tbsp butter in a sauteuse or a large frying pan, add the shallots, carrots, celery and mushrooms, cover and cook over a moderate heat, shaking the pan occasionally, until just soft. Remove the lid and cook the vegetables more rapidly to evaporate the moisture.

Push the vegetables to one side. Season the beef, add to the pan and cook for about 3 minutes each side. Stir the vegetables occasionally to prevent them from burning. Transfer the beef to a warmed dish, season, cover and keep warm.

Carefully remove the excess fat from the surface of the pan, then stir in the port and boil until reduced to a syrupy glaze. Stir in the stock and tarragon and reduce by three quarters. Pass through a sieve, pressing down well on the vegetables to extract as much liquid as possible. Return to the rinsed pan and reheat gently.

Meanwhile, prepare the potato galettes and glaze the vegetables for the garnish.

Gradually swirl the remaining butter into the sauce, making sure that each piece is completely incorporated before adding the next. Season and keep warm but do not allow to boil.

Slice the beef. Spoon the sauce over 4 warmed plates, arrange the beef on top and add the vegetables. Garnish with sprigs of parsley.

BEEF WITH BASIL AND TOMATOES

INGREDIENTS *(serves 4)*
4 fillets of beef, approximately 5-6 oz
salt and freshly ground black pepper
2 tbsp butter
½ *cup full bodied dry white wine*
1 cup veal stock, boiled down to ½ cup
½ *cup crème fraîche*
1½ *tbsp finely chopped fresh basil*
flesh from one large tomato, chopped

FOR THE GARNISH
small basil leaves

A simple dish that has the unmistakable flavor of the South of France.

Season the beef, heat the butter, add the beef and cook for about 3 minutes each side until rare. Transfer to a warmed plate, cover and keep warm.

Pour the excess fat from the pan, stir in the wine and stock and reduce by half. Stir in the crème fraîche and simmer until slightly thickened.

Reduce the heat to very low and stir in the basil and tomatoes. Season.

Cut the beef diagonally into slices, reform and keep warm.

Divide the sauce between 4 warmed plates. Place the beef on top and garnish with small basil leaves.

STEAK WITH OYSTER AND

MUSHROOM FILLING

INGREDIENTS (serves 4)
6 tbsp butter
2 shallots, finely chopped
3 cups button mushrooms, chopped
8 oysters
6 tbsp dry white wine
1½ tbsp lemon juice
1 tsp chopped thyme
salt and freshly ground black pepper
4 fillet steaks, approximately 6 oz
⅔ cup dry oloroso sherry
⅔ cup brown veal stock
celeriac purée (see p.301)

FOR THE GARNISH
4 oysters

Picture: page 239

The Australian carpetbag steak provided the inspiration for this dish.

Heat 2 tbsp butter, add the shallots, cover and cook over a moderate heat, shaking the pan occasionally, until softened. Stir in the mushrooms and cook, stirring occasionally, until softened.

Meanwhile, open and drain the oysters (see p.61). Heat the wine, add the oysters and poach for 30 seconds. Remove with a slotted spoon, cut each oyster into 4 and, off the heat, add to the mushrooms with the lemon juice, thyme and seasoning.

With a small, sharp knife, cut a pocket in each steak and fill with the mushroom mixture. Cover and chill.

Heat 2 tbsp butter, season the steaks, add to the pan and cook for about 3 minutes each side. Transfer to a warmed plate, cover and keep warm.

Tip the surplus fat from the pan, stir in the sherry and stock and reduce by three quarters. Reduce the heat to very low, dice the remaining butter and gradually whisk in, making sure that each piece is completely incorporated before adding the next. Season. Keep warm, but do not allow to boil.

Place the celeriac purée on 4 warmed plates, spreading it out to make circles that are larger than the steak and thicker around the edge than in the center. Add the steaks and spoon the sauce around. Place an oyster on each steak.

FILLETS OF BEEF WITH SOFT

GARLIC SAUCE

INGREDIENTS *(serves 4)*
8 cloves of garlic
1 cup dry white wine
½ cup white wine vinegar
2½ cups whipping cream
1 cup butter
salt and freshly ground white pepper
4 fillets of beef, approximately 6 oz
    trimmed

FOR THE GARNISH
sprigs of broccoli
meat glaze (see p.74)

Picture: page 242

Cooking garlic in this way produces a very delicate flavored sauce without any trace of harshness or bitterness. A simpler, yet still most effective way to garnish the dish with meat glaze is to trickle a thin stream around the edge of the sauce and plate or around the beef.

Boil the garlic cloves for 2 minutes, then refresh and drain. Repeat 4 times.

Reduce the wine and wine vinegar to about 1 tbsp, then stir in the cream and simmer for 3-4 minutes. Mix 2 tbsp butter with 6 of the garlic cloves in a food processor or blender for 30 seconds. Pass through a fine sieve. Season. Keep warm, but do not allow to boil.

Heat the remaining butter in a large sauteuse or frying pan, season the beef and cook for about 3 minutes each side to keep it rare.

Remove with a slotted spoon, cover and keep warm.

Cook the broccoli for the garnish until just tender, refresh and drain well. Gently warm the glaze in a small saucepan or bowl placed over a pan of hot water.

Spoon some of the sauce over 4 plates. Arrange the beef on top and garnish with the sprigs of broccoli and the glaze.

BEEF WITH ZUCCHINI AND

TOMATO PLATTERS

INGREDIENTS *(serves 4)*
1 lb 6 oz piece of fillet of beef
salt and freshly ground black pepper
½ cup butter
2 zucchini, quite thinly sliced
3 small firm tomatoes, peeled, seeded
    and sliced
3 tsp finely chopped thyme
⅓ cup dry vermouth
1¼ cups veal stock

FOR THE GARNISH
¼ cup small lima beans
sprigs of chervil

Heat the oven to 425°F.

Season the beef. Heat 3 tbsp butter, add the beef and sear evenly. Place in the oven for 15 minutes. The beef will be rare. Transfer to a warmed plate, cover and keep warm.

Meanwhile, blanch, refresh and drain the zucchini.

Arrange overlapping slices of zucchini and tomatoes in a single layer over the bases of 4 small buttered, ovenproof dishes, sprinkle with thyme and seasoning, cover, then place on the bottom rack of the oven for 10 minutes.

Pour the excess fat from the pan then stir in the vermouth, bring to the boil and reduce by half. Stir in the stock and reduce to about ⅔ cup. Pass through a sieve, then reheat in a clean saucepan over a very low heat, dice the remaining butter, and gradually whisk in, making sure each piece is fully incorporated before adding the next. Season and keep warm but do not allow to boil.

Meanwhile, cook the beans for the garnish in simmering salted water until just tender. Refresh and drain well then pop the tender centers from the outer skin by pressing between thumb and forefinger.

Cut the beef into 20 slices, reform and keep warm.

Carefully turn the zucchini and tomato platters onto 4 warmed plates, keeping them in shape. Spoon the sauce over the plates, add the slices of beef and garnish with the lima beans and chervil.

FILLET OF BEEF WITH PARSLEY

INGREDIENTS (serves 4)
4 fillets of beef, approximately
    6 oz
salt and freshly ground black pepper
6 tbsp butter
$\frac{3}{4}$ cup red wine
$\frac{2}{3}$ cup brown veal stock
$\frac{1}{4}$ cup sercial madeira
1 bay leaf
a sprig of thyme
$\frac{1}{2}$ cup parsley leaves
$1\frac{1}{2}$ tsp butter

FOR THE GARNISH
tiny flowerets of cauliflower

Picture: page 243

Season the fillets on both sides. Heat three quarters of the butter and cook the fillets for 3 minutes each side so that they remain pink inside. Transfer to a warmed plate, cover and keep warm.

Tip the butter from the pan. Stir the wine into the pan and reduce to 2 tbsp. Stir in the stock, madeira, bay leaf and thyme and simmer until reduced by a quarter. Pass through a sieve, then reheat gently, dice the remaining butter and gradually whisk in, making sure each piece is completely incorporated before adding the next. Season and keep warm.

Gently cook the parsley in a very little water until tender, boiling rapidly at the end of the cooking to evaporate off excess moisture if necessary. Purée, then blend in the butter. Season.

Blanch the cauliflower flowerets for the garnish, then refresh and drain well.

Cut the fillets into 6 slices. Spoon the sauce over 4 warmed plates, place a spoonful of parsley purée in the center and arrange the cauliflower around. Arrange the slices of beef on the sauce.

Fillets of beef with soft garlic sauce
Recipe: page 240

Fillet of beef with parsley
Recipe: page 241

BEEF WITH SPRING VEGETABLES

INGREDIENTS (serves 4)
¾ cup full bodied dry white wine
4 shallots, freshly chopped
3¼ cups veal stock
¾ cup veal stock
2½ tbsp Dijon mustard
⅔ cup whipping cream
1½ tbsp coarse grain mustard
1½ tsp freshly chopped chervil
1½ tsp finely chopped chives
1 tsp finely chopped tarragon
salt and freshly ground white pepper
1¼ lb fillet of beef
8 small carrots, turned
8 small turnips, turned
1 small zucchini, turned
1 cup French beans

A dish that shows off the first of the new season's vegetables to their best advantage. Choose whichever vegetables are the best and freshest to make a colorful display.

Reduce the wine with the shallots by half. Add ¾ cup stock and the Dijon mustard and reduce by half again. Stir in the cream and simmer for 3 minutes. Pass through a sieve into a clean pan. Add the coarse grain mustard, herbs and seasoning.

Bring the remaining stock to the boil. Cut the beef into 4, season, add to the stock, reduce the heat and poach the beef for 3—4 minutes until rare. Drain well, cover and keep warm. Meanwhile blanch, refresh and drain all the vegetables separately.

Reheat the sauce gently but do not boil.

Cut each piece of beef in half, reform and keep warm.

Spoon the sauce over 4 warmed plates. Arrange the beef and the vegetables in the sauce.

FILLET OF BEEF WITH RED CURRANTS

INGREDIENTS (serves 4)
1 cup red currant vinegar
1 onion, chopped
1 carrot, chopped
2 tbsp oil
2 bay leaves
2 sprigs of marjoram
8 black peppercorns, crushed
1 lb 6 oz fillet of beef
2 tbsp butter
salt and freshly ground black pepper
1½ cups red currants

FOR THE SAUCE
2 tbsp butter
2 tbsp finely chopped shallot
1 tbsp finely chopped carrot
2 tbsp finely chopped leek
2 cups veal stock
2 tbsp currant jelly

Bring the vinegar, onion, carrot, oil, bay leaves, marjoram and peppercorns to the boil, then leave to cool. Pour over the beef, cover and leave in a cool place to marinate for 24 hours, turning occasionally.

For the sauce heat the butter, add the shallot, carrot and leek, cover and cook over a moderate heat until soft and very lightly colored, shaking the pan occasionally. Stir in the stock, bring to the boil then reduce to 1¼ cups. Stir in the red currant jelly and ¾ cup strained marinade. Simmer until reduced to about 1¼ cups.

Meanwhile, heat the oven to 450°F.

Dry the beef very well. Heat half the butter, add the beef and sear evenly all over. Season the beef, then place in the oven for 7—8 minutes until rare.

Remove the beef, cover and keep warm.

Stir the sauce into the pan in which the beef was cooked, dislodging the sediment, then reduce until slightly thickened. Pass through a sieve then return to a very low heat and swirl in the remaining butter and the red currants. Season and keep warm, but do not boil.

Cut the beef into 12 slices, reform, cover and keep warm. Spoon the sauce over 4 warmed plates. Arrange the beef on the sauce.

FILLET OF BEEF WITH TURNIPS

AND MORELS

INGREDIENTS (serves 4)
1¼ lb fillet of beef
2 tbsp olive oil
2 sprigs of thyme
salt and freshly ground black pepper
6 tbsp butter
1¼ cups sercial madeira
1¼ cups brown veal stock
3 shallots, finely chopped
3¾ cups morels
12 baby turnips with green tops,
  turned (see p.65)
2 tbsp demerara sugar

FOR THE GARNISH
parsley leaves

The simple olive oil and thyme marinade ensures the beef is succulent and imparts an additional depth to the flavor.

———————

Marinate the beef with the olive oil, thyme and seasoning, covered, in a cool place overnight.

Heat the oven to 450°F.

Remove the beef from the marinade and dry well.

Heat 2 tbsp butter in a roasting pan, add the beef and sear evenly, then place in the oven for about 7 minutes. It will be rare.

Transfer the beef to a warmed plate, cover and keep warm.

Stir the madeira into the roasting pan and reduce by just over two thirds. Stir in the stock and reduce by half. Keep warm.

Heat 2 tbsp butter, add the shallots, cover and cook over a moderate heat, shaking the pan occasionally, until soft. Add the morels and cook for 3 minutes. Strain in the reduced stock. Season and keep warm.

Meanwhile, cook the turnips in gently boiling salted water until just tender. Refresh and drain.

Dissolve the sugar in the remaining butter over a low heat, add the turnips and carefully turn in the butter/sugar until evenly glazed.

Cut the beef into 24 slices. Reform, cover and keep warm. Remove the morels from the sauce with a slotted spoon. Spoon the sauce over 4 warmed plates. Place the morels in circles around the center, then arrange the slices of beef around the outside. Add the turnips and finish with the parsley.

POULTRY

AND GAME

◆ The term 'poultry' encompasses two quite different but equally delicious types of bird - chicken and duck - that require a different method of preparation and cooking in order to make full use of their unique characteristics. Light, lean chicken benefits from gentle cooking and responds well to steaming and poaching, while duck, with its richer flesh, responds better to short, fiercer cooking. Likewise, chicken is enhanced by light flavored and textured accompaniments, while duck benefits from ingredients that have a sharp note to them, such as spinach and sorrel. All game is lean but there are quite marked differences between the flavors and textures of animals and birds. No game should be hung for so long that it becomes 'high'. Not only will this mask the flavor but it may also deter people from eating it.

CHICKEN WITH FENNEL SAUCE

INGREDIENTS (serves 4)
4 chicken breasts
salt and freshly ground black pepper
2 tbsp butter

FOR THE SAUCE
1 small bulb of fennel with some
    feathery leaves
¼ cup parsley leaves
4 tbsp butter
1 shallot, finely chopped
⅓ cup dry white wine
½ cup chicken stock
1 cup whipping cream
salt and freshly ground white pepper
a squeeze of lemon juice

FOR THE GARNISH
broccoli purée (see p.62)
sprigs of fennel

Picture: page 250

Parsley not only adds color to the sauce, and therefore the dish, but also gives a new dimension and 'roundness' to the flavor of fennel.

For the sauce, chop ½ cup from the center of the fennel bulb. Chop the fennel leaves with the parsley very finely and mix with a very little water to give a soft purée.

Heat half the butter in a heavy pan, add the shallot, cover and cook over a moderate heat until soft. Add the chopped fennel, cover and cook over a low heat for 6-7 minutes until the fennel is soft.

Stir in the wine and stock and reduce to 3 tbsp, then stir in the cream and simmer for 2-3 minutes. Purée and simmer again if necessary, to give a smooth sauce.

Wrap the parsley/fennel purée in a cloth and squeeze the juice into the sauce to give a delicate green color. Over a very low heat, gradually swirl in the remaining butter. Season, adding a little lemon juice if necessary. Keep warm, but do not allow to boil.

Beat the chicken breasts to flatten them slightly. Season.

Heat the butter, add the chicken and cook for about 3 minutes each side.

Remove with a slotted spoon and drain on paper towels. Cut into slices. Heat the broccoli purée.

Spoon the sauce over 4 warmed plates and arrange the slices of chicken on top. Garnish with sprigs of fennel and add the broccoli purée, formed into mounds.

STUFFED POUSSINS

INGREDIENTS (serves 6)
3 oz chicken breast meat
salt and lemon juice
½ tbsp dry vermouth
½ egg white
¾ cup whipping cream, chilled
freshly ground white pepper
6 poussins, approximately 14 oz each
freshly ground black pepper
¼ cup red pepper, skinned, blanched
    and diced
4 tbsp finely chopped basil
4½ cups chicken stock

FOR THE SAUCE
lettuce sauce (see p.261) or
light mustard sauce (see p.224)

Purée the chicken breast meat in a food processor or liquidiser until smooth. Add salt and lemon juice and vermouth, then mix in the egg white. Pass through a sieve into a bowl placed over a bowl of ice, then gradually beat in the cream and season. Cover and chill for at least 30 minutes.

Cut through the poussins' legs at the first joint — use the ends for stock. Place the poussins breast downwards and cut along the backbone with a small sharp knife. Then cut the flesh away from the carcass with short clean movements, taking care not to pierce the skin. Cut out the thigh bones but leave the lower leg and wingbones in place

Mix the red pepper into the chicken mixture, then divide between the poussins, spreading it out evenly. Sprinkle the basil along the length of the mixture, adding just enough to give a green center to the slices when the poussins are sliced. Tuck the skin over the filling, reshape the birds and tie them up securely with string, but do not pull the string too tightly,

FOR THE GARNISH
basil leaves
whipping cream

Picture: page 251

so that the filling can expand during cooking.

Bring the stock to the boil in a saucepan that is large enough to hold all 6 birds, or use 2 smaller ones. Reduce the heat to simmering, lower in the poussins, cover with wax paper and poach for 10 minutes.

Prepare the sauce.

Remove the poussins from the poaching liquor. Drain them in a cloth, then trim the legs. Place them on a large warmed plate, cover and leave in a warm place for 3-4 minutes. Then remove the string and cut into neat slices.

Spoon the sauce over 6 large, warmed plates, carefully arrange the slices, overlapping, on the plates and garnish with basil leaves. Swirl thin lines of cream in the sauce.

CHICKEN BREASTS WITH PINK

LEEK SAUCE

INGREDIENTS *(serves 4)*
1 tbsp butter
white park of 1 leek, sliced
1 tsp finely chopped shallot
2 tbsp dry vermouth
1 cup chicken stock
½ cup whipping cream
salt and freshly ground black pepper
6 chicken breasts, skinned
1 tbsp skinned red pepper, chopped
2 egg yolks

FOR THE GARNISH
diced red pepper
small sprigs of thyme

A small amount of red pepper is used to lift the color of the light sauce without spoiling the delicacy of the flavor.

———————

Heat the butter in a heavy flameproof casserole, add the leek and shallot, cover and cook over a low heat, shaking the pan occasionally, until softened. Stir in the vermouth, stock and cream and simmer for 10 minutes.

Season the chicken breasts. Place in the casserole, cover and poach for 8-10 minutes.

Transfer the chicken breasts to a warmed plate, cover and keep warm.

Purée the contents of the casserole with sufficient red pepper to give a light pink color. Pour into a saucepan and reduce to 1¼ cups. Reduce the heat and keep warm.

Whisk the egg yolks with 3 tbsp cold water until foamy. Pour into the hot, but not boiling pink leek liquor, whisking constantly. Season.

Cut the chicken breasts into slices, reform and keep warm.

Divide the sauce between 6 warmed plates. Arrange slices of chicken breasts on the sauce. Garnish with diced red pepper and sprigs of thyme.

Chicken with fennel sauce
Recipe: page 248

250

Stuffed poussins
Recipe: page 248

CHICKEN WITH CARROT SAUCE

INGREDIENTS *(serves 4)*
2 large chicken breasts, cut in half
salt and freshly ground black pepper
3 tbsp butter
2 tbsp Pernod

FOR THE SAUCE
2 tbsp butter
2 cups baby carrots, finely
chopped
⅓ cup finely chopped tart apple
2 shallots, finely chopped
½ stalk of celery, finely chopped
bouquet garni of 6 parsley sprigs,
sprig of fresh thyme, ½ bay leaf
and 3 tsp fennel seeds, crushed
salt and freshly ground black pepper
1 cup chicken stock
¼ crème fraîche

FOR THE GARNISH
slim corkscrews of apple peel
feathery leaves from the carrots
'turned' carrots

Picture: page 254

For the sauce, heat the butter, add the carrot, apple, shallots, celery, bouquet garni and salt and pepper, cover and cook over a moderate heat, shaking the pan occasionally, for 5 minutes.

Stir in the stock and simmer for 10 minutes, stirring occasionally, until the vegetables are tender. Remove the bouquet garni and purée the carrot mixture in a food processor or blender, then pass through a fine sieve. Return to the rinsed food processor or blender and, with the motor running, slowly pour in the crème fraîche.

Season the chicken breasts. Heat 2 tbsp butter, add the chicken breasts and cook for 3 minutes each side.

Transfer the chicken breasts to a warmed plate, cover and keep warm.

Stir half the Pernod into the cooking juices, dislodging the sediment, then stir in the carrot sauce and simmer gently for 5 minutes.

Reduce the heat and stir in the remaining butter. Season. Add the remaining Pernod, if necessary, then spoon over 4 warmed plates. Arrange the chicken breasts on top and garnish with the apple peel corkscrews, carrot leaves and 'turned' carrots.

CHICKEN BREASTS WITH

ARTICHOKES AND SNOW PEAS

INGREDIENTS *(serves 4)*
4 tbsp butter
4 chicken breasts, skinned
salt and freshly ground black pepper
2 tbsp chopped shallots
1 cup chicken stock, boiled down to
½ cup
½ cup dry vermouth
4 tsp chopped basil
2 cooked artichoke bottoms (see p.64)
sliced
1 cup snow peas
⅓ cup pistachio nuts

Heat half the butter. Beat the chicken breasts to flatten them slightly. Season the chicken and the butter, cook for about 3 minutes each side until just cooked through. Transfer to a warmed plate with a slotted spoon, cover and keep warm.

Stir the shallots into the pan and cook over a moderate heat, stirring frequently. Stir in the stock, vermouth and basil and reduce to ¾ cup. Pass through a sieve into a clean pan and reheat gently. Over a very low heat gradually swirl in the remaining butter.

Lay the slices of artichoke in the top of a steamer and place over a pan of simmering water to warm.

Blanch the snow peas, refresh and drain well.

Slice the chicken breasts and arrange on 4 warmed plates. Spoon the sauce around and arrange the snow peas, slices of artichoke and pistachio nuts.

BREASTS OF CHICKEN WITH

PERNOD

INGREDIENTS (serves 4)
⅔ cup full bodied white wine
⅔ cup fino sherry
bouquet garni of 2 sprigs of fennel,
*   4 basil leaves, 4 mint leaves, sprig*
*   of lemon thyme, small strip of*
*   lemon peel and 2 sprigs of tarragon*
4 chicken breasts, skinned
salt and freshly ground black pepper
1 tbsp Pernod
2 bay leaves
1¼ cups whipping cream

FOR THE GARNISH
cucumber balls
puff pastry fleurons (see p.79)
leaf shapes of cucumber skin
sprigs of fennel

Picture: page 255

Only a little Pernod is used so that its fairly pervasive flavor enchances the other flavors without dominating them.

———————

Gently heat the wine, sherry and bouquet garni to just below simmering point in a covered pan. Remove from the heat and leave to infuse for about an hour. Remove and reserve the bouquet garni.

Beat the chicken breasts to flatten slightly, then season. Lay in a single layer in a heavy flameproof casserole and pour the wine/sherry and Pernod over. Add the bay leaves, cover with foil and poach gently for 7-10 minutes until tender.

Transfer the chicken breasts to a warmed plate, cover and keep warm.

Return the bouquet garni to the poaching liquor and reduce by three quarters. Stir in the cream and simmer until slightly thickened. Remove the bay leaves and bouquet garni. Season and keep warm.

Meanwhile, steam the cucumber balls for 2 minutes and warm the puff pastry fleurons.

Cut the chicken breasts into slices. Spoon the sauce over 4 warmed plates, arrange the chicken breasts on top and garnish with the cucumber balls, cucumber 'leaves', sprigs of fennel and fleurons.

ABOVE *Chicken with carrot sauce*
Recipe: page 252
OPPOSITE *Breasts of chicken with Pernod*
Recipe: page 253

SMALL CHARTREUSE OF PIGEON

AND CHICKEN

INGREDIENTS (serves 4)
⅔ cup (4 oz) chicken breast meat,
*   chopped and chilled*
salt and freshly ground black pepper
4 tbsp butter
¼ cup whipping cream
1 egg yolk
pinch of freshly grated nutmeg
2 pigeons
2 sprigs of thyme
2 tbsp oil
½ cup carrots, julienned
½ cup French beans, julienned
½ cup celery, julienned
¼ cup ruby port
2¼ cups chicken stock
½ cup chicken liver parfait

FOR THE GARNISH
julienned strips of carrot, celery and
*   French beans*
individual leaves of herbs

Picture: page 258

This is a good illustration of how Cuisine Vivante has adapted a traditional dish to fall into line with modern trends of eating. If serving this dish for a dinner party, choose recipes that do not require too much last minute attention for the other courses.

Heat the oven to 425°F.

Mix the chicken, seasoning, 2½ tbsp butter, the cream, egg and nutmeg together in a food processor until smooth. Cover and chill.

Season the pigeons, place a sprig of thyme inside each one, spoon the oil over and roast for 15 minutes until they are pink inside and still moist.

Remove the pigeons and drain the excess oil from the roasting pan.

Blanch, refresh and drain the vegetables.

Cut the breasts and legs from the pigeons and chop up the carcasses. Stir the port into the roasting pan, add the carcasses and simmer until reduced by half. Stir in the chicken stock and reduce again to one third. Strain, then stir in half the chicken liver parfait and season.

Arrange the vegetables alternately in the bottom and sides of 4 buttered individual serving dishes and chill for 10 minutes.

Carefully spoon a layer of the chicken mixture into the bottom of the dishes.

Cut the pigeon breast and leg meat into neat rounds, to fit the dishes, and place on top of the chicken with the remaining parfait. Moisten with a little of the sauce, then cover with the remaining chicken mixture.

Place the dishes in a baking or roasting pan, pour boiling water around them, then place in the oven for 20 minutes.

Gently reheat the remaining sauce over a very low heat. Gradually swirl in the remaining butter, keep the sauce warm, but do not allow it to boil.

Blanch, refresh and drain the vegetables for the garnish.

Leave the chartreuse to stand for a few minutes before unmolding onto 4 warmed plates. Spoon the sauce around, arrange the vegetables neatly in stacks and garnish with herb leaves.

CHICKEN BREASTS WITH VEGETABLE

FILLING AND VEGETABLE SAUCE

INGREDIENTS (serves 4)
2 chickens, approximately 1 lb each
1 carrot, chopped
1 onion, quartered
1 stalk of celery, chopped
1 leek, chopped
1 tomato, peeled, seeded and chopped
1 sprig of tarragon
1 sprig of thyme

FOR THE SAUCE
2 cups crème fraîche
1 carrot, julienned
$\frac{1}{2}$ small fennel bulb, julienned with
　a little green left on
3 snow peas, julienned
salt and 1 tsp green peppercorns,
　crushed
8 morels, chopped

FOR THE FILLING
salt and freshly ground black pepper
1 small carrot, julienned
$\frac{1}{2}$ small leek, julienned
$\frac{1}{2}$ stalk of celery, julienned
1 tsp finely chopped parsley
1 tsp finely chopped chives
8 morels
2 tbsp butter

Picture: page 259

Slit the chickens along the breast bone, remove the skin and wish bone. Cut off the fillet from the breasts and reserve. Cut off the legs and use in another dish. Remove and chop the wings and chop the carcass. Remove all visible fat.

Place the carcasses and the remaining ingredients in a large saucepan, cover with water, cover the pan and bring to the boil. Simmer for 1 hour.

For the sauce, strain off 3 cups of stock (reserve the remainder) and boil until reduced by half. Stir in the crème fraîche and reduce again to $1\frac{1}{2}$ cups.

Blanch the vegetable julienne, refresh, drain and dry very well, then add to the reduced stock with salt, green peppercorns and morels. Remove from the heat but keep warm.

With the point of a sharp knife, cut a horizontal pocket in each chicken breast, leaving $\frac{1}{2}$ inch at each end. Sprinkle salt and pepper inside the pocket.

Blanch the carrot, leek and celery for the filling. Refresh and drain well. Mix with the parsley and chives.

Divide the vegetables between the pockets in the chicken and top each with 2 morels. Close carefully and secure with a toothpick. Place a small knob of butter on each breast, then wrap securely in foil, but do not pull the foil too tightly across the breasts. Poach for 8-10 minutes, turning carefully twice.

Remove the breasts from the heat and leave for a few minutes before cutting each breast into 4 slices.

Spoon some of the sauce onto 4 warmed plates, then arrange the pieces of chicken on top.

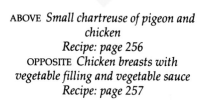
ABOVE *Small chartreuse of pigeon and chicken*
Recipe: page 256
OPPOSITE *Chicken breasts with vegetable filling and vegetable sauce*
Recipe: page 257

259

CHICKEN BREASTS WITH SHERRY VINEGAR SAUCE, WHITE WINE SAUCE AND WILD MUSHROOMS

INGREDIENTS *(serves 4)*
4 chicken breasts skinned
salt and freshly ground black pepper
5 tbsp butter
1 scallion, finely chopped
½ cup dry white wine
3¾ cups chicken stock
⅔ cup whipping cream
1 tbsp oil
2 cups chanterelles or other wild mushrooms
1 tbsp chopped parsley

FOR THE SHERRY VINEGAR SAUCE
¼ cup sherry vinegar
¾ cup dry white wine
1¼ cup chicken stock
4 tbsp butter
salt and freshly ground black pepper

FOR THE GARNISH
parsley sprigs

Picture: page 262

A wet meat cleaver will do just as well as a meat bat for beating the chicken breasts. Beat them firmly but take care not to break the flesh fibers.

Beat the chicken breasts to flatten them slightly. Season.

Heat the butter in a sauteuse or a large frying pan. add the scallion in a single layer, cover and cook over a moderate heat, shaking the pan occasionally until they are soft. Place the chicken breasts on top and cook until they have just stiffened. Remove.

Tip off excess fat, stir in the wine and reduce to 2 tbsp. Stir in the stock. Bring to the boil, lower the heat, add the chicken and poach until tender. Remove the chicken, cover and keep warm.

Pour the liquor from the pan and reserve.

For the sauce, stir the vinegar and wine into the pan and reduce to 2 tbsp. Stir in the stock and boil until it coats the back of a spoon. Pass through a sieve, then reheat gently. Dice the butter and gradually whisk in, making sure each piece is completely incorporated before adding the next. Season and keep warm but do not allow to boil.

Reduce the cooking liquor by half. Stir in the cream and simmer for 2-3 minutes. Pass through a fine sieve, then reheat gently and gradually whisk in the remaining butter. Season and keep warm.

Heat the oil, add the chanterelles and parsley and cook, shaking the pan occasionally for 3-4 minutes. Remove with a slotted spoon and drain on paper towels.

Spoon the vinegar sauce over one half of 4 warmed plates and spoon the white wine sauce over the other. Slice the chicken breasts. Arrange the chicken breasts on top.

Add the mushrooms and garnish with parsley sprigs.

CHICKEN BREASTS WITH LIGHT TOMATO SAUCE

INGREDIENTS *(serves 4)*
6 tbsp butter
1 shallot, very finely chopped
flesh of 2 tomatoes, chopped

Heat 1 tbsp butter in a small saucepan and add the shallot. Cover and cook over a moderate heat, shaking the pan occasionally, until the shallot is soft. Stir in the tomatoes and simmer gently until reduced to about ¼ cup. Pass through a

salt and freshly ground black pepper
4 chicken breasts, skinned
2 tbsp cognac
⅔ cup medium bodied dry white wine
¼ cup dry vermouth
¾ cup chicken stock

FOR THE GARNISH
celery leaves
julienned celery

sieve. Season

Season the chicken breasts. Heat 2 tbsp butter in a sauteuse or large frying pan, add the chicken and cook for 3 minutes each side. Transfer to a warmed plate with a slotted spoon, cover and keep warm.

Pour the excess fat from the pan, stir in the cognac and ignite with a taper. When the flames have died down, stir in the wine, vermouth, stock and tomato and reduce to about ½ cup. Reduce the heat to very low. Dice the remaining butter and gradually swirl in, making sure each piece is fully incorporated before adding the next. Season.

Meanwhile, blanch and refresh the celery julienne and drain well.

Cut the chicken breasts into slices, reform and keep warm.

Divide the sauce between 4 plates. Arrange the slices of chicken overlapping down the center of the plates. Garnish with celery leaves and the celery julienne randomly in piles.

BREAST OF CHICKEN WITH
LETTUCE SAUCE AND THYME

INGREDIENTS (serves 4)
½ cup wild rice
15 sprigs of thyme
salt and freshly ground pepper
4 chicken breasts, skinned

FOR THE SAUCE
3 tbsp butter
1 shallot, finely chopped
½ cup Iceberg lettuce, shredded
1 large leaf spinach, shredded
1 cup chicken stock
½ cup dry white wine
½ cup whipping cream
salt and freshly ground pepper

FOR THE GARNISH
sprigs of thyme
tomato 'diamonds'

Picture: page 263

Bring a pan of salted water to the boil, add the wild rice, stir once, cover and boil for 40-45 minutes until just tender.

Lay half of the sprigs of thyme in the bottom of a steamer or colander. Season the chicken breasts and place them on top of the thyme, place the remaining thyme on top then cover with wax paper.

Place the steamer or colander over a pan of simmering water and steam the chicken for 15-20 minutes until tender.

Meanwhile, for the sauce, heat 1 tsp butter, add the shallot, cover and cook over a moderate heat, shaking the pan occasionally, until soft. Stir in the lettuce, spinach, stock and wine and cook until tender then boil to evaporate off the excess moisture. Stir in the cream and simmer for 2-3 minutes. Purée then pass through a sieve. Return to the rinsed pan and reduce further if too thin. Reduce the heat to very low. Dice the remaining butter and gradually stir in, making sure each piece is fully incorporated before adding the next. Season and keep warm but do not boil.

Strain the wild rice. When the chicken is cooked, remove it from the heat, keep covered and warm for a few minutes before cutting into slices.

Spoon the sauce over 4 warmed plates. Arrange the chicken on top of the wild rice and garnish with the sprigs of thyme and tomato 'diamonds'.

ABOVE *Chicken breasts with sherry
vinegar sauce, white wine sauce and
wild mushrooms*
Recipe: page 260
OPPOSITE *Breast of chicken with lettuce
sauce and thyme*
Recipe: page 261

STEAMED POUSSINS WITH SHERRY SAUCE

INGREDIENTS *(serves 4)*
2 leeks, sliced lengthwise
2 carrots, chopped
2 shallots, chopped
2¼ cups chicken stock
1 cup fino sherry
6 sprigs of chervil
2 cloves
salt and freshly ground white pepper
4 poussins
4 strips of lemon peel
4 tbsp butter

FOR THE GARNISH
concassé tomatoes
fresh chervil

Put the leeks, carrots, shallots, stock, sherry, chervil, cloves and seasoning into the base of a steamer and bring to the boil.

Season the poussins inside and out and put a strip of lemon peel in each cavity. Place in the top of the steamer.

Put the top of the steamer in place on the base, cover and steam the poussins for 20-25 minutes. Transfer the poussins to a warmed plate, cover and keep warm.

Simmer the liquid for about 5 minutes, pass through a conical sieve, then reduce to about ½ cup. Reduce the heat to very low. Dice the remaining butter, then gradually swirl in, making sure that each piece is fully incorporated before adding the next. Season and keep warm but do not boil.

Remove the strips of lemon peel from the poussins. Spoon the sauce over 4 warmed plates. Place a poussin in the center of each and garnish the birds and the sauce with concassé tomatoes and chervil.

DUCK BREASTS WITH CALVADOS SAUCE AND NUTMEG SAUCE

INGREDIENTS *(serves 4)*
2 ducks
1 carrot, chopped
1 onion, chopped
2 stalks of celery, chopped
bouquet garni of a sprig of thyme
*   3 sprigs of chervil, 3 parsley*
*   sprigs and a bayleaf*
3 tbsp butter
2 tbsp finely chopped shallots
½ cup dry cider
¼ cup calvados

FOR THE NUTMEG SAUCE
1 cup dry white wine
1 cup veal stock
¾ cup whipping cream
a pinch of grated nutmeg
2 tbsp butter
salt and freshly ground black pepper

FOR THE GARNISH
1 crisp apple
2 tbsp sugar

Picture: page 266

This recipe is a development of the traditional theme of apples, cream and nutmeg, the characteristic flavors of Normandy. The base for the calvados sauce can be prepared in advance.

———————

Remove the breasts and legs from the ducks (keep the legs for another dish). Chop the carcasses, put them in a roasting pan and brown under a hot broiler. Transfer the carcasses to a large pan and pour off the excess fat from the roasting pan. Put the vegetables into the roasting pan, brown under a hot broiler, then add them to the carcasses with the bouquet garni and about 3¾ cup water. Bring to the boil slowly, skin the fat from the surface and simmer for 2-3 hours, skimming the surface occasionally.

Strain the stock and reduce by three quarters.

Heat 1 tbsp butter, add the shallot, cover and cook over a moderate heat, shaking the pan occasionally, until soft. Stir in the cider and reduce by half. Add the calvados and reduce to ¼ cup. Stir in the stock and simmer until syrupy. Remove from the heat.

Heat the broiler.

Season the duck breasts and cook under the broiler, skin

side up, for 3-4 minutes. Turn over and cook the other side for 3-4 minutes.

Meanwhile, reduce the wine to 2 tbsp. Stir in the stock and reduce by three quarters. Stir in the cream and nutmeg and simmer for 2-3 minutes. Reduce the heat and gradually swirl in the butter, making sure that each piece is completely incorporated before adding the next. Season and keep warm, but do not allow to come to the boil.

When the duck is cooked, transfer to a warmed plate. Cover and keep warm.

'Turn' the apple for the garnish (see p.65). Heat the sugar, add the apple and cook for about 2 minutes, shaking the pan frequently so that the apple cooks evenly. Remove with a slotted spoon and drain on paper towels.

Pass the calvados sauce through a sieve and reheat gently. Reduce the heat to very low and swirl in the remaining butter. Season.

Remove the skin from the duck and cut the breasts into slices. Arrange them on 4 warmed plates. Spoon the calvados sauce over one half of each plate, the nutmeg sauce over the other. Garnish with apple shapes.

BREAST OF DUCK WITH COGNAC AND PINK PEPPERCORN SAUCE AND CRISPY DUCK SALAD

INGREDIENTS (serves 4)
4 large duck breasts
salt and freshly ground pepper
½ tbsp oil
1½ tbsp pink peppercorns
1 cup cognac
1¼ cups whipping cream
4 tbsp butter
1 tsp soy sauce

FOR THE SALAD
lamb's lettuce
julienned red pepper
julienned zucchini
julienned fennel
small sprigs of chervil
vinaigrette dressing (see p.76))

Heat the oven to 450°F. Remove the excess fat from the duck breasts and reserve. Season the breasts.

Heat the oil, add the breasts skin side up, and cook over a high heat until just browned. Transfer to a rack placed in a roasting pan and place in the oven for about 4 minutes.

Transfer the breasts to a warmed plate and keep warm. Pour the excess fat from the roasting pan. Add the peppercorns and stir in the cognac. Stir in the cream and reduce until the sauce coats the back of the spoon. Gradually whisk the butter into the boiling sauce, making sure each piece is fully incorporated before adding the next. Season and keep warm but do not allow to boil.

Arrange small portions of salad on 4 side plates.

Remove the skin from the breasts. Shred it, then cook in a small pan over a high heat until golden brown. Pour off the excess fat. Add the soy sauce and toss over the heat. Divide between the salads.

Slice the duck breasts thinly. Reform and keep warm.

Spoon the sauce over 4 warmed plates. Arrange the duck breasts in a fan shape on the sauce. Spoon some of the dressing over the salads and serve with the duck.

◆
ABOVE *Duck*
breasts with Calvados
sauce and nutmeg sauce
Recipe: page 264
OPPOSITE *Breast of duck with spinach*
filling and tarragon sauce
Recipe: page 268

BREAST OF DUCK WITH SPINACH
FILLING AND TARRAGON SAUCE

INGREDIENTS (serves 4)
2 ducks
1 duck liver
1 tbsp cognac
salt and freshly ground black pepper
2 tbsp butter
¼ cup celery, finely chopped
½ cup shallot, finely chopped
½ cup spinach, shredded
¼ cup Iceberg lettuce, shredded

FOR THE SAUCE
1 shallot, finely chopped
1 tbsp lemon juice
4 tbsp finely chopped tarragon leaves
⅓ cup whipping cream
6 tbsp butter
salt and freshly ground black pepper

FOR THE GARNISH
tarragon leaves

Picture: page 267

A little Iceberg lettuce added to the spinach mellows and softens its flavor without destroying that characteristic sharp note that blends so well with duck.

———————

Heat the oven to 425°F.

Remove the breasts, whole, from the ducks.

Mash the duck liver with the cognac and season. Spread in the natural cavities formed by the two halves of the breasts.

Heat the butter, add the celery and shallot, cover and cook over a moderate heat, shaking the pan occasionally until the shallot is just soft. Stir in the spinach and lettuce, cover and cook, shaking the pan frequently until the spinach has 'fallen'. Remove from the heat, season and leave to cool.

Divide the spinach mixture between the breasts and secure the two halves of each breast together with trussing string.

Score the skin with the point of a sharp knife. Heat the remaining butter, add the duck breasts and sear evenly all over, then place in the oven for about 15 minutes.

Transfer the breasts to a warmed plate, cover and keep warm.

For the sauce, cook the shallot in the lemon juice over a moderate heat for 3 minutes, then boil to evaporate the liquid. Stir in the tarragon and cream and simmer for 1 minute. Reduce the heat to very low, dice the butter and gradually swirl in making sure that each piece is completely incorporated before adding the next. Season and keep warm but do not allow to boil.

Remove the trussing string from the breasts and cut them into slices. Arrange on 4 warmed plates, add the sauce and garnish with tarragon leaves.

DUCK WITH FLEURIE

INGREDIENTS (serves 6)
4 duck breasts
salt and freshly ground black pepper
small pinch of grated nutmeg
1½ tbsp butter

FOR THE SAUCE
3 tbsp butter
2 tbsp shallot, finely chopped
2 cups Fleurie
½ cup sauternes
2 sage leaves
2 sprigs of thyme
¾ cup duck stock
salt and freshly ground black pepper

FOR THE GARNISH
2 tbsp butter
1½ cups chanterelles
green grapes, peeled, seeds removed,
*   quartered*

Picture: page 270

Fleurie is the most charming and feminine of the single villages Beaujolais and is well worth looking for for this recipe. However, if your searches should prove unsuccessful, Chiroubles or Juliennas could be used instead.

———————————

For the sauce, heat 1 tbsp butter, add the shallot, cover and cook over a moderate heat, shaking occasionally until soft. Stir in the Fleurie, sauternes and herbs and reduce by half. Stir in the stock and reduce to 1½ cups. Remove from the heat.

With the point of a sharp knife, slash the skin of the duck breasts in a lattice pattern. Season and sprinkle with a little nutmeg. Heat the butter, add the duck breasts and sear the skin side for 30 seconds. Remove and tip the fat from the pan. Return the breasts to the pan and cook for 3-4 minutes each side until still pink in the center. Transfer to a warmed plate with a slotted spoon. Cover and keep warm.

Meanwhile, remove the herbs from the sauce, then purée the sauce and pass it through a sieve. Reheat gently. Dice the remaining butter and over a very low heat, gradually stir in, making sure that each piece is completely incorporated before adding the next. Season and keep warm but do not allow to boil.

For the garnish, heat the butter, add the chanterelles and cook for about 3 minutes, shaking the pan occasionally. Remove with a slotted spoon,

Remove the skin from the duck breasts. Slice the breasts, reform and keep warm. Spoon the sauce over 4 warmed plates. Arrange the slices of duck on top and place the chanterelles and grapes around the edge of the plate.

Breast of duck with figs
Recipe: page 272

ROAST DUCK WITH ESSENCE OF MUSHROOMS

INGREDIENTS *(serves 4)*
2 ducks, legs, wings and backbones removed
7 tbsp butter
2½ tbsp cognac
4 shallots, chopped
flesh of 2 tomatoes
2 cups red wine
2¼ cups brown veal stock, reduced by a half
bouquet garni of a bay leaf, sprig of thyme, sprig of rosemary, 4 parsley sprigs
salt and freshly ground black pepper
⅓ cup whipping cream
5 cups wild mushrooms
¼ cup ruby port
2 tbsp finely chopped parsley

FOR THE GARNISH
short, slim batons of carrot
parsley sprigs

Chop the duck legs, wings and backbones. Heat 1½ tbsp butter, add the bones and brown them. Drain off the excess fat. Ignite the cognac and pour over the bones. Stir in 3 of the shallots, the tomatoes, wine, reduced stock and bouquet garni. Bring to the boil and simmer for 1 hour, skimming the surface, if necessary.

Heat the oven to 425°F. Pass the stock through a conical sieve, pressing down well on the bones to extract as much liquid as possible.

Heat 1 tbsp butter. Season the duck and cook with breasts downward, for 1-2 minutes until they are slightly golden and crisp. Place in the oven for 5 minutes until the breasts are pink. Transfer to a warmed dish, cover and keep warm.

Pour the stock into a clean pan and reduce to ⅔ cup. Stir in the cream and simmer until slightly thickened. Season and keep warm, but do not allow to boil.

Cook the mushrooms in their own juices in a covered pan for 2 minutes. Drain well. Heat the remaining butter, add the remaining shallot and the mushrooms and cook for 2-3 minutes. Stir in the port and cook rapidly until the moisture has evaporated. Stir in the parsley and season.

Blanch, refresh and drain the carrot batons.

Slice the duck breasts, reform and keep warm.

Spoon the sauce over 4 warmed plates. Place the mushrooms in the center and arrange the duck breasts on top. Garnish with the carrot batons and parsley.

BREAST OF DUCK WITH FIGS

INGREDIENTS *(serves 4)*
4 duck breasts, skinned
salt and freshly ground black pepper
8 medium size figs, sliced
2 tbsp eau-de-vie de framboises
1 tsp confectioner's sugar
½ cup good quality dessert wine
1 cup duck stock
4 tbsp butter

FOR THE GARNISH
kumquats, cut into wedges

Picture: page 271

When kumquats are not available, small segments of orange, with every last trace of pith and peel removed, can be used instead.

Heat the broiler.

Season the duck breasts and cook, skinned side upper most, under the hot broiler for 1 minute. Turn over and cook for a further minute, then turn over and cook for 1 minute more. Remove from the heat, cover and keep warm.

Poach the slices of fig in the framboises, sugar and dessert wine for about 2 minutes, then carefully remove with a slotted spoon, cover and keep warm.

Boil the poaching liquor to reduce it slightly, then stir in the stock and reduce by one third. Dice the butter, reduce the heat to very low, then gradually whisk in the butter, making sure that each piece is completely incorporated before adding the next. Season.

Cut the duck breasts into thin slices. Arrange them on 4 warmed plates. Spoon on the sauce, arrange the figs and garnish with the kumquats.

DUCK WITH TURNIPS

INGREDIENTS (serves 4)
2 ducks
salt and freshly ground black pepper
4 tbsp butter
2 shallots, finely chopped
⅔ cup sherry vinegar
2½ cups duck stock
4 small even size turnips, peeled
⅓ cup spinach, trimmed
1 tbsp whipping cream

FOR THE GARNISH
½ quantity of white butter sauce (see p.66)

Heat the oven to 425°F.

Season the duck, then place in the oven for 25 minutes until very pink and moist inside.

Cut the legs and the breasts in one piece from the carcasses. Cover and keep warm.

Heat 2 tbsp butter, add the shallots and carcasses, then cook over a moderately high heat. Stir in the vinegar, then the stock and reduce to ⅔ cup.

Meanwhile, cut the tops off the turnips and hollow out the turnips slightly. Decorate the outside with a cannelle knife or ordinary knife. Place in the top half of a steamer or colander.

Bring some water to the boil in the bottom half of the steamer; put the top half of the colander in place, cover and cook for about 10 minutes until tender.

Wash the spinach, shake off the water, then cook in a small, covered saucepan over a low heat until soft. Purée with the cream. Season and return to the rinsed pan and keep warm.

Pass the sauce through a conical sieve, pressing down well on the carcasses to extract as much flavor as possible. Reheat over a very low heat and stir in the remaining butter, making sure that each piece is completely incorporated before adding the next. Season and keep warm, but do not allow to boil.

Prepare the white butter sauce for the garnish.

Place the duck legs and breast, skin side uppermost, under a hot broiler for a minute or two. Cut the breasts into slices. Reform and keep warm. Divide the spinach between the hollows in the turnips. Keep warm.

Spoon the sauce over 4 warmed plates. Add the duck breasts and legs. Place a circle of white butter sauce that is larger than the turnips on each plate and place a turnip in each circle so that there is a halo of sauce around it.

ABOVE *Duck quenelles with duck breasts*
Recipe: page 276
OPPOSITE *Wild duck with summer fruits*
Recipe: page 277

DUCK QUENELLES WITH DUCK

BREASTS

INGREDIENTS (serves 4)
8 oz duck leg meat, chopped
salt and lemon juice
1 egg white
1 cup whipping cream
1 tbsp ruby port
1 tsp finely chopped thyme
freshly ground black pepper
2 duck breasts
½ tbsp red currant jelly, melted
3¾ cups chicken stock

FOR THE SAUCE

2½ cups duck stock
½ cup raspberry vinegar
a strip of lemon peel
¾ cup butter
salt and freshly ground black pepper
1-2 tbsp eau-de-vie de framboise

FOR THE GARNISH
4 filo tart shell (see p.81)
flageolet purée (see p.62)
petits pois
mint leaves

Picture: page 274

The quenelle part of this dish is an especially useful addition to the cook's repertoire as it calls for the use of duck leg meat, and many Cuisine Vivante recipes only use the breast.

———————————

Purée the duck leg meat in a food processor or blender. Mix in the salt and lemon juice followed by the egg white. Pass through a sieve into a bowl over a bowl of ice and gradually work in the cream. Lastly, add the port, thyme and pepper. Cover and chill.

Heat the broiler.

Season the duck breasts and brush the skin with melted red currant jelly. Broil, skin side up, for 4—5 minutes. Turn over and broil for a further 4—5 minutes. Transfer to a warmed plate. Cover and keep warm.

Meanwhile, heat the chicken stock in a shallow pan until just simmering. Use 2 tablespoons to shape the duck leg mixture into 8 ovals and carefully lower them into the stock. Poach gently for about 3—4 minutes. Turn over and poach for another 3—4 minutes. Lift out with a slotted spoon and drain on a cloth.

For the sauce, boil the stock, raspberry vinegar and strip of lemon peel until reduced by three quarters. Remove the lemon peel and reduce the heat to very low. Dice the butter and gradually stir in, making sure that each piece is completely incorporated before adding the next. Season and keep warm but do not allow to boil.

Meanwhile, warm the tart shells and flageolet purée separately and blanch, refresh and drain the petits pois. Fill the tarts with flageolet purée.

Ignite the framboise and spoon over the duck breasts. Cut into slices and arrange on warmed plates. Spoon on some of the sauce. Add the quenelles and tartlets, then the petits pois. Finish with the mint leaves.

WILD DUCK WITH SUMMER FRUITS

INGREDIENTS (serves 4)
2 wild ducks
3 tbsp butter
1 carrot, chopped
1 onion, chopped
1 stalk of celery, chopped
3 juniper berries, crushed
bouquet garni of a sprig of thyme
     sprig of rosemary and 1 bay leaf
1 tbsp sugar
1 tbsp red wine vinegar
1 cup cognac
$\frac{1}{2}$ cup ruby port
$1\frac{1}{4}$ full bodied dry white wine
juice of 4 oranges
$\frac{1}{2}$ cup meat glaze (see p.74)
$1\frac{3}{4}$ cups duck stock
1 tbsp lemon juice
1 tbsp red currant jelly
salt and pepper

FOR THE GARNISH
apricots, halved and stoned
sweet white wine
red currants
sliced figs
orange rind julienne

Picture: page 275

The fruits can be varied according to what is available; the dish illustrated on p.275 shows kiwi fruits, plums and strawberries.

———————————

Remove the legs, backbones and wishbones from the ducks.

Melt 2 tbsp butter, add the duck legs, backbones and wish bones and cook until well browned. Add the vegetables and cook until lightly browned, stirring occasionally. Add the juniper berries, bouquet garni, sugar and vinegar and boil rapidly until the liquid has evaporated. Stir in $\frac{1}{2}$ cup cognac, the port and the wine. Reduce by half.

Boil the orange juice until reduced by half. Strain onto the bones. Add the meat glaze and stock and simmer for 2 hours, skimming the surface occasionally.

Heat the oven to 450°F. Pass the stock through a conical sieve, pressing down well on the bones to extract as much liquid as possible. Remove the fat from the surface then reduce to $1\frac{1}{2}$ cups. Add lemon juice, currant jelly and seasoning to taste.

Heat the remaining butter. Season the duck and cook, breast downwards for 1-2 minutes until lightly golden and crisp. Place in the oven for 5 minutes until pink and moist.

Lightly poach the apricots in the wine then add the red currants and sliced figs to cook very slightly.

Drain off the surplus fat from the roasting pan, ignite the remaining cognac and pour over the duck. Remove the breasts in one piece then carve into thin slices. Reform, cover and keep warm.

Remove the fruits from the wine with a slotted spoon and arrange on four warmed plates with the orange julienne. Spoon the sauce over the plates and arrange the slices of duck breast on the sauce.

OPPOSITE *Breast of guinea fowl in an*
apple jacket
Recipe: page 281
ABOVE *Breast of pheasant with white*
wine and orange
Recipe: page 289

279

PIGEON BREASTS WITH PORT SAUCE

AND CHESTNUTS

INGREDIENTS (serves 4)
4 pigeons
salt and freshly ground black pepper
5 tbsp butter
2 carrots, finely chopped
2 leeks, finely chopped
2 shallots, chopped
2½ cups chicken stock
1 bay leaf
4 sage leaves
6 black peppercorns
1 tbsp very finely chopped shallot
5 black peppercorns, crushed
4 tbsp red wine vinegar
¼ cup ruby port
¼ cup crème de cassis
1 tbsp red currant jelly
3 tbsp orange juice
chestnut purée (see p.300)
1½ tbsp sugar
6 cooked chestnuts

FOR THE GARNISH
½ cup cranberries

Young wild wood pigeon are ideal in this full flavored dish. The sauce can be prepared in advance up to the addition of the butter, and the purée up to the addition of the cream and butter.

———————————

Carefully remove the breasts from the pigeons, skin the breasts and beat lightly to flatten them. Season.

Heat 2 tbsp butter, add the carrots, leeks and shallots and cook over a moderate heat, stirring occasionally, for 4-5 minutes. Add the pigeon carcasses, stock, bay leaf, sage leaves and peppercorns. Bring to the boil, remove the scum from the surface, then simmer gently for about 45 minutes. Reduce to ½ cup. Pass through a conical sieve, pressing down well on the bones to extract as much liquid as possible.

Gently simmer the chopped shallots with the crushed peppercorns in the vinegar, port, crème de cassis and stock until the shallots are softened, then reduce the liquid by half, stir in the red currant jelly and the orange juice. Simmer briefly then reduce the heat to very low, dice the butter and gradually swirl in 2 tbsp, making sure each piece is incorporated before adding the next.

Heat the remaining butter, add the pigeon breasts and cook for 30 seconds on each side. Transfer to a warmed plate, cover and keep warm.

Prepare the cranberries and warm the chestnut purée.

Dissolve the sugar in a little water in a small saucepan, then stir in the chestnuts to coat them in syrup and heat through.

Slice the pigeon breasts, reform and keep warm.

Spoon the sauce over 4 warmed plates. Arrange the breasts on the sauce and place the purée in neat mounds around the breasts.

Chop the chestnuts and place on the mounds. Remove the cranberries from the liquid with a slotted spoon, drain well and scatter over the sauce.

BREAST OF GUINEA FOWL IN AN APPLE JACKET

INGREDIENTS (serves 4)
4 breasts, from guinea fowl,
    approximately 2 lb each
guinea fowl carcasses and trimmings,
    coarsely chopped
½ cup butter
2 shallots, chopped
1 carrot, chopped
1 tbsp tomato paste
1 cup dry white wine
¼ cup ruby port
salt and freshly ground black pepper
2 tbsp sirop de framboise
2 crisp dessert apples
2 tbsp sugar
⅓ cup calvados
4 pâte brisée tart shells (see p.80),
    cooked
¾ cup raspberries
1 tsp confectioner's sugar
⅓ cup full bodied dry whilte wine

FOR THE GARNISH
mint leaves

Picture: page 278

The skin of apple slices keeps the breasts of guinea fowl beautifully moist and gives them an additional succulence. The sauce can be prepared in advance but the apples must be left whole until they are required.

Heat 6 tbsp butter, add the carcasses and trimmings, shallots and carrot and cook, stirring occasionally, until well browned. Stir in the tomato paste, wine and port and sufficient water to cover the bones. Simmer for about one hour until the liquid is reduced by half, skimming the surface occasionally.

Pass through a conical sieve, pressing down well on the bones and vegetables to extract as much liquid as possible. Reduce the liquid to about ⅔ cup. Season and add the sirop. Keep warm.

Heat the oven to 400°F.

Heat the remaining butter, add the guinea fowl breasts and cook, skinned side down, for 30 seconds, turn over and cook for one minute. Turn over again, cover and place in the oven for about 6 minutes until pink and moist. Transfer to a warmed plate, cover and keep warm.

Peel, core and slice the apples. Gently dissolve the sugar in the calvados, add the apple slices and poach until just becoming tender.

Put the tart shells into the oven to warm through but do not allow to burn.

Carefully lift the apple slices from the liquid with a slotted spoon and arrange neatly over the guinea fowl breasts to cover them like a jacket. Brush the apples lightly with the calvados syrup and place the breasts in a hot oven for a few minutes.

Gently warm the raspberries, lightly sweetened with confectioner's sugar, in the wine in a covered pan, then remove with a slotted spoon, allowing the excess juice to drain off. Place in the tart shells and garnish with the mint leaves.

Transfer the guinea fowl breasts to 4 warmed plates. Add the raspberry tarts. Spoon the sauce around.

OPPOSITE
*Medallions of hare
with blackberry
sauce*
Recipe: page 292
ABOVE *Medallions
of rabbit with basil*
Recipe: page 290

LEFT *Medallions of
hare with beets*
Recipe: page 293

GROUSE WITH ENDIVE

INGREDIENTS (serves 4)
3 shallots, chopped
1 stalk of celery, chopped
1 carrot, chopped
3 juniper berries, crushed
4 coriander seeds, lightly toasted and
    crushed
2 cups brown veal stock
4 young grouse, trussed
salt and freshly ground black pepper
4 strips of bacon
2 tbsp butter
1 cup full bodied red wine

FOR THE ENDIVE
3 tbsp butter
4 heads of endive, thickly sliced
1 tsp sugar
salt and freshly ground black pepper
$\frac{1}{3}$ cup whipping cream

FOR THE GARNISH
16 endive leaf tips
4 tsp tomato concassé

For how to choose chicory see p.31. This recipe mellows the natural bitterness of chicory.

––––––––––––––

Simmer the shallots, celery, carrot, juniper berries and coriander seeds in the stock for an hour until the stock is reduced to 1 cup.

Heat the oven to 425°F.

Meanwhile, heat half the butter for the endive, add the endive and sugar and cook, stirring frequently until very soft and lightly colored. Turn into a cast iron flameproof casserole, cover with water, add the remaining butter and cook over a moderate heat for 15 — 20 minutes until tender.

Season the grouse inside and out and tie a strip of bacon over the breasts.

Heat the butter in a roasting pan, add the grouse and sear evenly. Cover closely with buttered wax paper and place in the oven for 10 minutes. Remove the grouse from the pan with a slotted spoon, cover and keep warm.

Pour most of the fat from the pan, then stir in the wine and reduce by half. Stir in the stock and reduce to 1 cup. Season.

Meanwhile, drain the endive well, then turn into an ovenproof dish that it just fits, season and pour over the cream. Put into the oven for about 10—15 minutes until the cream has almost evaporated.

Blanch, refresh and drain the endive leaf tips for the garnish.

Cut the legs from the grouse and cut off the lower part of the leg at the joint. Remove the breasts in one piece, then carve into slices. Reform and keep warm with the thighs.

Divide the sauce between 4 warmed plates. Arrange the grouse, endive and endive tips, placing the concassée tomatoes on the stems of the tips.

PARTRIDGE WITH JUNIPER SAUCE

AND CABBAGE

INGREDIENTS *(serves 4)*
4 partridges, trussed
salt and freshly ground black pepper
4 sprigs of thyme
4 strips of bacon
1 tbsp olive oil

FOR THE SAUCE
½ cup sercial madeira
1¼ cups full bodied red wine
5 juniper berries, crushed
a sprig of thyme
1 bay leaf
1 cup chicken stock
¼ cup whipping cream
2 tbsp butter
salt and freshly ground black pepper

FOR THE CABBAGE
1 tbsp butter
approximately 3 cups hard white
  cabbage, finely shredded
½ cup bual madeira
salt and freshly ground black pepper

Heat the oven to 425°F.

Season the partridges inside and out. Place a sprig of thyme in the cavity of each and tie a strip of bacon over the breasts.

Heat the oil, add the partridges and sear evenly. Place in the oven and cook for 10 minutes. Remove the bacon and cook for a further 5 minutes.

Meanwhile, heat the butter for the cabbage, add two thirds of the cabbage and the madeira, cover tightly and cook over a very low heat until softened, shaking the pan occasionally. Season.

Transfer the partridges to a warmed plate, cover and keep warm.

For the sauce, stir the madeira into the partridge cooking juices and reduce by half. Stir in the wine, add the juniper berries, thyme and bayleaf and reduce the liquid to about 3 tbsp. Stir in the stock and reduce by half. Stir in the cream and simmer briefly. Pass through a sieve into a clean pan. Reheat gently, over a very low heat, and gradually stir in the butter. Season, and keep warm, but do not allow to boil.

Blanch and refresh the remaining cabbage and drain well.

Divide the sauce between 4 warmed plates. Place the cooked cabbage in the centers to form a bed and place the partridges on the beds. Scatter the remaining cabbage on the sauce.

OPPOSITE
*Medallions of
venison with apples
and celeriac*
Recipe: page 294
ABOVE *Loin of
venison with pears
and cranberries*
Recipe: page 295

LEFT *Venison
medallions in port
jelly and beet
purée*
Recipe: page 296

RABBIT WITH CELERIAC AND APRICOTS

INGREDIENTS (serves 4)
12 dried apricots soaked in 1 cup
    medium bodied dry white wine
    for at least 4 hours
1 large head of celeriac
4 tbsp butter
1½ tbsp lemon juice
salt and freshly ground black pepper
2 large saddles of rabbit
⅓ cup white wine vinegar
1½ tbsp finely chopped shallot
2½ cups brown veal stock

FOR THE GARNISH
sprigs of chervil

Simmer the apricots in the wine until tender.

Heat the oven to 425°F.

Peel the celeriac and scoop into balls with a melon baller, or cut into cubes. Place immediately in a saucepan with 1 tbsp butter, the lemon juice, salt and sufficient water to cover. Bring to the boil, cover then simmer until tender.

Meanwhile, heat half the remaining butter in a roasting pan. Season the rabbit, add to the pan and sear evenly. Place in the oven for about 15 minutes until pink and moist in the center. Transfer to a warmed dish with a slotted spoon, cover and keep warm.

Pour the excess fat from the pan, stir in the wine vinegar and shallot and reduce by two thirds. Stir in the stock and reduce to ¾ cup. Remove from the heat and gradually swirl in the remaining butter. Pass through a sieve, season and reheat gently, but do not allow to boil.

Remove the fillets from the saddles and cut each one diagonally into slices. Reform and keep warm. Remove the apricots from the wine with a slotted spoon and cut into quarters.

Spoon the sauce over four warmed plates. Place the slices of rabbit down the center of each one. Arrange the apricot quarters and balls of celeriac in groups around the slices. Garnish the rabbit with sprigs of chervil.

SALMIS OF PHEASANT

INGREDIENTS (serves 4)
2 cups Beaujolais
3 shallots, chopped
1 leek, sliced
1 carrot, sliced
12 juniper berries, crushed
bouquet garni of 4 parsley sprigs
    1 sprig of marjoram, 1 bay leaf
2 basil leaves
4 tbsp good quality Marc de
    Bourgogne
2 hen pheasants
½ cup seedless muscat or other
    white grapes, peeled, halved and
    seeded, if necessary
½ cup black grapes, peeled, halved
    and seeded
½ cup butter
2 cups game stock
2 tbsp whipping cream
salt and freshly ground black pepper

Bring the wine, shallots, leek, carrot, juniper berries and bouquet garni to the boil then simmer until reduced by a quarter. Leave to cool then stir in 2 tbsp Marc. Pour over the pheasants, cover and leave in a cool place for 12-18 hours turning the pheasants over occasionally.

Marinate the grapes separately in the remaining Marc for 2 hours at room temperature.

Remove the pheasants and the vegetables separately from the marinade. Drain and dry well.

Heat the oven to 425°F. Heat 4 tbsp butter in a roasting pan, add the pheasants and sear evenly. Place in the oven for 20 minutes, basting occasionally. Remove with a slotted spoon and pour most of the fat from the pan.

Add the vegetables to the pan and cook over a moderate heat, stirring frequently until lightly browned. Stir in the marinade, bring to the boil and reduce to ¾ cup. Stir in the stock and reduce to 1 cup. Stir in the cream then pass through a conical sieve. Reheat gently and then, over a very low heat

FOR THE GARNISH
4 small spinach leaves or larger ones,
    neatly trimmed

gradually stir in the remaining butter. Season and keep warm but do not allow to boil.

Meanwhile remove the grapes from the Marc with a slotted spoon, place in a single layer on a warmed plate, cover and put in the oven to warm. Remove the trussing strings from the pheasant. Cut each bird into quarters. Remove all the bones except the main ones in the legs and wings. Pack the pieces of pheasant, skin side up, in a large, heavy, buttered casserole. Cover and keep warm.

Heat a deep fat frying pan of oil to about 400°F, spread two of the spinach leaves out in the basket, lower them into the oil and fry briefly until crisp. Remove and drain on paper towels. Cook the remaining leaves in the same way.

Arrange the pheasant on 4 warmed plates. Spoon some of the sauce over half of the pheasant and spoon the remainder over most of the plates. Place the spinach leaves on the parts of the plates without sauce.

Garnish the plates with black and green grapes.

BREAST OF PHEASANT WITH WHITE WINE AND ORANGE

INGREDIENTS (serves 6)
6 tbsp butter
2 shallots, finely chopped
4 oranges, rind julienned, juice
    squeezed
1 cup full bodied dry white wine
breasts of 3 young pheasants
8 tbsp cognac
5 tbsp good quality bitter orange
    marmalade
salt and pepper

FOR THE GARNISH
orange segments, skin and white
    removed
strips of blanched orange rind
individual watercress leaves

Picture: page 279

Heat the oven to 425°F.

Heat the butter in a heavy flameproof casserole, add the shallots and cook over a low heat, stirring frequently, until soft but not colored. Remove with a slotted spoon.

Increase the heat to moderate, then stir in half the orange juice. Season the pheasant breasts and place, skin side down, in the orange butter for 1 minute. Turn them over to coat them and remove with a slotted spoon.

Stir half the wine into the casserole and boil it until almost evaporated. Place the pheasant breasts, skin side up, in the casserole, cover closely with buttered wax paper, cover the casserole and cook in the oven for 4—5 minutes. They should be still pink and moist.

Transfer the pheasant breasts to a warmed plate, cover and keep warm.

Place the casserole on a high heat, pour in the cognac and remaining wine and boil rapidly. Scrape down the sides and add the remaining orange juice and the orange julienne. Boil until the sauce is dark, then whisk in the marmalade.

Pass the sauce through a sieve, pressing down well on the orange julienne to extract as much flavor as possible. Season.

Cut the breasts into slices and arrange them on 4 warmed plates. Pour the sauce around and garnish with orange segments, orange rind and watercress leaves.

RABBIT MILLE FEUILLES

INGREDIENTS (serves 4)
10 oz puff pastry (see p.79)
salt and freshly ground black pepper
2 small saddles of rabbit
4 tbsp butter
⅓ cup cider vinegar
½ cup full bodied dry white wine
2¼ cups rabbit stock
½ piece of stick cinnamon
½ cup whipping cream
1 tbsp clear honey
2 crisp juicy apples
lemon juice

FOR THE GARNISH
sage leaves
corkskrews of caramelized orange peel

Divide the pastry in half, roll each half out very thinly to a rectangle about 13 × 5 inches. Trim the edges with a sharp knife, then carefully transfer each piece to a wet baking tray. Prick the top well with a fork to minimize the amount of rising. Cover and leave in a cool place for at least 30 minutes.

Heat the oven to 425°F.

Uncover the pastry and bake for 12—15 minutes until crisp and golden.

Season the rabbit. Heat half the butter in the roasting pan, add the saddles and sear evenly. Place in the oven for about 20 minutes. They should be still pink and moist. Transfer to a warmed plate, cover and keep warm.

Stir the vinegar and wine into a roasting pan then reduce to about 1 tbsp. Stir in the stock and cinnamon stick and reduce to ⅓ cup. Stir in the cream and honey then pass through a sieve into a clean saucepan. Reheat gently, then over a very low heat gradually swirl in the remaining butter. Season and keep warm but do not boil.

Meanwhile, core and slice the apples and brush with lemon juice. Lay in a single layer in the top half of a steamer or a colander. Cover and place over a pan of simmering water for about 2 minutes — they should remain crisp. Then remove from the heat.

With a large, sharp knife cut each piece of pastry into 6 rectangles approximately 4 × 2 inches. Then remove the fillets from the saddles and carve into slices along their length. Trim the slices to fit the pastry.

Place a rectangle of pastry on each of 4 warmed plates, cover with rabbit slices and spoon a little sauce over the rabbit. Then repeat the layering ending with a rectangle of pastry. Spoon the remaining sauce around the pastries. Arrange some of the apple slices on the pastry and arrange the remaining slices in the sauce. Garnish with sage leaves and corkscrews of caramelized orange peel.

MEDALLIONS OF RABBIT

WITH BASIL

INGREDIENTS (serves 4)
2 saddles of rabbit, filleted
salt and freshly ground black pepper
2 tbsp butter

FOR THE SAUCE
⅔ cup sercial madeira
12 basil leaves

Blackcurrants and cranberries can be added to the garnish for extra color and richness.

Cut each piece of rabbit into 12 medallions. Season.

Heat the butter, add the rabbit and cook for about 2—3 minutes each side so the medallions remain pink inside.

$\frac{2}{3}$ cup dry white wine
1$\frac{1}{4}$ cups veal stock
1$\frac{1}{4}$ cups whipping cream
6 tbsp butter
salt and freshly ground black pepper

FOR THE GARNISH
basil leaves

Picture: page 283

Transfer to a warmed plate with a slotted spoon, cover and keep warm.

Tip the excess fat from the pan. Stir in the madeira, basil and wine and reduce to about 3 tbsp. Stir in the stock and reduce by three quarters. Stir in the cream and simmer until slightly thickened. Reduce the heat to very low. Dice the butter then gradually whisk in, making sure each piece is fully incorporated before adding the next. Season.

Spoon the sauce onto 4 warmed plates, arrange the rabbit on top and garnish with the basil leaves.

SADDLE OF HARE WITH CELERIAC

MOUSSES AND ORANGE

INGREDIENTS (serves 4)
celeriac mousse (see p.309)
2 tbsp oil
2 saddles of hare
1 cup ruby port
$\frac{1}{4}$ cup brandy
$\frac{1}{3}$ cup sercial madeira
2 sprigs of thyme
3 tbsp orange juice
8 juniper berries, crushed
3 black peppercorns, crushed
1 cup game stock
julienned orange rind cut into short
   strips
2 tbsp butter
salt and freshly ground black pepper

Only a very simple vegetable accompaniment is necessary to complete this main course. To minimize last minute preparation, prepare the orange rind in advance and have the dishes for the mousses set ready in the baking pan.

Prepare the celeriac mousse, cover and keep cool.

Heat the oven to 450°F.

Heat 1$\frac{1}{2}$ tbsp oil, add the saddles, sear evenly, then cook in the oven for 9—10 minutes until pink and still moist in the center. Reduce the heat to 350°F.

Transfer the saddles to a warmed plate, cover and keep warm.

Pour the excess fat from the roasting pan, stir in the port, brandy and madeira and heat to simmering point. Stir in the thyme, orange juice, juniper berries, peppercorns and stock and reduce to about 1 cup.

Divide the celeriac mousse mixture between 4 small buttered dishes, and place the dishes in a roasting or baking pan. Surround with boiling water, cover with buttered wax paper and place in the oven for 15—20 minutes until just set.

Heat the remaining oil, add the orange rind and cook until beginning to curl. Remove with a slotted spoon and drain on paper towels.

Pass the sauce through a sieve, then reheat gently. Gradually swirl in the butter over a low heat. Season and keep warm but do not boil.

When the mousses are set, remove them from the heat and leave to stand for a few minutes. Cut the saddles lengthwise into slices. Reform and keep warm.

Unmold the mousses onto 4 warmed plates, spoon the sauce around. Arrange the slices of hare on the sauce. Place some of the orange julienne on the mousses and scatter the remainder over the sauce.

MEDALLIONS OF HARE WITH

BLACKBERRY SAUCE

INGREDIENTS (serves 6)
4 strips of bacon
4 saddles of hare, trimmed and
　　seasoned
2 tbsp oil

FOR THE SAUCE
3 cups blackberries
½ cup granulated sugar
12 sugar lumps
2 tbsp red wine vinegar
1 cup game stock
1 tbsp butter

FOR THE GARNISH
blackberries
mint leaves

Picture: page 282

If the saddles of hare are large, 3 will be sufficient — unless appetites are very hearty. It is important to keep on tasting the sauce when the stock is being added to get the right balance of flavors.

Heat the oven to 420°F.

Tie a strip of bacon over each saddle. Heat the oil in a roasting pan, add the saddles and seal quickly all over. Place in the oven for 15—20 minutes — the meat should remain pink inside. Transfer the saddles to a warmed plate, cover and keep warm.

Barely cover the blackberries with water, add the sugar and poach for 8—10 minutes, then pass through a fine sieve.

Heat the sugar lumps in a small, heavy based pan, then stir in the vinegar and simmer for 2—3 minutes. Stir in the blackberry purée and reduce until fairly syrupy.

Stir a spoonful of stock at a time into the blackberry sauce, checking constantly to avoid adding too much, as the flavor should be rich yet still with a tang to it. When the right amount has been added, simmer for 3—4 minutes. Remove from the heat and swirl in the butter.

Cut each saddle into 5—6 slices and arrange on 6 warmed plates. Spoon the sauce around and garnish with blackberries and mint leaves.

MEDALLIONS OF VENISON WITH

HARLEQUIN PEPPERCORN SAUCE

INGREDIENTS (serves 4)
5 cups game stock
bouquet garni of 4 parsley sprigs
　　1 bayleaf, a sprig of thyme, 2 sprigs
　　of chervil, a sprig of tarragon
1 small leek, sliced
2 shallots, chopped
1 small carrot, chopped
3 tomatoes, chopped
¾ tsp black peppercorns, finely crushed
¾ tsp white peppercorns, finely
　　crushed
4 venison steaks, approximately
　　5 oz and 1 inch thick
salt
6 tbsp butter

Simmer the stock with the next 5 ingredients for 2 hours, then reduce to about 1 cup. Pass through a conical strainer, pressing down well on the vegetables to extract as much liquid as possible. Measure out ¾ cup.

Mix the black and white peppercorns together. Season the venison with salt and the mixed peppercorns.

Heat 3 tbsp butter in a sauteuse or large frying pan. Add the venison and cook for about 3—4 minutes each side until pink and moist inside. Transfer to a warmed plate with a slotted spoon, cover and keep warm.

Pour the excess fat from the pan. Pour the cognac into the pan and ignite with a taper. When the flames have died down, stir in the reduced stock and reduce again by half. Stir in the cream and boil again until slightly thickened. Reduce the heat

3 tbsp cognac
⅓ cup whipping cream
1 tsp green peppercorns
1 tsp pink peppercorns

FOR THE GARNISH
cooked flageolet beans * (see p.305)
½ quantity of white butter sauce (see
   p.196)

* if not available, use navy beans or
   small lima beans

to very low. Dice the remaining butter and gradually stir in, making sure that each piece is completely incorporated before adding the next. Stir in the green and pink peppercorns and add salt to taste.

Meanwhile, warm the beans in a steamer. Prepare the white butter sauce.

Cut each piece of venison into 6 slices. Reform and keep warm. Spoon the sauce over 4 warmed plates. Arrange the slices of venison, overlapping, so that they form three quarters of a circle. Place the flageolet beans in a single layer in the semi-circular space formed in front of the venison. Carefully spoon the sauce around the circumference of the venison.

MEDALLIONS OF HARE WITH BEETS

INGREDIENTS (serves 4)
2 saddles of hare, trimmed
salt and freshly ground black pepper
2 tbsp oil

FOR THE MARINADE
2¼ cups red wine
1 large carrot, diced
1 onion, chopped
bouquet garni of a sprig of thyme,
   a sprig of rosemary, a bayleaf and
   4 parsley stalks
8 black peppercorns, crushed
8 juniper berries, crushed
2 cloves

FOR THE SAUCE
1 tbsp chopped shallot
1 tbsp red wine vinegar
¾ cup freshly cooked beets
   chopped
⅓ cup whipping cream
1 tsp creamed horseradish

FOR THE BEETS
½ cup freshly cooked small
   beets thinly sliced
2 tsp red wine vinegar

FOR THE GARNISH
½ cup plain noodles
1 tbsp oil
sprigs of chervil

Picture: page 283

A dish that succeeds even when hare is not quite at its best. Start the preparation the day before it is to be served and do be sure to dry the hare well after removing it from the marinade.

Mix the ingredients for the marinade together. Pour over the saddles, cover and leave in a cool place for 24 hours, turning occasionally.

Heat the oven to 450°F.

Remove the saddles from the marinade with a slotted spoon, drain and dry well. Strain the marinade.

Season the saddles. Heat the oil, add the saddles and sear all over, then cook in the oven for 9—10 minutes, so they are pink inside and moist. Transfer to a warmed plate, cover and keep warm.

Tip most of the oil from the pan in which the saddles were cooked.

Stir in the shallots and vinegar into the pan, cover and cook over a moderate heat, shaking the pan occasionally until the shallots have softened. Add the beets and 3 tbsp of the marinade and reduce by three quarters. Stir in the cream and reduce by half. Stir in the horseradish and seasoning. Keep warm.

Meanwhile, cook the noodles in boiling salted water with the oil until just tender. Drain well.

Gently warm the beet slices in the vinegar in a covered pan.

Cut the saddles into slices and arrange on 4 plates. Divide the sauce between the plates and arrange the slices on the sauce, then finish with a small mound of noodles on each plate and garnish with sprigs of chervil.

MEDALLIONS OF VENISON

WITH APPLES AND CELERIAC

INGREDIENTS (serves 6)
2½ lb saddle of venison, boned
bones and trimmings from the saddle
4 carrots, chopped
4 small leeks, chopped
2 stalks of celery, chopped
10 juniper berries, crushed
rind of 1 orange
bouquet garni of 3 sprigs of thyme
  1 bay leaf and 6 parsley sprigs
salt and freshly ground black pepper
3¼ cups (26 fl oz bottle) of fruity
  dry white wine
4 tbsp butter
¼ cup calvados
1¼ cups crème fraîche
⅓ cup red currant jelly
2 crisp green dessert apples
¼ cup Scotch apple liqueur, or
  fruity dry white wine
2 inch piece of stick cinnamon

FOR THE GARNISH
julienned celeriac

Picture: page 286

The tang of crème fraîche is essential for this dish, so if you are unable to buy it, make your own according to the method on p.51.

———————————

Cut the venison into 6 lean medallions, place in a shallow dish, add 2 carrots, 2 leeks, 1 stack of celery, the juniper berries, orange rind, bouquet garni and seasoning and pour half the wine over it. Cover and leave in a cool place for 18 hours, turning occasionally.

Place the bones, remaining carrots, leeks and celery in a roasting pan and brown under a hot broiler, turning occasionally. Tip the bones and vegetables into a large saucepan. Stir the remaining wine into the roasting pan and bring to simmering point, stirring. Pour into the saucepan with about 4½ cups water and season. Bring to the boil, skim the scum from the surface and simmer for about 12 hours. Leave to cool and remove the fat from the surface.

Pass through a conical sieve, pressing down well to extract as much flavor as possible. Reduce to 1¼ cups.

Remove the venison from the marinade with a slotted spoon and dry well.

Heat the butter in a large sauteuse or frying pan and cook the medallions for about 3 minutes each side so that they remain pink and moist. Remove with a slotted spoon, place on a warmed plate, cover and keep warm.

Tip the surface fat from the pan. Stir in the calvados and ignite with a taper. Stir in the sauce and reduce by half. Stir in the crème fraîche and red currant jelly. Season. Keep warm but do not boil.

Meanwhile, peel, core and slice the apples and poach for about 5 minutes in the Scotch apple liqueur, or wine, with the piece of stick cinnamon. Remove the apple slices with the slotted spoon and drain.

Blanch, refresh and drain the celeriac.

Spoon the sauce over 6 warmed plates. Arrange the venison on top and add the apple slices and celeriac julienne.

LOIN OF VENISON WITH

PEARS AND CRANBERRIES

INGREDIENTS (serves 4)
1½ lb loin of venison
bones from the loin
1 carrot, chopped
1 onion, chopped
10 cups veal stock
10 juniper berries, crushed
3 sprigs of thyme and 3 sprigs of
  chervil, tied together
2 tbsp tomato paste
4 tbsp butter
salt and freshly ground black pepper
½ cup cranberries
1½ tsp sugar
2 tbsp brown sugar
⅓ cup Gewürztraminer wine
2 tbsp poires William
2 pears

Picture: page 287

The stock can be prepared in advance. If a Gewürztraminer wine is not available, another full bodied, fruity dry white wine could be used instead; in place of poires William you could use cognac.

Brown the venison bones under a high broiler, then stir in the vegetables and brown these. Tip into a large saucepan, stir in the stock, juniper berries, herbs and tomato paste and bring to the boil, skimming off the scum as it rises. Simmer for 2½ hours, removing the scum occasionally.

Strain the stock and reduce to one third. Leave to cool and remove the excess fat from the surface.

Heat the oven to 425°F.

Heat half the butter, add the venison and sear all over, then place in the oven for 15—20 minutes until pink and moist inside.

Meanwhile, put the cranberries into a saucepan and pour 3 tbsp boiling water over. Cover and leave for 15 minutes. Bring to simmering point and simmer for 3 minutes. Turn off the heat and leave for 15 minutes. Stir in the white sugar.

Remove the venison from the roasting pan, cover and keep warm.

Bring the venison sauce to the boil, reduce if necessary, then reduce the heat to very low and gradually whisk in the remaining butter. Season and keep warm, but do not allow to boil.

Dissolve the brown sugar in the wine and poires William over a gentle heat. Peel, core and cut the pears into batons. Add to the wine and cook gently for 2 minutes. Remove with a slotted spoon and reduce the liquor until syrupy. Remove from the heat and return the pear batons to the pan.

Cut the venison into slices and arrange on 4 warmed plates. Spoon the sauce around. Remove the cranberries and pears from their liquors with a slotted spoon and arrange on the sauce.

VENISON MEDALLIONS IN PORT

JELLY WITH BEET PUREE

INGREDIENTS (serves 6)
12 oz boned venison saddle,
trimmed
salt and freshly ground black pepper
2 tbsp butter
2½ cups game stock (see p.76)
1 cup red wine
1 cup ruby port
1½ tsp gelatin
1 tbsp sugar
2 tsp red wine vinegar
1½ tsp pink peppercorns

FOR THE PUREE
¾ cup freshly cooked beets
chopped
2 tsp red wine vinegar
⅓ cup whipping cream
¾ tsp horseradish cream
salt and freshly ground black pepper

FOR THE GARNISH
crème fraîche

Picture: page 287

This is a very versatile recipe as it can be served as a fairly substantial first course, a main course, as part of a buffet or as part of a picnic. Pack the venison unmolded and the purée in a sealed container. A cobweb design of cream can be piped into the sauce for color contrast.

Heat the oven to 425°F.

Tie the venison into a neat cylindrical shape. Season. Heat the butter in a roasting pan, add the venison and sear evenly. Place in the oven and cook for 10—15 minutes, until pink and moist in the center. Remove with a slotted spoon and leave to cool on a wire rack.

Reduce the stock, wine and port by half. Cool slightly, then stir a little into the gelatin. Stir until the gelatin has dissolved, then pour back into the reduced liquid.

Dissolve the sugar in the vinegar, then stir into the reduced stock. Leave to cool.

Spoon a layer of the cold reduced liquor into 6 cold individual dishes. Sprinkle the peppercorns around the circumferences of the dishes. Leave in the refrigerator for 1 hour.

Cut the venison into six ½—¾ inch slices and place one in each dish. Spoon sufficient stock into the dishes to just cover the venison and leave in the refrigerator for 2 hours.

For the purée, warm the beets in the vinegar, then purée with the cream. Add the horseradish cream and seasoning. Cover and chill lightly.

Unmold the venison onto 4 cold plates. Spoon the sauce around and swirl in the crème fraîche.

MEDALLIONS OF VENISON WITH

TURNIP MOUSSES AND PORT SAUCE

INGREDIENTS (serves 4)
12 medallions, approximately 1½ oz
    each, from a saddle of venison
2¼ cups full bodied red wine
8 juniper berries, crushed
5 coriander seeds, toasted and
    crushed
a sprig of thyme
salt and freshly ground black pepper
½ cup butter, diced
1 cup ruby port
2¼ cups game stock, boiled down
    to 1 cup

FOR THE TURNIP MOUSSES
1 lb small turnips, halved
salt
2 egg whites
1 tbsp butter, just melted
3 tbsp whipping cream
freshly ground white pepper
a small pinch of grated nutmeg

FOR THE GARNISH
3 tsp concassé tomato

Do not leave the medallions in the marinade for long. Be sure to dry them well before cooking.

Mix the wine, juniper berries, coriander, sprig of thyme and seasoning together. Pour over the venison and leave to marinate for 30 minutes.

Cook the turnips in simmering salted water until tender. Drain very well, pressing down well on the turnips to extract as much water as possible. Purée, then leave the purée to drain through a sieve.

Heat the oven to 350°F.

Remove the venison from the marinade and dry well.

Heat 4 tbsp butter in a sauteuse or large frying pan, add the venison and cook for about 2 minutes each side until they are pink and moist in the center. Transfer to a warmed plate with a slotted spoon. Cover and keep warm.

Turn the turnip purée into a bowl of ice. Gradually beat in the egg whites, then the butter, cream, pepper and nutmeg. Divide between 4 small buttered individual dishes. Place the dishes in a roasting or baking pan, surround with boiling water and place in the oven for 18—20 minutes.

Pour the excess fat from the sauteuse, stir in the port and reduce by half. Add the reduced stock and reduce by half again. Reduce the heat to very low. Dice the remaining butter and gradually stir in, making sure that each piece is completely incorporated before adding the next. Season and keep warm but do not allow to boil.

Leave the mousses to stand for a minute or two before unmolding onto 4 warmed plates. Spoon the sauce around. Arrange the medallions and place a little concassé tomato on the top of each mousse.

VEGETABLE
DISHES

◆ It is a mistake to view vegetables as merely accompaniments to more important main courses. Cuisine Vivante vegetable dishes have a much more positive role to play in complementing the texture, color, flavor and style of the main course. When combining a vegetable dish with a main course, whether it be fish, shellfish, meat, poultry or game, make sure that the method of preparation and cooking is one that will combine to bring out the best in both dishes. Vegetables should always be thoroughly drained and the plates and dishes warmed before serving. ◆

P E A   P U R E E

INGREDIENTS *(serves 4)*
2 tbsp butter
3 scallions, finely sliced
1 scant cup petit pois
1¼ cups water
5 round lettuce leaves, finely shredded
2 tbsp whipping cream
salt and freshly ground pepper

Heat the butter, add the scallions, cover and cook over a moderate heat, shaking the pan occasionally until they are softened. Stir in about 1¼ cups water, bring to the boil, add the peas and lettuce and return to the boil for 1 minute.

Drain well then pass through a sieve into a clean saucepan. Reheat gently, beat in the cream and seasoning.

PEA AND MINT PUREE
Add 2 tbsp finely chopped mint with the lettuce.

C H E S T N U T   P U R E E

INGREDIENTS *(serves 4)*
1½ lb chestnuts
2¼ cups milk
6 tbsp butter
a pinch of sugar
salt and freshly ground black pepper
1—2 tbsp cognac, optional

Split the chestnut skins with the point of a sharp knife.

Put the chestnuts into a heavy based saucepan or flameproof casserole and place over a moderate heat, turning them over constantly, until the skins dry and crack.

As soon as the chestnuts are cool enough to handle, peel off the skins.

Simmer the chestnuts in the milk for 20 minutes, then pass through a fine sieve.

Reheat the purée in a clean saucepan and beat in the butter. Add a pinch of sugar, seasoning and cognac to taste.

T U R N I P   P U R E E

INGREDIENTS *(serves 4)*
1 lb (approximately 3 cups) small
    turnips, peeled and thinly sliced
salt and freshly ground white pepper
2 tbsp butter
¼ cup whipping cream, lightly
    whipped

Turnips can produce a surprising amount of water, even when small and young. So to make a good purée it really is important to dry it thoroughly before adding the butter and cream.

_____

Cook the turnips in the minimum of simmering salted water until tender but not falling apart.

Drain very well, then purée. If the purée is too moist, turn it into a frying pan and boil rapidly, stirring, to evaporate the excess moisture.

Over a low heat, beat in the butter and pepper then fold in the cream.

CAULIFLOWER PUREE

INGREDIENTS (serves 6)
1 medium size cauliflower, trimmed
    and broken into flowerets
salt
2 tbsp butter
¼ cup whipping cream
freshly ground black pepper
a pinch of grated nutmeg

Cook the cauliflower in simmering salted water until tender.
Drain well and refresh under cold running water. Drain again and dry in a cloth or on paper towels.
Pass through a mouli-légumes.
Melt the butter in a nonstick pan. Stir in the cauliflower then beat in the cream and reheat gently. Season and add a pinch of nutmeg.

CELERIAC PUREE

INGREDIENTS (serves 4)
1½ lb (approximately 3 cups)
    celeriac, peeled and chopped
salt
1¼ cups milk
2 tbsp butter
2 tbsp whipping cream

Cook the celeriac in the salted simmering milk until tender.
Drain well, reserving the milk.
Pass the celeriac through a mouli-légumes or sieve.
Heat the butter in a nonstick pan, add the celeriac purée, then beat in the cream and sufficient of the cooking milk to give a creamy consistency. Reheat gently. Season.

ZUCCHINI PUREE

INGREDIENTS (serves 4)
2 lb (approximately 8 large) zucchini
salt
2 tbsp butter
3 tbsp whipping cream
freshly ground white pepper
a squeeze of lemon juice, optional

Peel the zucchini and chop finely. Place in a colander, sprinkle with salt and leave to drain for 30 minutes.
Rinse under cold running water. Drain well.
Heat the butter, add the zucchini and cook over a moderately low heat for 3—4 minutes. Stir in sufficient water to just cover, cover the pan and simmer gently until tender.
Drain well, then purée. Return to a nonstick pan and heat gently, to drive off excess moisture if necessary. Beat in the cream and season, adding a squeeze of lemon juice, if liked.

SAFFRON RICE TIMBALES

INGREDIENTS
a pinch of saffron threads
2 tbsp dry vermouth
2 tbsp long-grain rice per person
a pinch of salt

Adjust the amount of rice needed for each portion according to whether the timbales are to be used to garnish a dish or as a vegetable accompaniment.
Soak the saffron threads in the vermouth.
Measure water to three times the volume of the rice. Bring the water, with a pinch of salt, to the boil. Add the rice and saffron, with its liquid, return to the boil, stir once, cover, lower the heat and simmer for about 12—15 minutes until the rice is just tender and the liquid has been absorbed. Pack the rice into oiled molds. Leave to stand in a warm place for a minute or two then unmold onto warm plates.

CARROT PUREE

INGREDIENTS *(serves 4)*
1 lb (approx 4 cups) carrots, peeled
  and sliced
salt
2 tbsp butter
¼ cup whipping cream
freshly ground black pepper
a pinch of sugar

Cook the carrots in simmering salted water until tender.

Drain well and pass through a mouli-légumes into a bowl lined with a double thickness of cheesecloth. Fold the cheesecloth over the puréed carrots and squeeze out the excess moisture.

Heat the butter in a nonstick pan. Stir in the carrot purée then beat in the cream and reheat gently, stirring. Season and add a pinch of sugar to taste.

BRUSSELS SPROUTS PUREE

INGREDIENTS *(serves 4)*
1 lb (approx 3 cups) Brussels sprouts,
  trimmed
salt
2 tbsp butter
⅓ cup whipping cream
freshly ground black pepper

Blanch the Brussels sprouts for 2 minutes. Refresh then cook in simmering salted water until tender.

Drain well, dry on paper towels then pass through a mouli-légumes.

Heat the butter in a nonstick pan, add the Brussels sprouts, then beat in the cream and reheat gently. Season.

FRESH TOMATO PASTE

INGREDIENTS *(serves 4)*
1½ tsp butter
2 shallots, very finely chopped
flesh from 3 lb ripe tomatoes, chopped
  (approx 4½ cups)
bouquet garni of 3 parsley sprigs, a
  sprig of chervil, a sprig of thyme
  and a bay leaf
salt and freshly ground black pepper
a pinch of sugar or squeeze of lemon
  juice to taste

The flavor of the tomatoes used for this recipe *must* really be good — see the notes on p.31.

Heat the butter in a heavy based saucepan, add the shallots, cover and cook over a moderate heat, shaking the pan occasionally, until the shallots are soft.

Stir in the tomatoes and bouquet garni and simmer gently until the moisture has evaporated. Remove the bouquet garni. Season and add sugar or lemon juice to taste. Leave to cool and store in a covered glass or earthenware container in a cool place.

POTATO BASKETS

INGREDIENTS *(serves 4)*
1 lb (approx 3 cups sliced) even size
  floury potatoes
oil for frying
salt and freshly ground black pepper

The small baskets used here can be bought from good Chinese stores, hardware or kitchen stores or department stores.

Slice the potatoes very thinly in a food processor or with a mandolin cutter, then julienne slices.

Line a wire mesh ladle about 2-2½ inches in diameter with a thin layer of potato julienne and hold them in place by placing

302

another ladle on top.

Heat a deep fat frying pan to 400°F, lower in the ladle and cook the potatoes for 1—2 minutes until crisp and golden. Carefully remove the potato basket from the ladle. Sprinkle with salt and pepper and keep warm while preparing the remaining baskets.

♦ ZUCCHINI CUPS WITH PEAS

INGREDIENTS (serves 4)
4 fat courgettes, approximately 5-7 cm/2-2½ inch diameter, about 9 cm/ 3½ inches long
7 g/¼ oz butter, diced
2 tsp finely chopped shallot
6 tbsp petits pois
1 tsp finely chopped mint
salt and finely ground white pepper
a squeeze of lemon juice

FOR THE GARNISH
small mint leaves

Peel lengthwise strips from the zucchini to create a striped appearance with a knife or potato peeler.

Cut the ends from the zucchini and cut them into 1½ inch lengths. Remove balls of the flesh with a small melon baller, leaving a narrow border.

Heat the butter, add the shallot and cook over a moderate heat, shaking the pan occasionally until soft. Add the balls of zucchini and cook, stirring occasionally for 3 minutes until the flesh is just beginning to soften.

Add the peas, mint, seasoning and a squeeze of lemon juice and heat for about 1 minute, shaking the pan occasionally. Meanwhile, cook the zucchini cups in simmering salted water for about 4 minutes until just tender. Refresh and drain well.

Spoon the zucchini balls and peas into the zucchini cups. Garnish with mint leaves.

♦ POTATO GALETTES

INGREDIENTS (serves 4)
1 lb (approx 3 cups sliced) potatoes
olive oil
salt and freshly ground black pepper

Picture: page 306

Peel the potatoes, then slice thinly with a mandolin or in a food processor.

Heat some oil in a small frying pan over a high heat. Arrange a quarter of the potato slices in a single layer, overlapping, in a circle in the pan and fry on both sides until crisp and golden.

Quickly drain on paper towels. Cut into a neat circle with a plain 2 inch cookie cutter.

Keep warm while preparing the remaining galettes. Sprinkle with salt and freshly ground black pepper just before serving.

POTATO FANS

INGREDIENTS (serves 4)
1 lb (approximately 3-4 cups) sliced
   potatoes
1 tbsp oil
1 tbsp butter
sea salt and freshly ground black
   pepper

Heat the oven to 400°F.

Peel the potatoes and cut into even shapes about $2\frac{1}{2}$ inches long. Slice the potatoes across their width at $\frac{1}{4}$ inch intervals, cutting almost to the base, but leaving the sides joined. Rinse in cold water and drain well.

Heat the oil and butter in a roasting pan until very hot. Add the potatoes, turn them in the fat to coat them evenly, season well, then place in the oven for 50—60 minutes until crisp and golden and soft in the center, turning them occasionally and basting.

POTATO CASTLES

INGREDIENTS (serves 4)
1 lb (approximately 3 cups, sliced)
   potatoes
oil
salt and freshly ground black pepper

Heat the oven to 375°F.

Peel the potatoes and trim to the width of a mold. Cut into slices about $\frac{1}{8}$ inch thick.

Heat a thin layer of oil in a frying pan. Add a few potato slices at a time and cook for 1—2 minutes until soft but not colored. Remove with a slotted spoon and drain on paper towels.

When all the slices have been fried, line the sides and base of 4 buttered molds with potato. Season well, then fill the centers with the remaining potato slices, packing them down well and doming the top slightly, as they will shrink when cooked.

Place the molds in a baking or roasting pan of hot oil and place in the oven for about 20 minutes until the sides are golden and have shrunk away from sides of the molds.

Run the point of a sharp knife around the edges of the molds, then invert onto warmed plates.

ARTICHOKE AND POTATO GALETTE

INGREDIENTS (serves 4)
2 potatoes, about 6 oz each
6 tbsp clarified butter
2 tsp finely chopped thyme
salt and freshly ground black pepper
3 large or 5 small cooked artichoke
   bottoms, thinly sliced

FOR THE GARNISH
short snow pea pieces, julienned

Heat the oven to 425°F.

Peel the potatoes and, using a mandolin or food processor, cut into very thin slices.

Over a moderate heat, heat a very thin layer of clarified butter in 4 small flameproof dishes or one large round dish. Arrange half the potato slices in concentric circles in the bottom of the dishes or dish, shaking occasionally to prevent the potato from sticking. Sprinkle half the thyme over. Season.

Cover the potato slices with slices of artichoke, sprinkle the remaining thyme over, season then cover with the remaining potato, continuing to shake occasionally. Season again and trickle 1—2 tsp clarified butter over the potatoes. Cover with foil and cook for 5 minutes to brown the bottom.

Place in the oven and cook for about 25 minutes for small dishes, or 20—25 minutes for a large one, until the potatoes are tender.

Blanch the snow peas for the garnish, refresh and drain well.

Invert the galettes onto a warm plate and place a few snow pea julienne on the top of each one. If a large dish is used, cut the galette into slices to serve.

VEGETABLE SPIRALS

INGREDIENTS (serves 4)
2 carrots, approximately 7 oz each
2 turnips, approximately 7 oz each
1 cucumber, approximately 4 oz

Single-coloured spirals can be prepared in the same way using just one type of vegetable.

Blanch the carrots and turnips for 3 minutes. Refresh and drain well.

Cut each carrot into a $2\frac{1}{4}$ inch long cylinder then, with a very sharp, thin bladed knife, peel off long strips around each cylinder. If the strips break, it does not matter as short pieces can still be used.

Repeat with the turnips and cucumber, but only cut down as far as the cucumber seeds.

Carefully blanch the strips in boiling water for 1 minute, then remove with a slotted spoon.

Lay the strips together to form long tricolored strips. Roll them together then fasten with thread or fine string.

Cook in boiling salted water for 5 minutes.

Lift the coils out from the water with a skimmer or slotted spoon and drain on paper towels.

Place on 4 warmed plates. Remove the threads or string. Unroll a short length of each coil and spread it out on the plate.

FLAGEOLET BEANS

INGREDIENTS (serves 4)
$\frac{3}{4}$ cup flageolet beans,* soaked overnight in cold water
1 large shallot, quartered
a sprig of summer savory
2 tbsp butter
salt

* use navy or small lima beans if flageolet not available.

Drain the beans well. Put into a saucepan with the shallot, summer savory and butter, add plenty of water and bring to the boil. Simmer for about an hour until tender but still retaining their shape.

Drain well, remove the pieces of shallot and sprinkle salt over the beans.

TOP LEFT *Flageolet beans in potato baskets*
Recipes: page 305 & 302
TOP RIGHT *Potato galettes*
Recipe: page 303
CENTRE *Spinach, cauliflower and carrot mousselines*
Recipe: page 308

DOME OF CAULIFLOWER AND

BROCCOLI

INGREDIENTS (serves 6)
1 lb (approximately 4 cups)
   trimmed broccoli, broken into
   flowerets
1 cauliflower, approximately 1 lb
   (approximately 4 cups) broken into
   flowerets
salt
2 tbsp butter, diced
1 shallot, finely chopped
freshly ground black pepper

A useful recipe to bear in mind for the occasions when serving a main course that requires a fair amount of last-minute attention to detail.

Cook the broccoli and cauliflower separately in simmering salted water until only just tender. Refresh and drain well.

Trim off the stems and cut them into 5 mm/¼ inch slices.

Heat the butter, add the shallot, broccoli and cauliflower stems and cook over a moderate heat, stirring occasionally until the shallot is soft. Season.

Place a large broccoli floweret, stem side up, in the bottom of a 5 cup glass bowl. Arrange a circle of small cauliflower flowerets around it, with the stems pointing towards the center of the bowl. Continue arranging alternating rows of broccoli and cauliflower. Fill the center with any remaining flowerets and the sliced stems.

Place a plate that is slightly smaller than the inside of the bowl on top of the vegetables and place a 1 lb weight on top.

Thirty minutes before required, place the bowl in a large saucepan and surround with boiling water. Cover the saucepan and place over a very low heat for 30 minutes.

Invert the bowl onto a warmed plate and carefully lift away from the dome of cauliflower and broccoli.

SPINACH MOUSSELINE

INGREDIENTS (serves 4)
1½ (approximately 3 cups) spinach
2 tbsp butter
1 shallot, finely chopped
salt and freshly ground black pepper
1 egg beaten with 1 egg yolk
¼ cup whipping cream, lightly
   whipped

Picture: page 306

Heat the oven to 350°F.

Blanch and refresh the spinach. Drain well, pressing down firmly on the spinach with the back of a spoon to extract as much liquid as possible.

Heat the butter and add the shallot. Cover and cook over a moderate heat shaking the pan occasionally, until the shallot is soft. Stir in the spinach and heat through, stirring, to drive off the last of the moisture.

Purée, season, beat in the eggs, then fold in the cream.

Strain into 4 buttered individual dishes or molds. Place in a baking or roasting pan and surround with boiling water. Cover the top of the molds with buttered wax paper, place in the oven and cook for 15-20 minutes.

Remove the molds from the heat and leave to stand for a minute or two before unmolding onto warmed plates.

POTATO AND CELERIAC CAKES

WITH CHESTNUTS

INGREDIENTS (serves 4)
1 head of celeriac, approximately
   1 lb (approximately 4 cups diced)
8 oz (approximately 2 cups) potatoes
4 tbsp butter
salt and freshly ground black pepper
4 cooked chestnuts, halved

Peel the celeriac, dice, putting the dice into acidulated water as soon as they are prepard. Simmer for about 20 minutes until tender.

Peel and dice the potatoes and simmer in salted water for about 20 minutes until tender.

Drain the vegetables well, purée, then reheat together in a nonstick frying pan, stirring to drive off as much water as possible. Beat in half the butter and the seasoning.

Divide the mixture into 8. Form each piece into a flat cake enclosing a chestnut half in the center. Mark the tops in a diamond pattern with the point of a sharp knife.

Heat the remaining butter in a frying pan, add the potato and celeriac cakes and cook until golden on each side.

CELERIAC MOUSSES

INGREDIENTS (serves 4)
1 head of celeriac, approximately
   1½ lb (approximately 6 cups diced)
2 tbsp clarified butter
1 shallot, finely chopped
2 leaves of sage
1½ cups chicken stock
¼ cup medium bodied dry white wine
1 whole egg and 2 egg yolks, beaten
   together
¼ cup whipping cream, lightly
   whipped
salt and freshly ground white pepper

For a flavor variation the sage leaves can be omitted and a pinch of freshly grated nutmeg added instead.

Heat the oven to 350°F.

Peel the celeriac and cut into approximately 1 inch cubes. Put the cubes into acidulated water as soon as they are prepared.

Cook the celeriac in simmering acidulated water for 5 minutes. Drain.

Meanwhile, heat the butter, add the shallot, cover and cook until soft, shaking the pan occasionally. Stir in the celeriac, sage, stock and wine. Bring to the boil, then simmer for about 15 minutes until the celeriac is tender. Drain, reserving the liquid.

Boil the liquid until reduced to about 2 tbsp.

Remove the sage, then purée the celeriac with the reduced liquid. Beat in the eggs and fold in the cream. Season, then divide between 4 small buttered molds.

Place the dishes in a roasting pan and surround with boiling water. Cover the tops of the molds with buttered wax paper and place in the oven for 15-20 minutes until just set.

Leave the mousses to stand for a minute or two before unmolding.

DESSERTS

The dessert is as important as any other element in a Cuisine Vivante meal. If the rest of the meal has been well balanced the thought of a dessert will not be daunting. 'Dessert' is not a synonym for very rich, sweet cakes, pastries, creams and such creations but can, and should, be light, airy, refreshing and palate cleansing. Desserts need present the cook with few problems since the majority can be largely prepared in advance. Any decorations that need to be added at the last minute can be completed in the pause that is usually welcome between the main or cheese course and the dessert.

APRICOTS AND ICE CREAM

INGREDIENTS (serves 4)
5-6 ripe apricots, depending on size
1¼ cups dessert wine
2½ cups raspberries
2 tbsp sifted confectioner's sugar
1-2 tbsp kirsch
1¼ cups vanilla ice cream (see p.336)

FOR THE GARNISH
orange segments
4 tiny sprigs of mint
1-1½ cups small, firm strawberries halved

Picture: page 314

A little cream can be piped into the sauce in a cobweb design for extra effect.

Cut the apricots into halves, remove the stones and poach in the wine for about 8 minutes until just becoming tender. Leave to cool in the wine, then remove with a slotted spoon. Drain well, peel and cut into quarters. Cover and chill.

Purée, then sieve the raspberries. Sweeten with confectioner's sugar and add kirsch to taste. Chill.

About 30 minutes before serving, transfer the ice cream to the main part of the refrigerator. Chill 4 plates.

Place balls of ice cream in the center of the plates. Arrange apricot slices on top of the ice cream. Spoon the raspberry purée around the ice cream and arrange the strawberries with the sprigs of mint around the edge of the plates.

WHITE WINE GRANITA WITH

APRICOT ICE CREAM

INGREDIENTS (serves 4)
⅓ cup sugar
1¼ cups good quality dessert wine
1 tbsp strained orange juice
½ quantity of apricot ice cream (see p.313)
2 oranges
2 pears
lemon juice

FOR THE SAUCE
2 egg yolks
½ cup crème fraîche
¼ cup Grand Marnier
2 tbsp strained orange juice
1 tsp finely grated lemon rind

FOR THE GARNISH
mint leaves
chocolate shapes

Picture: page 315

Dissolve the sugar in ⅓ cup water, bring to the boil and boil for one minute. Leave to cool, then stir in the wine and fruit juices.

Pour into a shallow metal container and freeze until just firm, forking through the mixture occasionally from the outside to the middle so that the mixture forms a mass of small crystals.

For the sauce stir all the ingredients together in a bowl over a pan of hot water and continue to stir until the mixture thickens. Remove from the heat and leave to cool, stirring frequently. Cover the surface with cling film and chill lightly.

When the granita is nearly ready, about 30 minutes before serving, transfer the apricot ice cream to the refrigerator.

Thinly pare the rind from one of the oranges, cut into julienne strips then blanch for 4 minutes. Refresh and drain.

Peel the oranges and divide into segments, removing all the white and skin. Quarter and core the pears and cut each quarter into lengthwise slices. Dip in lemon juice diluted with water to prevent discoloration.

Spoon a thin layer of the sauce over 4 cold plates. Place scoops of the apricot ice cream and white wine granita on the sauce. Dry the fruit well and arrange attractively. Garnish with mint leaves and chocolate shapes.

APRICOT ICE CREAM

INGREDIENTS (serves 4)
1¼ lb ripe apricots
a squeeze of lemon juice
¾ cup confectioner's sugar
1¼ cups crème fraîche or
*   whipping cream*

Remove the stones from the apricots, purée and sieve the flesh.

Add lemon juice and sugar to the purée to give the right balance of sweetness and freshness, bearing in mind that freezing masks sweetness. Cover and chill for 1 hour.

Lightly whip the crème fraîche or cream, then carefully fold in the chilled purée until just evenly blended. Freeze in a sorbetière or ice-cream maker for 15—20 minutes, then spoon into a container, cover and place in the freezer. Or spoon the mixture into a shallow metal container, cover and freeze for 45 minutes. Tip the mixture into a cold bowl and beat well with a cold whisk. Return to the container, cover and chill for 45 minutes. Repeat the beating, return to the freezer, covered, and freeze until firm.

Transfer the ice cream to the refrigerator about 30 minutes before serving.

ORANGE CUSTARD WITH APRICOT PUREE

INGREDIENTS (serves 6)
2¼ cups cereal cream
zest of 6 tangerines or mandarins
*   (about 1 lb fruit)*
1 vanilla pod
⅓ cup sugar
2 eggs
2 egg yolks
1 lb fresh apricots, halved and
*   stoned*
sugar
a squeeze of lemon juice

Pour the cream into the top of a double boiler or a bowl placed over a pan of hot water. Stir in the fruit zest and vanilla pod and heat gently to just below simmering point. Remove from the stove, cover and leave to infuse for 20 minutes. Remove the vanilla pod and leave for 40 minutes.

Heat the oven to 325°F.

Add the sugar to the cream and stir until dissolved.

Beat the eggs and egg yolks together then stir into the cream. Strain the liquid into a nonstick or lightly oiled 7 inch sandwich cake pan. Place the pan on a pad of newspaper in a roasting or baking pan, surround with boiling water, cover and place in the oven for 40-50 minutes until just set.

Poach the apricots in the minimum of water until tender. Purée, then pass through a sieve. Add sugar and a squeeze of lemon juice to taste. The purée must be very thick — if necessary reheat it, stirring to drive off the excess moisture. Leave to cool then cover and chill.

Remove the custard from the roasting pan, carefully loosen around the edge and leave to cool, uncovered.

Carefully unmold the custard onto a cold serving plate just before serving. Gently spoon the purée over the surface. Cut into wedges to serve.

OPPOSITE *Apricots
and ice cream
Recipe: page 312*
ABOVE *White wine
granita with apricot
ice cream
Recipe: page 312*

LEFT *Gratin of
fruits
Recipe: page 317*

STRAWBERRIES AND ORANGE CREME

INGREDIENTS (serves 4)
⅔ cup crème fraîche
1 egg white
2 tsp confectioner's sugar, sifted
1 lb (approx 3 cups) strawberries,
    hulled and halved

FOR THE DECORATION
small mint leaves

Picture: page 318

The whipped crème can just be spooned over the plates and the strawberries arranged on it for a very simple effect, or the crème can be piped over the plates, as in the photograph, for a more ornate appearance.

Very lightly whip the crème fraîche with the egg white and sugar, then fold in the orange juice.

Pipe the flavored crème into the center of 4-5 cold plates. Arrange layers of pink grapefruit and orange segments around the crème and decorate with strawberries and mint leaves.

STRAWBERRY MOUSSES WITH

COCONUT SAUCE

INGREDIENTS (serves 4)
1 lb (approx 2½ cups) strawberries
bare ½ cup confectioner's sugar
a squeeze of lemon juice
2½ tsp gelatin
2 egg whites
1¼ cups whipping cream, whipped

FOR THE SAUCE
¼ cup sugar
⅔ cup milk
¼ cup coconut cream
1¼ cups whipping cream, whipped

FOR THE GARNISH
strawberries, sliced
mint leaves

Picture: page 319

Do not prepare the light, airy mousses more than a few hours in advance. Keep them covered with plastic wrap until they are to be served.

Purée the strawberries then pass through a sieve. Add sugar and lemon juice to taste.

Dissolve the gelatin in 4 tbsp water in a small bowl placed over a pan of hot water. Leave to cool.

Whisk the egg whites until stiff but not dry.

Gradually whisk the gelatin into the strawberry purée, then fold in the cream, followed by the egg whites. Spoon into individual molds and leave to set.

For the sauce, pierce 2 of the coconut eyes and drain out all the milk. Crack the coconut and scoop out the flesh. Cut the flesh into small pieces then cook over a low heat with the coconut milk, sugar, milk and coconut cream until soft. Pass through a fine sieve, then fold in the cream.

Unmold the mousses onto 4 cold plates, spoon the sauce over and decorate with sliced strawberries and mint leaves.

STRAWBERRY COOKIE GATEAUX

INGREDIENTS (serves 4)
¾ *cup all purpose flour*
2 egg whites, very lightly beaten
scant ¾ *cup confectioner's sugar, sifted*
5 tbsp butter, melted
1 cup strawberries
1—2 tbsp sugar
squeeze of lemon juice
⅓ *cup crème pâtissière (see p.81)*
2 tbsp marzipan
1½ tbsp kirsch
⅔ *cup whipping cream, whipped*
approx 2½ cups wild strawberries, or
  small strawberries
confectioner's sugar

Picture: page 318

To ensure the cookies bake evenly it may be necessary to turn the baking sheets in the oven and swap shelves. Raspberries could replace all or some of the strawberries.

Heat the oven to 350°F.

Mix the flour, egg whites and confectioner's sugar together, then stir in the melted butter. Spoon the mixture into 12 even circles on greased cookie sheets and bake for about 10 minutes until golden.

Remove the circles quickly from the cookie sheets and leave to cool.

Purée the strawberries, then pass through a sieve and add sugar and lemon juice to taste.

Mix the crème pâtissière, marzipan and kirsch together in a food processor or blender, then fold in the cream. Cover and chill.

Cut the wild strawberries into halves or slice the strawberries. Reserve some for the decoration.

Place 4 of the circles on individual plates. Spread with a layer of the marzipan mixture, then cover with wild strawberries.

Place another cookie circle on these and repeat the layering, but, before putting on the final cookie, sprinkle it liberally with confectioner's sugar and mark a pattern with a vey hot skewer. Spoon the sauce around and decorate with the reserved strawberries.

GRATIN OF FRUITS

INGREDIENTS (serves 4)
2-4 sweet, juicy grapefruit, preferably
  pink
2-4 sweet, juicy oranges
confectioner's sugar
2 egg yolks
1 tbsp sugar
1 cup champagne or good quality
  sparkling dry white wine

FOR THE DECORATION
fresh fruits, eg Cape gooseberries,
  strawberries
mint leaves

Picture: page 315

Adjust the number of oranges and grapefruit according to their size and the size of the portions you wish to serve.

Peel the grapefruit and oranges then divide into segments, making sure all the pith and membrane have been removed. Arrange on 4 plates.

Whisk the egg yolks and sugar together in a bowl placed over a pan of hot water. Whisk in the champagne or sparkling wine and continue to whisk until the mixture is light, fluffy and slightly thickened. Remove from the heat and whisk until cold.

Heat the broiler to very high.

Spoon the sauce over the fruits. Sprinkle lightly with confectioner's sugar and place briefly under the very hot broiler until lightly colored.

Decorate with the fruits and mint leaves.

ABOVE *Strawberries*
and orange crème
Recipe: page 316
RIGHT *Strawberry*
cookie gâteaux
Recipe: page 317

OPPOSITE
Strawberry mousses
with coconut sauce
Recipe: page 316

NOUGAT GLACE WITH PASSION

FRUIT

INGREDIENTS *(serves 6)*
$\frac{1}{3}$ *cup sugar*
2 egg whites
3$\frac{3}{4}$ cups crème fraîche
3 tbsp Cointreau
$\frac{1}{3}$ cup crystallized orange peel, chopped
$\frac{1}{3}$ cup crystallized lemon peel, chopped
3 passion fruit
1 tbsp sugar
a squeeze of lemon juice

Picture: page 322

The light, fresh, citrus orange flavor of the nougat glacé combines exceptionally well with the flavor of the passion fruit sauce. If preferred, it can be frozen in individual decorative molds.

————————

Dissolve about $\frac{1}{3}$ cup of the sugar in 2 tbsp water, bringing it to the boil. Boil until the temperature reaches 250°F.

Meanwhile, whisk the egg whites with the remaining sugar until stiff but not dry, then slowly pour in the boiling syrup, whisking constantly. Continue whisking until the mixture is cold.

Whip the crème fraîche lightly with the Cointreau, then fold into the meringue with the crystallized peels.

Spoon into an oblong loaf pan, cover and freeze until firm.

Remove the pulp and seeds from the passion fruit. Dissolve the sugar in a little water, then simmer briefly to make a light syrup. Stir in the passion fruit pulp and seeds. Add a squeeze of lemon juice and adjust the sweetness. Leave to cool, then chill.

About 20 minutes before serving, unmold the ice cream and leave in the refrigerator.

Spoon the passion fruit over the mold and serve in slices.

ORANGE SHERBET

INGREDIENTS *(serves 4)*
$\frac{1}{2}$ *cup sugar*
finely grated rind of 2 oranges
2 cups strained fresh orange juice
lemon juice

Picture: page 323

Dissolve the sugar in $\frac{1}{2}$ cup water and bring to the boil. Leave to cool, then stir in the orange rind, orange juice and lemon juice to taste.

Freeze in sorbetiére or ice cream maker for 10— 12 minutes, then transfer to the freezer, covered. Or, alternatively, pour into a shallow metal container, cover and chill for 1 hour, then place in the freezer for 45 minutes. Tip the mixture into a cold bowl and beat well with a cold whisk. Return to the container, cover and freeze for 30 minutes. Repeat twice, then leave to freeze until firm.

Transfer the sherbet to the refrigerator about 40 minutes before serving.

APPLE AND BLACK CURRANT

TERRINE

INGREDIENTS (serves 6)
1lb (approx 2⅔ cups) dessert apples,
    peeled, cored and sliced
2 slices of lemon
1 tbsp sugar
4 tbsp gelatin
3 tbsp calvados, optional
1¼ cups crème fraîche, lightly whipped
1 large egg, separated
1lb (approx 4 cups) black currants
1-2 tbsp sugar

FOR THE SAUCE
2 cups black currants
1-2 tbsp confectioner's sugar
lemon juice

Blackberries or raspberries can be used in this terrine instead of black currants. You could make it in an large decorative ring mold — simply form a deep channel in the apple mixture in the same way.

Cook the apples very gently with the slices of lemon, sugar and 1 tbsp water in a covered saucepan for 30 minutes. Remove the slices of lemon and purée the apples.

Dissolve 3 tbsp gelatin in the calvados, or water, in a small bowl over a pan of hot water. Remove from the heat, leave to cool, then beat into the apple purée.

Gently fold the crème fraîche into the apple mixture.

Whisk the egg white until stiff but not dry, then gently fold into the apple cream, cover and chill for one hour.

Cook the black currants with 1-2 tbsp water in a covered pan over a very low heat for about 10 minutes until softened, purée, then pass through a sieve and add sugar to taste.

Bring the black currant purée to the boil and simmer for 2-3 minutes to drive off excess moisture. Blend half of the hot purée with the egg yolk in a bowl. Place the bowl over a pan of hot water and cook, stirring until the mixture thickens slightly. Remove from the heat and beat in the remaining purée. Leave to cool slightly.

Dissolve the remaining gelatin in 2 tbsp of the purée in a small bowl over a pan of hot water. Remove from the heat and leave to cool.

Blend the black currant gelatin into the black currant purée, cover and chill.

Spoon the partially set apple mixture into a terrine rinsed out with cold water, pushing the mixture up the sides to coat them and leaving a deep channel down the center. Spoon the black currant mixture into the channel. Cover and refrigerate until set.

For the sauce, gently cook the black currants with 1 tbsp water in a covered pan for about 10 minutes. Purée, pass through a sieve, then stir in confectioner's sugar and lemon juice to taste, cool, cover and chill.

To serve, loosen around the edge of the apple mixture with the point of a sharp knife, then invert onto a cold plate. Spoon the sauce over 6 cold plates. Cut the terrine into slices and place one on each side.

OPPOSITE *Nougat glacé with passion fruit* Recipe: page 320
Orange sherbet Recipe: page 320

BELOW *Black currant rings* Recipe: page 324

BLACK CURRANT RINGS

INGREDIENTS (serves 4)
2 cups black currants
¼ cup sugar
2 egg yolks
½ cup milk
1 tsp gelatin
2 tbsp crème de cassis
lemon juice
⅔ cup whipping cream, whipped

FOR THE DECORATION
whipped cream
mint leaves

Picture: page 323

Cook the black currants very gently in a covered saucepan with 1 tbsp water and 1 tbsp sugar for a few minutes until they are just softened but still whole.

Whisk the egg yolks with the remaining sugar until thick and light.

Bring the milk to the boil in a double boiler or a bowl placed over a pan of hot water, then pour onto the egg yolks in a slow stream, whisking continuously. Pour back into the double boiler or bowl and cook over hot water, stirring continuously until thickened. Strain into a bowl and leave to cool, stirring occasionally to prevent a skin forming.

Strain the black currants. Reserve the juice. Purée half of the fruit, then pass through a sieve, pressing down well to extract as much juice as possible. Stir the purée and reserved juice into the cooled custard. Reserve the remaining blackcurrants.

Dissolve the gelatin in the crème de cassis in a bowl placed over a pan of hot water. Allow to cool slightly, then stir into the custard. Add lemon juice to taste. Place the custard over a bowl of ice and leave until it is just on the point of setting, stirring occasionally.

Fold in the cream.

Rinse 4 individual ring molds in cold w
with the black currant custard. Leave them to set.

Unmold the rings onto 4 cold plates and spoon some of the reserved black currants into the centers. Arrange the remaining black currants around the molds and decorate with whipped cream and mint leaves.

GRAPES IN GINGERSNAP BASKETS

INGREDIENTS (serves 4)
grated rind of 1 lemon
grated rind of 1 lime
1½ tbsp lemon juice
1½ tbsp lime juice
1½ tbsp granulated sugar
1¼ cups medium white wine
1 egg, separated
1 tbsp sugar
2 cups green grapes, peeled and seeds
    removed, if necessary
2 cups black grapes, peeled and seeds
    removed, if necessary
4 gingersnap baskets (see p.332)

FOR THE DECORATION
long twisted strips of lime and lemon
    peel
small scoops of vanilla ice cream
    (see p.336)

The only last minute preparation for this composite dessert is making the warm, frothy sauce. Vary the size of the baskets according to taste.

___

Stir the fruit rinds and juices, granulated sugar and wine together in a saucepan and heat gently until the sugar has dissolved. Bring to the boil and reduce by half. Cool slightly.

Put the grapes into a large shallow dish and pour the fruit syrup over. Cool completely then cover and chill for several hours.

Transfer the ice cream to the refrigerator 30 minutes before serving.

Just before serving strain the juices from the grapes and measure off 2 tbsp.

Whisk the egg yolk with the sugar in a small bowl placed over a pan of hot water until thick and pale, then very gradually whisk in the 2 tbsp of juice from the grapes.

Whisk the egg white until just beginning to hold shape, then fold into egg yolk mixture.

Place the gingersnap baskets onto 4 dessert plates. Place small scoops of vanilla ice cream in the bottom, add the grapes and spoon the sauce over.

ICE CREAM WITH PEACHES

INGREDIENTS (serves 4)
6 egg yolks
¾ cup confectioner's sugar
¼ cup kirsch
vanilla flavoring
2¼ cups whipping cream
5 peaches
2 slices of orange, white and skin removed
2¼ cups sauternes
bare 1 cup sugar
¼ tsp peach brandy
juice of ½ orange

Picture: page 327

A recipe to choose for a special summertime occasion.

────────────

Whisk the egg yolks with the confectioner's sugar and kirsch until light and fluffy, then whisk in 1 or 2 drops of vanilla flavoring. Gently fold in the cream and divide the mixture between 4 freezerproof dishes. Cover and freeze for 2 hours.

Poach 2 of the peaches and the orange slices in the wine with ½ cup sugar and a few drops of vanilla flavoring for 10 minutes. Leave to cool in the syrup.

Peel and slice the remaining peaches.

Heat the remaining sugar in a small, heavy based saucepan until it begins to turn golden brown. Remove from the heat and stir in the peach poaching liquor. Heat gently, stirring to make sure all the caramel has dissolved. Add the sliced peaches and peach brandy and simmer for 10 minutes. Liquidize, then pass through a sieve and add sugar and orange juice to taste.

Peel the whole poached peaches, cut into halves and remove the stones.

Unmold the ice cream onto 4 cold plates. Cut almost across the center and ease the 2 halves apart. Spoon the sauce around the ice cream. Lay a peach 'tail' on top of the ice cream and garnish the edge of the plate with whipped cream and dots of Grenadine.

Poached apples
Recipe: page 328

Ice cream with peaches
Recipe: page 325

POACHED APPLES

INGREDIENTS (serves 4)
4 dessert apples
½ cup sugar
⅔ cup dry cider
2 cups water
a strip of lemon peel
1 vanilla pod
½ cup red Loire wine or Beaujolais
*   Villages*
4 egg yolks
½ cup sugar
1 tsp gelatin
1 tsp sirop de fraises
lemon juice

FOR THE DECORATION
mint leaves
black currants

Picture: page 326

A soft red wine that is low in tannin must be used, otherwise the flavor of the dish will be spoilt.

———————

Peel, halve and core the apples.

Dissolve the sugar in the cider and 2 cups water. Bring to the boil, add the apples, lemon peel and vanilla pod. Reduce the heat and poach the apples for about 8 minutes. Leave to cool in the liquid, then remove with a slotted spoon and drain well. Cover and chill.

Boil the wine until it is reduced by half.

Whisk the egg yolks, sugar and wine together in a bowl over a pan of hot water until light and thickened. Remove from the heat and whisk until cold.

Dissolve the gelatin in the sirop and 1 tbsp water in a bowl placed over a pan of hot water. Remove from the heat and leave to cool slightly, then lightly fold into the sauce. Taste and add a little lemon juice if necssary to 'lift' the flavor.

Spoon the sauce over 4 plates and leave to set — this will not take long.

Arrange the apple slices on the sauce and decorate with mint leaves and black currants.

PILLOWS OF FRESH PEAR

INGREDIENTS (serves 4)
2 pears
⅔ cup water
½ cup sugar
1½ tbsp lemon juice
¼ cup poires William
6 oz puff pastry (see p.79)
beaten egg
2 cups black currants
1 cup sugar
pinch of ground cinnamon
crème pâtissière made from 1¼ cups ¹⁄₄)
*   milk and 2 egg yolks (see p.81)*

FOR THE DECORATION
mint leaves
slices of peeled pear, dipped in lemon
*   juice*

Picture: page 330

The pastry can be cut into different shapes — round, diamond, square, scalloped, flower or heart.

———————

Peel, core and halve the pears lengthwise, then poach them in ⅔ cup water, with the sugar, lemon juice and poires William, for 5—10 minutes, until tender. Leave to cool in the liquor, then remove with a slotted spoon and drain well.

Meanwhile, roll out the pastry to ¼ inch thick. Trim and straighten the edges, then cut into 4 rectangles, about 4 × 3 inches. Transfer to a baking tray, cover and chill for at least 30 minutes.

Heat the oven to 425°F.

Brush the pastry with beaten egg, mark a pattern with the point of a sharp knife, and bake for about 7 minutes until crisp, golden and risen. Transfer to a wire rack to cool.

Purée the black currants with 1¼ cups of the poaching liquor, the sugar and cinnamon. Pass through a sieve, then chill.

Split the puff pastry rectangles in half lengthways. Carefully remove any pastry that is soft. Place the bottom halves on 4 cold plates. Reserve a little of the crème pâtissière for the decoration, then spread a layer onto each base. Arrange the sliced pears on top, then drop the lids in place.

Spoon the black currant sauce around. Spoon the reserved crème pâtissière into a wax paper pastry bag, snip off the end and pipe a pattern on the sauce. Decorate with the mint leaves and slices of pear.

MANGO SHERBET

INGREDIENTS (serves 4)
½ *cup sugar*
¼ *cup water*
1 *cup mango flesh, puréed and sieved*
juice of 1 lemon, strained

Picture: page 331

Dissolve the sugar in ¼ cup water and bring to the boil. Leave to cool.

Blend the syrup with the mango purée and lemon juice. Freeze in a sorbetière or ice cream maker for about 15 minutes, then transfer to the freezer. Alternatively, pour into a shallow metal container. Cover and chill for 1 hour, then place in the freezer for 45 minutes. Tip the mixture into a cold bowl, beat well with a cold whisk, then return to the container, cover and freeze for 30 minutes. Repeat the beating and freezing twice more. Leave the sherbet to freeze until firm.

Transfer the sherbet to the refrigerator about 30 minutes before serving.

MANGO ICE CREAM WITH

COCONUT SAUCE

INGREDIENTS (serves 4)
2 *egg yolks*
bare ½ *cup confectioner's sugar*
1 *very large or 2 smaller ripe mangoes*
lemon juice
⅔ *cup whipping cream, whipped*
coconut sauce (see p.316)

FOR THE DECORATION
grated coconut

Picture: page 330

Whisk the egg yolks and confectioner's sugar together in a bowl over a pan of hot water until they are lukewarm. Remove from the heat and continue whisking until the mixture is cold and very thick and light.

Sieve the mango flesh and sharpen it with a little lemon juice.

Fold the mango flesh and cream together, then fold into the egg yolk mixture. Pour into a shallow metal container, cover and freeze until firm.

About 30 minutes before serving, transfer the ice cream to the main part of the refrigerator.

Spoon the sauce onto 4 cold plates. Scoop the ice cream into the center and decorate with grated coconut.

ABOVE *Pillows of fresh pear*
Recipe: page 328
RIGHT *Mango ice cream with coconut sauce*
Recipe: page 329

OPPOSITE *Mango sherbet*
Recipe: page 329

GINGERSNAP BASKETS

INGREDIENTS (makes 8—10)
4 tbsp corn syrup
4 tbsp butter
⅔ cup sugar
½ cup all purpose flour
1 tsp ground ginger
½ tsp finely grated lemon zest
½ tsp lemon juice

Heat the oven to 350°F.

Gently heat the syrup, butter and sugar until the sugar has dissolved. Remove from the heat and fold in the remaining ingredients.

Drop 3 spoonfuls of the mixture onto a lightly greased cookie sheet, leaving plenty of room for the mixture to spread.

Bake in the oven for 7—10 minutes until golden brown.

Quickly but carefully remove with a spatula and mold around an orange or apple or small bowl.

When set, remove from the molds and leave to cool on a wire cooling tray.

Bake the remaining mixture in the same way and shape as above.

WINE JELLY WITH PEACHES

INGREDIENTS (serves 4)
3 tsp powdered gelatin
2½ cups fruity dry white wine
½ cup sugar
juice of 1 lemon
strips of lemon peel
small mint leaves
4 peaches
2 tbsp poires William

Picture: page 334

Dissolve the gelatin in a little of the wine in a small bowl over a pan of hot water. Remove from the heat and leave to cool slightly.

Gently heat half the remaining wine with the sugar and lemon juice, stirring constantly until the sugar has dissolved. Remove from the heat, stir into the gelatin. Reserve ¼ cup of the remaining wine and stir the gelatin mixture into the rest of the wine. Spoon a very thin layer over 4 cold plates. Leave until just beginning to set. Leave the remaining jelly in a cool place until just becoming syrupy.

Cut shapes out of the lemon peel with aspic cutters. Reserve some of the shapes and some of the mint leaves. Arrange the remainder on the plates. Leave to set in place, then cover with a thin layer of syrupy jelly, taking care not to dislodge the decoration. Leave to set.

Peel the peaches, remove the stones and cut the flesh into slices. Sprinkle with the reserved wine, cover and chill.

Just before serving, whisk the reserved jelly with the poires William until frothy.

Place the unwhipped jelly in the center of the plates, then add the whipped jelly and arrange the slices of peach on top.

COUPELLES

INGREDIENTS (makes 8—10)
4 tbsp sweet butter
2 egg whites
¼ cup sugar
½ cup all purpose flour

The baked cookies set very quickly after they are removed from the oven, so it is advisable to cook only 3 at one time and to use 2 or 3 cookie sheets in rotation. Handle with care after shaping, as they are brittle. Store in an airtight container and do not fill or place on a sauce until just before serving.

Heat the oven to 400°F.

Slowly melt the butter then allow to cool.

Whisk the egg whites until frothy, then whisk in the sugar and continue to whisk for 2—3 minutes until thick. Gently fold in the flour together with the melted butter.

Drop 3 spoonfuls of the mixture onto a lightly greased cookie sheet and spread each one out to a circle 4 inches in diameter.

Bake in the oven for 5-7 minutes until the edges are light golden brown.

Carefully but quickly remove the cookies with a spatula and quickly shape around the bottom of an orange or apple or small dish.

When set to shape, remove from the mold and leave to cool completely on a wire cooling rack.

Cook the remaining mixture in a similar way, using a cool cookie sheet each time and shaping the cookies as above.

Store carefully in tins or airtight containers.

KIRSCH ICE CREAM IN COUPELLES

INGREDIENTS (serves 4)
¾ cup sugar
3 egg whites
3 tbsp good quality kirsch
1 cup whipped crème fraîche or
    whipping cream
4 coupelles

FOR THE DECORATION
whipped crème fraîche or whipping
    cream, optional
pieces of fresh pineapple
strawberries
mint leaves

Picture: page 335

The ice cream goes equally well with raspberries — either whole, instead of the other fruits in the coupelles, or as a sauce with the ice cream served simply on top.

Dissolve the sugar in ⅔ cup water, then bring to the boil and boil for 3-5 minutes until the temperature reaches 230-260°F.

Whisk in the kirsch, then carefully fold in the crème fraîche or whipping cream. Spoon into a shallow metal container, cover and chill for 30 minutes, then place in the freezer.

Whisk in the kirsch, then carefully fold in the crème fraîche or double cream. Spoon into a shallow metal container, cover and chill for 30 minutes, then place in the freezer.

About 20 minutes before serving, transfer the ice cream to the main part of the refrigerator.

Place the coupelles on 4 cold plates and scoop ice cream into the center. Garnish with the cream, if used, fruits and mint leaves.

Wine jelly with peaches
Recipe page 332

Kirsch ice cream in coupelles
Recipe: page 333

FLOATING ISLANDS ON BLACK

CURRANT SAUCE

INGREDIENTS (serves 4)
2 tbsp sugar
2 cups black currants
a squeeze of lemon juice
2 egg whites
¼ cup sugar

FOR THE DECORATION
mint leaves

Dissolve the sugar in 2 tbsp water, add the black currants and cook, covered, over a low heat for 2-3 minutes. Purée, then pass through a sieve and add lemon juice to taste.

Whisk the egg whites until stiff, then very gradually whisk in half the sugar, whisking well after each addition, and continue to whisk until the meringue is stiff. Whisk in the remaining sugar and whisk again until the meringue is very stiff.

Heat a wide pan of salted water until the water is just moving.

Form the meringue mixture into small mounds on a slotted spoon, then rest the spoon gently on the surface of the water. The mounds will gently float off the spoon onto the surface of the water. Cook for about 3-4 minutes, turning occasionally. Remove carefully with a slotted spoon and leave to drain on a cloth. Cook the remaining meringue in the same way.

Spoon the black currant sauce over 4 plates and carefully transfer the meringue mounds to the surface of the sauce. Decorate with mint leaves.

VANILLA ICE CREAM

INGREDIENTS (serves 4)
½ vanilla pod, split
2 cups whipping cream
4 egg yolks
⅓ cup sugar

Heat the vanilla pod with the cream in a heavy based saucepan to just below boiling point. Remove from the heat, cover and leave for 30 minutes.

Lightly whisk the egg yolks with the sugar in a bowl. Strain in the cream, whisking constantly. Rinse the saucepan and pour in the cream/egg yolk mixture. Place over a low heat and cook gently, stirring constantly, until the mixture thickens. Do not allow it to boil.

Remove from the heat and leave to cool, stirring occasionally to prevent a skin forming, then pour into a shallow metal container. Cover and place in the freezer until a 1 inch border of ice crystals have formed around the edge.

Tip the ice cream into a cold bowl and beat with a cold whisk to break up the ice crystals but do not allow the mixture to warm. Return the mixture to the container, cover and freeze until firm. Alternatively, freeze the ice cream in an ice cream maker.

About 35 minutes before serving transfer the ice cream to the main part of the refrigerator.

BAKED APPLES WITH BERRIES

INGREDIENTS (serves 4)
⅔ cup raspberries
½ cup strawberries
2½ tbsp eau-de-vie de Framboises
1 tsp sugar
1 tbsp lemon juice
4 large, crisp, dessert apples
3 tbsp butter
bare ½ cup confectioner's sugar
1 cup crème fraîche

FOR THE DECORATION
slices of small strawberries
mint leaves

Put the raspberries and strawberries into a small bowl. Sprinkle 2 tbsp Framboises and the sugar over. Cover and leave for 1 hour, very gently folding the fruit over 2 or 3 times.

Acidulate a bowl of cold water with the lemon juice.

Peel the apples, leaving the stalks on. Cut a slice from the top of each apple and remove the cores. Put each one in the acidulated water as soon as it is finished.

Heat the oven to 400°F.

Remove the apples from the water and dry well. Place in an ovenproof dish and fill the cavities with some of the raspberries and strawberries. Pour the juices over the apples and reserve the fruit that remains.

Divide half the butter between the apples and put the removed slices back in place. Sprinkle the apples with about ¼ cup confectioner's sugar. Scatter the remaining butter in the dish and surround the apples with about ¾ cup water.

Place in the oven and cook for 15-20 minutes.

Bake the apples with the cooking juices and sprinkle with a further ¼ cup confectioner's sugar. Return to the oven for another 15 minutes until just cooked throughout. Leave to cool then chill for 1 hour.

Purée the remaining raspberries and strawberries then pass through a sieve. Whisk lightly with the crème fraîche, remaining Framboises and remaining confectioner's sugar.

Remove the slices from the apples and spoon some of the berry sauce over the apples. Spoon the remaining sauce around the apples and decorate with strawberry slices and mint leaves.

CONVERSION CHARTS, GLOSSARY & INDEX

WEIGHTS AND MEASURES

SPOON MEASURES

In American recipes, when quantities are stated as spoons, 'level' spoons are meant. European recipes and those in this book usually call for rounded neither level, nor over-heaped) spoons, unless specifically stated otherwise. Also, American 'spoons' are standard cook's measuring spoons, whereas European 'spoons' tend to be any available kitchen or eating spoons. The best plan is to regard 2 American teaspoons or tablespoons as 1 English teaspoon or tablespoon. Dessertspoons are not often called for in recipes, but 1 dessertspoon is the equivalent of 2 teaspoons or half a tablespoon.

VOLUME

Metric	Imperial		American
5 ml	—	1 tsp	1 tsp
10 ml	—	2 tsp	2 tsp
20 ml	—	1 tbsp	1½ tbsp
30 ml	1 fl oz	1½ tbsp	2 tbsp
50 ml	2 fl oz	3 tbsp	¼ cup
60 ml	2½ fl oz (½ gill)	3½ tbsp	¼C+2 tsp
75 ml	3 fl oz	4 tbsp	½C(6 tbsp)
100 ml	4 fl oz	¼ pint	½C(¼ pint)
150 ml	5 fl oz (1 gill)	¼ pint	¾C
175 ml	6 fl oz	—	¾C
200 ml	7 fl oz	—	—
250 ml	8 fl oz	⅓ pint	1C(½ pint)
300 ml	10 fl oz (2 gills)	½ pint	1¼C
350 ml	12 fl oz	—	1½C
400 ml	14 fl oz	⅔ pint	1¾C
450 ml	15 fl oz	¾ pint	—
500 ml	16 fl oz	—	2C (1 pint)
550 ml	18 fl oz	—	2¼C
575 ml	20 fl oz	1 pint	2½C
600 ml	21 fl oz	—	2¾C
700 ml	25 fl oz	1¼ pint	3C
750 ml	27 fl oz	—	3½C
800 ml	28 fl oz	—	3⅔C
850 ml	30 fl oz	1½ pints	3¾C
900 ml	32 fl oz	1⅔ pints	4C
1 litre	35 fl oz	1¾ pints	4½C
1.1 litre	40 fl oz	2 pints	5C
1.3 litre	48 fl oz	2⅔ pints	6C
1.5 litre	50 fl oz	2½ pints	6¼C
1.66 litre	56 fl oz	2¾ pints	7C
1.75 litre	60 fl oz	3 pints	7½C
1.8 litre	64 fl oz	3¼ pints	8C
2 litre	72 fl oz	3½ pints	9C
2.1 litre	76 fl oz	3⅔ pints	9½C
2.2 litre	80 fl oz	3¾ pints	10C
2.25 litre	84 fl oz	2 quarts	10½C

WEIGHTS				LENGTH	

Metric	Imperial	Metric	Imperial
8 g	¼ oz	325 g	11 oz
15 g	½ oz	350 g	12 oz
20 g	¾ oz	375 g	13 oz
25 g	1 oz	400 g	14 oz
30 g	1 oz	425 g	15 oz
45 g	1½ oz	450 g	16 oz (1lb)
50 g	1¾ oz	550 g	1¼ lb
55 g	2 oz	675 g	1½ lb
75 g	2½ oz	700 g	1⅔ lb
85 g	3 oz	800 g	1¾ lb
100 g	3½ oz	900 g	2 lb
115 g	4 oz	1 kg	2¼ lb
125 g	4½ oz	1.35 kg	3 lb
140 g	5 oz	1.5 kg	3½ lb
150 g	5½ oz	1.8 kg	4 lb
170 g	6 oz	2 kg	4½ lb
175 g	6½ oz	2.3 kg	5 lb
200 g	7 oz	2.5 kg	5½ lb
210 g	7½ oz	2.7 kg	6 lb
225 g	8 oz	3 kg	6½ lb
250 g	8½ oz	3.2 kg	7 lb
255 g	9 oz	3.5 kg	8 lb
275 g	9½ oz	4 kg	9 lb
285 g	10 oz	4.5 kg	10 lb
300 g	10½ oz	5 kg	11 lb

LENGTH

Metric (cm)	Imperial (in)
0.3	⅛
0.6	¼
1	½
2	¾
2.5	1
5	2
15	6
30	12 (1 ft)
46	18
92	36 (1yd)
100 (1m)	39

TEMPERATURE

°C	°F	Gas mark	°C	°F	Gas mark	°C	°F	Gas mark
27	80		71	160		130	275	1
29	85		77	170		140	285	
38	100		82	180		150	300	2(c)
41	105		88	190		160	325	3(w)
43	110		93	200		180	350	4
46	115		96	205		190	375	5(m)
49	120		100	212		200	400	6(lh)
54	130		107	225	¼(vc)	220	425	7
57	135		110	228		230	450	8(h)
60	140		115	238		250	475	9(vh)
66	150		120	250	½	260	500	

GLOSSARY

Acidify To add vinegar or lemon juice to a sauce or cooked dish.

Acidulated water Water to which lemon juice or vinegar has been added. Used for blanching sweetbreads etc. Also lemon juice and water mixed in equal quantities and added to apples, bananas, artichokes etc. to prevent them from going brown.

Aiguilette Thin strips of meat, most likely from the breast of poultry or game.

Aspic Jelly made from calfs foot or the bones of meat, fish or poultry. Vegetables, fish or meat can be served in aspic.

Bain marie A water bath in which delicate foods are stood in their dishes to cook away from direct heat in the oven. Can also be used to keep foods hot without spoiling.

Bake To cook in dry heat in the oven.

Bake blind To bake an empty pastry case. So that the case keeps its shape, it is filled with blind beans, *see* below.

Bard To cover meat, game or poultry in strips of pork or fatty bacon to prevent it drying out during roasting. Reduces the need for basting.

Baste To spoon the cooking liquid over the food as it cooks to add flavor and prevent it drying out.

Batter A beaten mixture used to make cakes, puddings or pancakes or to coat foods to be fried. Usually a liquid made from flour, eggs and milk.

Bavarois Dessert made with cream and eggs and set with gelatin.

Beat To mix energetically with a wooden spoon or in an electric mixer, incorporating air so that the mixture is light and smooth.

Beignets Fritters.

Beurre manié Flour and butter creamed together into a paste and used as a thickening for sauces etc.

Beurre noir Butter heated until it is dark brown — *not* black.

Beurre noisette Butter heated until it is light brown. Take care not to burn it.

Bind To thicken soups or sauces with eggs, cream etc.

Bisque A creamy soup made with puréed fish or shellfish.

Blanch To heat briefly in boiling water or steam. This can be done to whiten sweetbreads etc., to facilitate peeling vegetables or shelling nuts, to remove a strong or bitter flavor from certain meats and vegetables, or to prepare fruit and vegetables for preserving or freezing.

Blanquette A casserole made without prior frying of the meat to seal it. The meat is usually chicken, veal or lamb and the sauce thickened with cream or egg yolk.

Blend To mix together thoroughly.

Blind beans Dried beans (or can even be pebbles or marbles) used to fill a pastry

case for baking blind. Can be stored and reused.

Boil To cook in liquid brought to boiling point and kept there. Pasta is cooked at a full rolling boil in an open pan so that the water is agitated as much as possible to help stop the pasta sticking together. A tablespoon of oil added to the water helps too.

Bouquet garni Bunch of herbs used to flavor food during cooking and removed before serving.

Braise To cook slowly on a bed of vegetables in a covered pan.

Bread To coat in flour, egg, then breadcrumbs before frying.

Brochette (*see* Skewer).

Brunoise Finely diced root vegetables simmered in butter and stock until soft. Used to flavor soups and sauces and some fish dishes.

Caramelize To melt sugar into a syrup, either by boiling in a pan and stirring continuously, or by heating under the broiler.

Chaudfroid A jellied white sauce made of butter and flour with egg yolks, stock, cream and gelatin. Used to give a white glaze to chicken etc. A brown chaudfroid is used on game and meat.

Chine To remove the backbone from a rack of ribs.

Chowder A fish stew or soup, often made with clams or oysters.

Clarified butter Butter that has been melted so that the clear oil can be separated from the milk particles and other impurities. It can then be heated to a higher temperature than unclarified butter without burning.

Clarify To clear a stock by adding lightly beaten egg whites and crushed egg shells. Bring the liquid to the boil, then cool and strain before using.

Cocotte A cast iron casserole with a lid, usually round or oval in shape. Also individual ovenproof dishes for baking eggs.

Collops Small slices of meat.

Cool To allow to stand at room temperature. *Not* to put in the fridge.

Court bouillon Specially prepared cooking liquor for poaching fish and shellfish, and sometimes vegetables and meat. Water acidulated with a little vinegar and containing also herbs and seasoning, onion, garlic, carrot, celery, wine, stock, oil etc.

Cream To beat together certain foods until smooth and creamy. To cream butter and sugar, beat together in a bowl with a wooden spoon until soft and fluffy and light in color, or use an electric mixer.

Croustade A bread case for hot savory mixtures that is dipped in fat and baked or fried until crispy.

Croûte Crust or pastry case enclosing a filling. Usually made of rich brioche dough.

Croûton Trimmed bread cut into neat shapes and fried. Used as a garnish.

Dariole Small castle shaped mold used for both sweet and savory mousses and sometimes for rice and cakes.

Deglaze To add boiling water, wine or stock to the meat sediment and cooking juices in the pan. Essential stage in making a sauce for fried meat.

Déglacer (*see* Deglaze).

Dégorger To remove strong or bitter tasting flavors from meat, fish or vegetables, usually by salting them, then soaking or washing. An alternative to blanching.

Dépouiller To add a little cold liquid to a pan of simmering stock, which will bring the fat and scum to the surface, making it easier to skim off.

Devil To broil food in a coating of butter and a hot sauce, such as Worcestershire.

Dice To cut into small cubes of even size.

Dredge To dust with flour, sugar etc.

Dropping consistency The consistency of a mixture that will fall reluctantly from a spoon when jerked — neither runny nor solid.

Duxelles A mixture of finely chopped mushroom and onion or shallot, sometimes mixed with ham. Used raw or cooked in butter until soft and dry to stuff or flavor poached fish, shellfish or meat, or to garnish a papillote.

Emulsion A stable suspension of fat and another substance. Mayonnaise is an emulsion.

Escalope A thin slice of meat, eg veal, often beaten flat to make it larger and thinner.

Farce Stuffing.

Fines herbes A combination of parsley, chives, tarragon and chervil.

Fillet A cut of prime meat or fish off the bone.

Flake To break down into small pieces with a fork.

Flamber To set light to alcohol poured over food. Adds flavor and drama to presentation.

Fold in To mix a heavy creamy mixture with a light and fluffy one, gently fold the first into the second with a large metal spoon in a three dimensional figure-of-eight motion. Do not beat or overwork, or you will lose all the air.

Fricassée Chicken or veal fried and then cooked in a sauce.

Fromage blanc Very soft low fat cheese.

Garniture Garnish or trimming. Neat shapes of vegetables, pasta, croûtons etc. used to enhance the flavor and appearance of a dish. An important part of presentation in Cuisine Vivante.

Giblets Gizzard, heart, neck and liver of poultry. The liver is very strong in flavor, but the others are often used in the making of stock.

Glacé de viande Concentrated meat glaze made by boiling brown stock to reduce. Used for coloring and flavoring sauces.

Glacé de poisson As above, but of fish. (*See also* fish fumet.)

Glaze A thin coating of syrup or aspic that gives a shine to a finished dish (eg jellied meat juices on turkey, or melted jam on a fruit pie).

Gluten Proteins found in wheat important in the making of bread.

Gratin A gratin dish is oval and ovenproof. Dishes cooked au gratin are dotted with butter, cheese and bread crumbs and browned in the oven.

Grill To cook by direct heat.

Infuse To steep or heat through to extract a flavor, eg vanilla in milk.

Julienne Fine needleshreds or matchstick lengths of vegetable etc.

Knead To work dough, pressing it and stretching it until it reaches the right elasticity and consistency, and to distribute the yeast if there is any.

Knock back To knead dough for a second time and expel the air once it has risen.

Knock up To separate the edges of raw puff pastry so that it rises during cooking with as much air between the layers as possible.

Lard To thread strips of pork or anchovy through meat before roasting to make it juicy and flavorsome.

Lardons Strips of port fat used to line pâté tins or to thread through meat, *see* above.

Leavening Agent used to make mixtures rise in cooking — yeast, egg white, baking powder.

Liaison Thickening agent for sauces, either flour and butter or egg yolk, cream or blood.

Macédoine Diced mixed fruit for a fruit salad, or diced mixed vegetables for a garnish or hors d'oeuvre.

Macerate To soften or steep food in a liquid, especially of fruit, to let the flavors mingle.

Marinade The liquid in which food is marinated. *See* below.

Marinate To tenderize and flavor food, especially meat, by steeping in a liquid, usually red or white wine or a mixture of oil and lemon juice, flavored with herbs and chopped vegetables.

Mask To cover food with a sauce.

Médallions Food trimmed into neat rounds, usually meat.

Mirepoix A bed of vegetables used for braising. Usually finely diced onion, carrot and celery, sometimes mixed with ham, which has been fried gently in butter until soft.

Mount (monter) To add butter to a sauce, waiting until each small piece is incorporated before adding the next, to thicken it and give it a velvety texture and a rich sheen.

Mousseline A light, creamy, frothy mixture, a sauce with a mousse-like texture or small molds of poultry or fish purée whipped with cream and served hot or cold.

Noisette Hazelnut. Used also to describe a quantity, eg a nut of butter, or a shape. A noisette of lamb is a neat round taken from the best end.

Panade A mixture thickened with flour and used as the base of a soufflé or cake.

Papilotte An oiled paper or foil case that envelops food while it is cooking and contains its aroma or flavor.

Parboil To boil briefly. *See* Blanch.

Poach To cook gently in barely trembling water.

Pound To reduce to a paste or a powder with a pestle and mortar.

Praline Almonds and sugar pounded together and cooked to a toffee. Used to coat cakes and puddings.

Prove (or Proof) To rise, of yeasted dough.

Purée To press through a fine meshed sieve or otherwise reduce food to a smooth, soft consistency.

Quark Very soft, almost liquid white cheese made from skimmed milk.

Quenelle Finely pounded food, most commonly fish, mixed with egg whites and cream to a very smooth paste over ice, formed into sausage shapes and poached in water or light stock.

Ragoût A stew made from even sized pieces of meat, fish or sometimes vegetables. They are usually sautéed first, then simmered gently in stock. Cuisine Vivante chefs have developed lighter types of ragoût that need less cooking.

Ramekin Small ovenproof dish used for cooking tiny individual portions.

Reduce To boil, uncovered, so that the liquid evaporates. It strengthens the flavor and improves the appearance of liquids to be used as sauces.

Refresh To stop vegetables continuing to cook and losing their color by submerging them briefly in cold water after they have finished cooking.

Relax To put pastry in the fridge in between rollings. The gluten in the flour will have expanded during rolling and this allows it to contract so that there is less danger of shrinkage in the oven.

Render To reduce fat to a liquid by melting over a gentle heat.

Rest Batter is set aside to rest so that the starch can expand. This makes it lighter when cooked.

Ribbon trail When a mixture has been whisked, it leaves a ribbon trail in the bowl when the whisk is raised out of the mixture. The thickness of the ribbon trail and the time it takes to disappear are indications of the consistency of the mixture.

Roast To cook meat in the oven by the action of direct heat and its own vapor.

Rouille Emulsion of garlic and oil for flavoring Mediterranean soups.

Roux An amalgamation of butter and flour cooked over a gentle heat and used as the basis for many sauces. Flour-based sauces are not favored by chefs of the Cuisine Vivante as they are heavy and tend to mask the flavors of the other ingredients.

Salmis Poultry or Game pieces, roasted in the oven until almost done, then cooked in a rich wine sauce.

Salpicon Finely diced meat, fish or vegetables, bound with a savory sauce and used to make rissoles, croquettes or stuffings for meat, vegetables or pastry shells.

Sauter Literally 'jump'. To fry food lightly in butter or oil, shaking and tossing it frequently.

Scald Mainly used of milk. To heat until just below boiling point.

Seal, sear, seize To brown the surface of meat quickly over a high heat to prevent the juices escaping during cooking.

Simmer To cook in liquid that is not quite boiling, so that only the occasional bubble rises to the surface.

Skewer To hold in place with metal or wooden sticks, pointed at one or both ends. Prawns etc. can be threaded onto a skewer or brochette and grilled over charcoal.

Slake To mix flour to a paste with water.

Steam Light method of cooking food over boiling waer much favored by Cuisine Vivante.

Suprême Poultry breast.

Sweat To cook gently in a closed pan without browning, either in butter or in the food's own juices.

Terrine A loaf-pan shaped baking dish. Also the food cooked in it — pâté or other minced mixtures baked or steamed and usually eaten cold and sliced.

Timbale Food cooked or served in a castle shaped mound.

Tomalley The liver of a lobster. Especially prized by the chefs of the Cuisine Vivante.

Tournedos Thick beef steaks from the narrow end of the fillet.

Turn Technique of cutting around vegetables to make them of even size and attractive in appearance.

Zest Finely grated lemon or orange rind. The colored part only is grated and used for flavorings.

INDEX

T

ACKNOWLEDGEMENTS

The publishers wish to thank the
following for the loan of china, glassware,
kitchen equipment and provisions:

The Reject China Shop, Beauchamp Place,
    London SW1
David Mellor (kitchen supplies), Covent
    Garden, London WC2
Moulinex Ltd.
Magimix Ltd.
Mr John Lawless, City Herbs, London
Mr Terry Connelly, Woodhouse Hume
    Ltd., London
L & E Fisheries Ltd., London
Donaldson's, London